THE KEYS TO THE PREDICTIONS OF NOSTRADAMUS

THE KEYS TO THE PREDICTIONS OF NOSTRADAMUS

Bardo Kidogo

foulsham
LONDON • NEW YORK • TORONTO • SYDNEY

foulsham

Yeovil Road, Slough, Berkshire SL1 4JH

ISBN 0-572-01964-5

Designed and typeset by Peter Constable Ltd, London.

Printed by St.Edmundsbury Press Ltd,
Bury St.Edmunds, Suffolk.

*We all stand on the shoulders
of earlier workers in our field.*

*This book is dedicated to all
those people whose contributions
preceded it and kept its subject alive.*

CONTENTS

PROLOGUE

"Was it then a god who penned these signs?"
pondered Goethe's Faust,
his copy of Nostradamus in his hands.

Dear Reader,

The purpose of this book is to encourage the reading of Nostradamus' prophecies and to help in understanding them. The one hundred and sixty-one quatrains used for this purpose are listed on page 178. Several deal with past events. Those have been selected so that Nostradamus' predictions can be compared with what has actually happened. This allows us to gauge his accuracy and study his techniques. Most of the verses listed, however, are about the future. This is because anyone wanting only to read history can open a history book. Whereas those who would read Nostradamus, want to know what is going to happen. To find out about this, and before reading on, you should obtain a complete edition of Nostradamus' prophecies. Several of the most easily obtained English translations are listed in Appendix One.

In the past it has been quite usual for his would-be readers soon to give up their attempts in disgust. His presentation, which was intended to confuse, had succeeded in doing so. But his cryptic style of writing is not in fact very difficult to understand. It is like a shoelace. Pull on the wrong ends, and the knot will only tighten. But pull on the right bits, and his riddles unravel like so many slip-knots.

This book is mainly about what still lies in the future. It can begin with the happy discovery that the future which Nostradamus predicts for us is not nearly as black as popular misconceptions had led us to believe. This reassurance is relevant. After all, if we are apprehensive about what will be revealed, we are not going to try all that hard to read the details. The facts about it are therefore separated from the fictions.

Then we will look at Nostradamus the man. For it is always best to weigh anything we are told, against who tells it to us. We will look at what made him tick, his motives and personal prejudices. And then at why he made predictions, and how he came by his apparent insights into the future.

When we have seen something of the man we will examine why he did not express himself in everyday language; why, at first sight, much of what he wrote was gobbledegook.

The nearest thing to difficulty about understanding what Nostradamus wrote arises from the sheer volume of his verses. There are almost a thousand of them, many of which are not self-contained and so, to make sense, have to be read with others. These need to be unscrambled before the right ones can be read together. A way in which this can be done is suggested.

Detailed analyses of all of Nostradamus' verses would fill a bookshelf and is not attempted here. Instead, what will have been discussed will be applied to sample verses. These have been selected for analysis in an order that allows us to proceed in easy stages from almost direct translations to a full interpretation.

This book ends with a dictionary of Nostradamus' meanings in his verses about the future. When this dictionary is used, even the best-intentioned of further discussion would hinder rather than be useful. And readers will then find how easily one can, with a sure eye, go it alone.

It only remains for me to wish you what I have gained from Nostradamus.

Which is a curiosity about the future satisfied,...and many hours of pleasure.

Yours sincerely,

BARDO KIDOGO.

Conventions

ABBREVIATIONS

C.   = CATALAN
GK. = GREEK
IT. = ITALIAN
L.   = LATIN
L.G. = LOW GERMAN
N.   = NORMAN OR OLD NORSE
O.F. = OLD FRENCH, LANGUE D'OC OR PROVENÇAL

TYPE

Small italics are used for English dialects and foreign words. Capital italics refer to entries in the dictionary in Part Four.

OTHER MARKS

Perpendicular brackets contain cross-references. Single inverted commas contain translations, short quotations or 'special' words.

MICHEL NOSTRADAMUS.
Médecin,
Né à St Remy, en Provence, le 14 Décemb. 1503,
Mort le 2 juillet 1566.

Paris chez Odieuvre Md d'Estampes, rue d'Anjou la derniere Pte Cochere à gauche entrant par la rue Dauphine, CPR

PART ONE

NOSTRADAMUS: THE MAN

*"To understand a Proverb, and the interpretation;
the words of the wise and their dark sayings."*
(PROVERBS I : 6.)

CHAPTER ONE

THE BACKGROUND
TO HIS PROPHECIES TODAY

"Time is what keeps the light from reaching us".
(MEISTER ECKHART. 13TH. CENTURY MYSTIC.)

THE NATURE OF TIME

One of the causes of Nostradamus' work having remained mysterious for so long has been man's concept of the time dimension. This was that time was linear. That is, that it just moved on from past to present to future, in a straight line as it were. By many people in the past nothing which contradicted that notion was therefore taken seriously. So, despite mounting evidence to the contrary from research centres and unnumbered personal experiences, seeing into the future was widely thought to be impossible. And for four centuries that belief degraded all attempts to understand Nostradamus.

Now, though, modern advances in physics have proved time to be merely relative. So we are at last free to use Nostradamus' glimpses of tomorrow before they flit through our today and can no longer be used as guides.

Gone, or at least ought to have been, the days when men had intellectual difficulties in believing his predictions. Predictions such as, in verse II 62, that "An Ayatollah will suddenly seize power from a Shah", with the result that, still holding onto that old hang-up, in 1979 they were surprised when the event happened. Today, being caught on the hop like that can be avoided simply by keeping an open mind on the subject of time.

THE VALUE OF HIS PROPHECIES TODAY

Much can be known in advance. Such as what will

otherwise happen at a major international sporting event, in the Channel Tunnel, in Eastern Europe, to Turkey, to a Western Task Force in the Persian Gulf, to an off-shore oil field, and to a British government of the day. And about attempts to release poisons into public water supplies and into the air in crowded places. Even the puppet-masters and methods of the terrorist groups responsible can be known before these megatrocities are committed.

But these events, including that which Nostradamus describes as "the worst crime in history", being merely acts of terrorism, will be preventable. The good news is that, contrary to what is often claimed, Nostradamus' prophecies do not tell of a Third World War. At worst they tell only of corruption, drug-trafficking, famine, pollution, racial and religious conflict and escalating terrorism; all of them matters with which mankind has already come to terms. It is a disappointing list for those who have had their expectations wetted by such nonsenses as that Nostradamus foretells the landing of flying saucers. He does not even say anything about the earthquake which seismologists expect in California and which pop-commentators on Nostradamus have therefore felt safe in claiming that he predicts.

NEVER MIND THE QUALITY, FEEL THE WIDTH

Churning out accounts of what Nostradamus allegedly foretells has become a thriving industry. The more fanciful the alleged prediction, the more blatantly it is intended to exploit human hopes or fears, the more blindly it seems to be accepted. *"Credo quia absurdum"*, "I believe because it is absurd", wrote Tertullian. He did not in fact mean quite what that sounds as if he meant; but never mind, because it makes the point. But not as well as does Descartes' axiom which was, *"De omnibus est dubitandum"*. That means, "Doubt everything."

MISREPRESENTATIONS

It is said that many of Nostradamus' verses are too vague to mean anything specific. This is true only insofar as those particular verses do not deal with specific events. They are for placing between quatrains which do contain the details. This is a technique which corresponds with the historian's use of similarly broad, sweeping statements between details of particular events. And it is largely due to this technique that by reading history books we can understand the past.

It is also said that some verses can be associated with more than one historical event. This too is true. It is a cliché that history repeats itself. And a fact of which Nostradamus made full use. He deliberately chose events the descriptions of which would fit later events as well or even better. In this way he would get recognition for two or occasionally more successful prophecies for the price of one.

It is claimed by many people that Nostradamus' prophecies do not make sense. "It will rain stones", or some such phrase, they quote, derisively. Yet these same people think nothing of looking up at a cloudy sky and announcing that, "It's going to rain cats and dogs"!

It is not always due to carelessness on the part of the reader that Nostradamus is misunderstood. There have been many deliberate distortions of what he wrote, usually for political purposes. One such was hatched under Dr. Goebbels during the Second World War. And in Sweden and the United States the Nazi sympathizers Karl Krafft and Norab were both active in this field.

EFFECTS OF PROPHECIES

Prophecy is an old tool of political activists of all persuasions because there lurks in everyone a suspicion that if something has been foretold it is somehow more likely to come about. During his ministry even Jesus was careful to live-out biblical prophecies.

In fact, an event is indeed more likely to happen if it has been foretold by someone like Nostradamus. This is because the prophecy itself implants the idea to do the thing, and implies that an attempt to do it will be successful. It is, however, a double-edged tool, because those who do not want the event to take place will have been forewarned of it and can take preventive measures. The overthrow of the Shah of Iran, mentioned above, which those who had understood the verse therefore expected, might have been aborted had the Shah's advisers used their side of the tool.

SORTING FACTS FROM FICTIONS

There is only one way to do this when dealing with Nostradamus. It is to go to what he wrote, for oneself, and have a look. All those books listed under Further Reading are serious studies, suitable for this purpose.

That done, it is next essential to get some grasp of Nostradamus the man; his outlook, his methods and his intentions. These are all grounded in his life, and can be recognised as responses to his personal experiences and social background. These facts have to be known because the difference between understanding what any ambiguous piece of writing could mean, and what it does mean, can depend completely on knowing sufficient about the writer.

CHAPTER TWO

HIS EARLY LIFE: THE LESSONS

*"There is no such thing as a miracle which violates natural law.
There are only events which violate our limited
knowledge of natural law."*
(ST. AUGUSTINE OF HIPPO. 354 - 430 A.D.)

HIS FAMILY HOME

As was to be expected of humble beginnings so long ago, records of Nostradamus' early life are sketchy. But it is generally agreed that he was born to Renée, an ex-doctor's daughter, at St. Rémy in Provence on 14 December in 1503. It was into a household of uncertain faith. His paternal grandfather Peyrot, a Jewish grain merchant, had married a Gentile. And faced with persecution by the Church their son Jacques, Nostradamus' father, became an at least nominal convert to Christianity. This probably accounts for some records showing that the infant Nostradamus was registered as "Jehan to be called Jean", and others as Michel the only forename he used in later life. Whenever it really was that his family acquired the surname de Notre Dame, - later corrupted in Michel's case to Nostradamus, - the expediency of choosing words carefully was something he would have absorbed with his mother's milk.

HIS EDUCATION

Michel proved to be such a bright child that his grandfathers insisted on taking over his early education themselves. They taught him mathematics, astrology, Hebrew, Greek and Latin.

But by the age of nineteen he had not learned to match his precision with words to equal care about who heard them. He was studying philosophy at Avignon when he was overheard suggesting that the earth moves round the sun. As Galileo was to be sentenced to life imprisonment for saying that, it was a serious mistake to do so. Michel was sent away, to study medicine at Montpellier university.

In 1529 he graduated from Montpellier. But after four years in the field, gaining experience in treating the plague, he returned to the university. This was to improve on his bachelor degree. And despite the faculty's suspicions about some of the ideas produced by his active mind, his outstanding abilities were so obvious that he emerged with a doctorate. He stayed on at the university as a teacher. But soon his opposition to the practice of bleeding patients who were already weak caused trouble, and he had to move away.

HIS TRAVELS

Practising medicine as he went, he travelled the plague-ridden districts of southern France until, at Toulouse, he received a letter from the renowned Giulio Cesare Scaligero. His reply so impressed Scaligero that the young doctor was invited to come and visit him at Agen. He did so, and then took lodgings in Agen so that they could continue to meet.

This was a crossroads in Nostradamus' life. Scaligero was a philosopher, poet, and well-known literary critic. He was distinguished in botany, mathematics and medicine. He also had one of the best brains in Europe, and had studied astrology under his fellow Italian Luca Gaurico about whom we are to hear again.

As his medical practice there prospered, Nostradamus settled down in Agen. He married well, to an Adriète de Loubéjac, and they had two children. But then, suddenly, everything went wrong for him. The 'Black Death' came to Agen; and when it killed his wife and children it finished his practice there as a doctor. For if he could not save his own family, his patients reasoned, he would not be much help to anyone else's. It was a hurtful public reaction, in which his contempt for stupid people, so clear from his writings later, may have had its origin.

Next, he and Scaligero quarrelled, and his dead wife's family sued him for her dowry back. That was not the end of his misfortunes. In 1538 the Inquisition issued a summons for him to appear before it to explain a remark he had been overheard making about a statue of the Virgin Mary. And also about his friendship with Antoine Philibert Sarazin, a Protestant. The latter was a doctor of medicine at Lyons who, when they too quarrelled, accused Nostradamus of practising witchcraft.

It was a sad time for Nostradamus. His life appeared to have come apart. Yet later, with hindsight, he may himself have recognised that the Fate which had seemed to conspire against him had really achieved something else. It had forced him out of a humdrum life into a new course for which he would prove uniquely qualified.

Reluctant to chance being tortured by the Inquisition, he took off, keeping near the German border, and then moving down Italy to Sicily. It was a route littered with many of the places the names of which he uses in his prophecies. And it was in Italy, with his circumstances keeping his recent traumas in his thoughts, that there occurred the first recorded instance of what he was going to develop into an ability to see into the future at will.

It happened one day in a street, when he noticed a young Franciscan monk, a swineherd from Ancona. Nostradamus greeted the young man who was named Felice Peretti as "Your Holiness". It is not known whether he gave any explanation to Peretti for addressing him in a way which might have been mistaken for sarcasm. But nineteen years after the strange Frenchman who had accosted him was dead, Peretti would have understood what he had meant. For the once rustic youth with no apparent expectations of advancement in the Church was elected pope, in 1585, as Sextus V.

HIS RETURN TO FRANCE

In 1544, having decided it should now be safe to do so, Nostradamus returned to France. He settled in Salon en Craux in

Provence. There, on 11 November, 1547, he wedded Anne Ponsarde Gemelle with whom he was to have three sons and three daughters who all outlived him. This marriage to the wealthy widow Gemelle may be seen by those who are superstitious about such things as another sign of the hand of a god in his life. For now, mature and many lessons learned, he could afford to devote his time to developing a technique for obtaining precognition. There is room for doubt about what that method was, so this will be discussed in a later chapter.

CHAPTER THREE

HIS LATER LIFE:
HIS LESSONS LEARNT

*"The slenderest knowledge that may be obtained
of the highest things is more desirable than
the most certain knowledge of lesser things."*
(ARISTOTLE. 384 - 322 B.C.)

HE PUBLISHES LES PROPHÉTIES

Nostradamus went into print cautiously. For the first five years from 1550 his almanacs predicted nothing more-controversial than local events and the weather. These having been accepted without trouble from the Church, there appeared the first edition of what had been ten years in preparation. In 1555 "Les Prophéties de Michel Nostradamus" was published by Mace Bonhomme, a printer at Lyons.

The ripples from it did not take long to spread. Trying to solve its puzzling verses became all the rage at the French court. And within a year its author was sent for to appear before the queen, Catherine de Medici.

When he returned from the court to Salon, though he still had to look over his shoulder for agents of the Inquisition, with an interview with the queen herself under his belt he could continue publishing with relative safety. The sympathetic attention which Nostradamus gives to monarchs in his verses reflects his gratitude for this protection which their interest afforded him. It contrasts with his ambiguous treatment of the Church, which later banned his books.

His success continued as more and more of his prophecies were connected with events which then happened. Two years after that first edition of Les Prophéties was published he had drafted a second, with twice as many predictions in it. And sleeping only four or five hours a night he kept working on another. To cope with this output and the visitors it produced, Nostradamus had to employ a secretary, Jean Aymes de

Chavigny, who later became his biographer.

Nostradamus now had so international a reputation that de Chavigny was to recall that "Those who came to France sought Nostradamus as the only thing to be seen there". And it occasioned little surprise when on the fifth of December 1560 the king, Francis II, died; nor when, before that month was out, the young heir of the junior branch of the Valois family also died. For at the beginning of that month the Tuscan ambassador to the French court had sent this report to Duke Cosimo of Florence.

"The health of the king is uncertain and Nostradamus, in his predictions for this month, says that the royal house will lose two young members from an unforeseen sickness."

A NEW PHENOMENON

There had been prophets around for thousands of years. They were either in the Bible or soon proved to be wrong, so even the Church was not greatly concerned. But Nostradamus soon proved to be a new phenomenon. He was a layman, and worse, his prophecies consistently turned out to have been correct. The political establishments of the day, as we have seen, were confident of their positions and merely found his predictions intriguing, even useful. But many lesser men felt their small worlds threatened, and sought to stir up their rulers against him. Such a man was William Fulke who, in London in 1560, went into print with this "Antiprognosticon that is to saye, an invective agaynst the vayn and unprofitable predictions of the astrologians". And in order to appreciate the stir which Nostradamus' accuracy caused during his own lifetime, even beyond France, it is worth reading this.

"Yea, this Nostradamus reigned here so like a tyrant with his soothsayings, that without the good luck of his prophecies, it was thought that nothing could be brought to effect. What - shall I speak of the common peoples' voice? 'This day the Bishop of Rome must be driven out of his parliament'; 'Tomorrow the Queen shall take upon her the name of Supreme Head'; 'After twenty days all things shall wax worse'; 'Such a day shall be the day of the Last Judgement' - that except the true preachers of God's holy word had sharply rebuked the people for crediting such vain prophecies, there should have been none end of fear and expectation."

Just under average height, Nostradamus was well built, with grey eyes deep-set in a wrinkled but ruddy and open face above a forked beard. He now had gout, and though his movements were quick so too was his temper. But behind these features, and a liking for listening to others rather than talking himself, there was still the excellent memory and subtle mind which was producing riddles half Christendom was now trying to decipher.

A PROPHET IN HIS OWN LAND

He had become an exception to the adage that no man is a prophet in his own land, and what happened in 1564 put this beyond doubt. At that time the entire royal court was on a two-year progress through France, to introduce the new king, Charles IX, to his people. In all the towns through which it passed the royal train was met with bunting and with proud and grateful speeches. People from other places had to make do with lining the route and cheering. The little town of Salon was one of the latter. Those of its citizens who had wanted to glimpse the famous people of their day had made their way to Avignon where the court had rested for a fortnight. They were therefore astonished when those of their neighbours who had gone to the main road to cheer the royal family as it passed, now rushed back into Salon with the news. At the turnoff to Salon the baggage train and the retinue had gone straight on. But the king himself, his brothers, his sister and their mother the dowager Catherine de Medici, had branched off and were at this very moment riding straight towards their town.

When this news was at last believed, confusion reigned. Carpenters were put to erecting a platform in the town centre, and the local haberdashery was ransacked for red and white velvet in which to deck it. While all this was going on, the delighted town fathers composed the most fulsome speeches they could come up with at short notice; and everyone rushed home to put on their best clothes. At last everything was ready. When word spread that the royal family was in sight, all that remained unsettled was the order in which the prominent citizens would address their king on this historic day. They need not have bothered. They all lost the argument. As soon as the first speech started it was interrupted by the young king himself.

"We've really come to see Nostradamus", he explained, bluntly. And wasting no more time, the royal family asked the way to the old man's house, where they all dined with him.

It was during this visit by the court to Salon that Nostradamus noticed a small boy among the retinue who, embarrassed at finding himself the object of sudden attention, ran away and hid. But the next morning the child was found and after examining moles on the boy's body the elderly doctor turned to Catherine and announced that one day this lad would be the king of France.

His words caused consternation, because Catherine had living sons, and the boy indicated was not even a Valois. Yet that the child with the moles was the young Henry of Navarre, who indeed later became King Henry IV of France, is less interesting in itself to the reader today than what the fact that he made such a prophecy illustrates. For it was a prediction which would not prove to have been accurate until 1589, which was twenty-three years after Nostradamus himself was dead. So he could not benefit from it, and in the meantime it could only upset his patron. Yet he made it; even after having a night in which to think it over. This suggests that by now his caution was being eroded by a perhaps superstitious belief that his gift automatically carried with it a duty to use it to the full, whatever the consequences.

Of course he had enjoyed the acclaim with which his work had been received, the material comforts which came with it; and doubtless, too, the feeling of "I told you so". Originally these things may have been all that he wanted. Before the first edition was published, however, his ambitions had almost certainly begun to extend far beyond such limits. Carried by thoughts not easily understood by men for whom the purpose of life is to close both hands round passing coins.

HIS OLD AGE

Charles IX gave Nostradamus the title of Counsellor and Physician to His Majesty. When the old man returned to Salon again, suffering now from dropsy, he retired to the room in which he both slept and worked. On 1 July 1566 he was found dead at his desk.

Years earlier he had written this. "Back from court, gift of the king, confined to place, nothing he will do with it. Nearest family of my blood and friends, find quite dead, near the bed and the bench. Will have gone to God."

It is worth conjecture as to whether his views on his own death gave him the courage to make his undiplomatic disclosure about Henry of Navarre. For his dedication of the first edition of Les Prophéties to his infant son Caesar parallels the giving by Enoch of his revelations about the future of mankind to his son Methusaleh. Because Enoch's passing was not death, and an end. Instead, he "walked with God".

CHAPTER FOUR

THE PROPHECIES

"Your sons and daughters shall prophesy, your old men shall dream dreams, your young men shall see visions."
(JOEL. II, 28.)

WHAT NOSTRADAMUS WROTE

He wrote history,....before it unfolded. Much of what he predicted in his four-line rhyming verses came true during his lifetime. But the real value of their immediate popularity was not in the material comforts this brought him, for which his wife's money was sufficient. Nor was it in the protection that Royal approval brought. It was that acclaim in his own lifetime was essential if his prophecies were not to be forgotten at his death. So although those verses are of little interest today, we owe to them the survival of the others, including those about events still to come.

He wrote only about Europe. The great events of the other continents are nowhere to be found, save insofar as Europe is directly involved. Hence the American Civil War, the Communist revolutions in Russia and China, the military then economic rise of Japan, and so on, are not mentioned; but we do find the execution of Charles I.

HOW HE WROTE

Nostradamus maintains his readers' interest by using words which will mean something, if not quite as much, in one century as another. A galley, for example, remains a ship even when there are no longer ships of that design. But that freedom with obsolete terms only works forwards. Technology has produced things, such as aircraft, of which our ancestors had no knowledge. So for their sakes Nostradamus speaks of these as birds. And because Nostradamus was not an ornithologist, the more intelligent of our ancestors knew he did not mean birds of the feathered kind; but things hidden from themselves in the future. And this is what puts today's readers in a different position from that of our predecessors. For there is nothing in Les Prophéties which awaits further technological innovations in order to be recognised. The period in which we live therefore appears to be the last about which Nostradamus wrote predictions.

However, Les Prophéties was unfinished when Nostradamus died, so there may be no significance in its ending where it does. He had randomly grouped his verses into ten chapters which he called 'Centuries', among which each hundred verses is similarly scattered without chronological order or connection one with the next. And the seventh 'century' is incomplete. But even had it been complete, it may be that only Nostradamus, rather than history, had run out of time. Certainly, verse VI 2 says no more than that, "Around 1905, a strange century will be in store".

WHY NOSTRADAMUS MADE PREDICTIONS

Millions of people have had extra-sensory experiences of one sort or another, including precognitions. Most accept premonitions as a feature of life and think little more about them. Nostradamus, though, had noticed that the earth goes around the sun and had wanted to know why. He was that rarity, a thinking man. So for him there had to be a reason for precognitions, a proper use for them. But beyond perfecting a technique to encourage them to come, he was faced with deciding what to do with them when they did. Either nothing; or to pass them on to other people in prophecies.

THE RIGHTS AND WRONGS OF PROPHESYING

The former course was counselled by the Church, whose dogma condemned prophecy and denied that it could have value. Isaiah XLIII carries this warning. "Let now the astrologers, the stargazers, the monthly prognosticators, stand up and save thee from the things that shall come upon thee. Behold, they shall be as stubble; the fire shall burn them." However, when in Acts VIII 13 and 14, Simon Magus offers to buy their trade secrets from the Apostles, and "Peter said unto him, 'Thy silver perish with thee, because thou hast sought to obtain the gift of God with money' ", Nostradamus can scarcely have failed to be suspicious. After all, Isaiah's outburst in particular was coming from a man who was a prophet himself, and was aimed at his lay rivals. And Peter's scolding of Simon Magus continues, "Thou hast neither part nor lot in this matter". That these curses were evidence only of there being one rule for insiders, and another for everyone else, was a natural conclusion.

Posed against hostile attitudes though, were the opinions of many of those men upon whose ideas Nostradamus had been brought up. Among these were Plato, who wrote of "Prophecy, the noblest of the arts", and Socrates who called it, "The special gift of heaven, and the source of the chiefest blessings among men". And many outstanding men of the Ancient World had displayed tacit approval of prophets, by consulting oracles. Among these were Alexander the Great who had done so at Ammon and Delphi, Germanicus at Clarus Apollo at Colophon, Hannibal at Ammon, Lycurgus at Delphi, Titus at the Paphian Venus on Cyprus, and Trajan at Heliopolis; and the last king of Rome, Tarquin, had paid a fortune for her books of prophecies to the sibyl of Cumae.

Even so, the Roman world as a whole furnished no more definite a guide as to the morality of prophesying than did the Bible. For though it was the patriotic duty of every Roman citizen to report any natural phenomenon which might be a heavenly portent of a future event, so that professional augurs and the priests in charge of the Sibylline Books could consider what action to take, there were also other opinions in Rome.

The milder ones merely considered that, assuming the future could be known, people would be happier without that knowledge. Others took a more critical line, as Tacitus records in his Annals. "The senate also ordered the expulsion of astrologers and magicians from Italy. One was thrown from the Tarpeian Rock; another executed by the consuls in traditional fashion to the sound of the bugle". And both Augustus and Tiberius had books of prophecy other than those of the Cumaean sibyl destroyed.

And had everyone agreed on the value of prophecy, there remained other factors to be weighed. There was the possibility that acting upon precognitions, using them as warnings, might interfere with God's plans for us. On the other hand, it could be argued that if God did not want premonitions to be acted on, He would not provide them. Even today, thoughtful men tend to balance such considerations with care. In the sixteenth century such matters were complicated by deeply held religious beliefs and superstitions.

In short, Nostradamus' position was much like that of the Persian officer about whom he had read in Herodotus. The Persian complains to Thersander that "The worst pain a man can have is to know much and to be impotent to act". But there was, too, another thread running through the argument. It was the possibility that on Judgement Day God sorts wheat from chaff according to spirituality, judged in tests set by precognitions. If this were so it might be crucial that he should turn his own into prophecies through which God might work His designs. In Nostradamus' case it may well have been this argument that tipped the scales. And hence his wish that;

> "Aprés la terriene mienne extinction,
> Plus fera mon écrit qu'a vivant".

> "After my earthly passing,
> My writ will do more than during life".

CHAPTER FIVE

DEVELOPING THE PRECOGNITION

"Tell me what a man dreams
and I will tell you what he is".
(ARAB PROVERB.)

HIS STATED METHOD

In the first two verses of Les Prophéties Nostradamus describes his technique for divination. Each night, in his study at the top of the house, he would wash from himself the smells associated with the workaday world and put on clean clothes. That done, he would sit down in front of a metal tripod on top of which rested a bowl of water. In the light cast by a single candle he would watch and occasionally disturb the water by moving the tripod with a wooden wand held between his legs. As he gazed, fixedly, at the water, visions would appear on its glassy surface.

This was a technique known as scrying. It had been described in De Mysteriis Egyptorum, a book by the fourth century writer Iamblichus, which had been republished at Lyons in 1547.

Nostradamus certainly did examine ideas associated with ancient Egypt. Shortly after De Mysteriis came out locally, he himself translated into French The Book of Orus Apollo, Son of Osiris, King of Egypt. This was, though, merely a work on ethics and not connected with occult practices.

Scrying with tripod and water was already a widely established technique. It was the method held to have been used at Delphi in Greece, where from 1,000 B.C. until 390 A.D. there had been the most famous of all oracles. At Delphi, from the basement 'place that must not be entered', having washed in the sacred spring Cassotis, the priestess-mediums issued, often written on leaves, predictions for which kings across the

Mediterranean and Near East would wait before sending orders to their armies.

But, in practice, consultations at Delphi were usually delayed by formalities. The visitors, isolated there among the mountains, were obliged to lodge with priests and other temple employees who were skilled at drawing information from their guests. And the siting of many state treasuries in the sanctuary of the temple precincts ensured that the priests already had a second-to-none knowledge of the current international situation. Add to these circumstances the fact that, with the excuse that this was necessary in order that the medium's advice be understandable by the client, the priests altered her words as they saw fit. And nowadays it would be judged naive to believe that the usually excellent advice given by the oracle really came from a woman looking at a bowl of water.

That Nostradamus really believed that it had done so is unlikely, especially after he had experimented himself. But if he did believe it, and practised scrying himself, that he would then give away his technique to all and sundry is most unlikely. The magician does not volunteer how he gets the rabbit from the hat.

Yet, with the Inquisition breathing down his neck, he had to be ready to say something. Safety lay in claiming merely to be following an old tradition. He could point out that Plutarch, whose Parallel Lives was among his literary sources, had actually been a priest at Delphi, an oracle mentioned in Caesar's Civil Wars and widely in classical literature. Also that Iamblichus' book had not been banned. And the method it outlined, also, conveniently, happened to be one which would explain why Nostradamus needed to be undisturbed at night.

USE OF DREAMS

And passing the nights alone would have been all that was necessary in order to protect his secret, if this was that his precognition came in directed dreams interrupted only while he recorded them before returning to sleep for more.

The latter technique is very simple, for far less active

brains than that of Nostradamus. In this, sleep is immediately preceded by a self-imposed light hypnotic trance which is induced in seconds. The chosen subject of the dream is thought about while in this state, and instructions are given to oneself to waken as soon as the dream has been presented. If the first dream does not furnish sufficient detail, or its symbolism is too involved, these doubts can be cleared up by further dreams. It is an extraordinarily easy process from the word go. And as Nostradamus gained experience his dreams would have become lucid. From then on he would have directed them from within the dreams themselves, asking what questions he wished from those people he was dreaming about.

That Nostradamus at least considered dreams as his route to precognition can safely be assumed, because they were widely accepted to have this purpose in the Classical World in which he was steeped. Admittedly, some writers had advised caution. In Herodotus he would have read what the Magi said to Astyages, that "Dreams - they often work out in something quite trivial". And in Sirach 34, "Unless the Most High has sent you the dream, pay no attention to it". Virgil too agreed that though dreams can furnish guidance, some do not. He wrote that they can sometimes provide visions of the future. But not always. As he put it, if they come through a gate of horn they are true, and if through a gate of ivory they are false.

Some people never found out which gate their dream had come through. Cicero was one. He was in the Capitol in Rome on this day, chatting about a dream he had had the night before. In his dream a young man had descended from the sky, down a golden chain, Cicero recounted. Suddenly he interrupted his story. "But there's the actual boy I dreamed of!" he exclaimed, staring across the crowded chamber at a then unknown youth. Though Cicero did not live to see his dream explained, the young Gaius Octavian at whom he had pointed was to become master of most of the known world as Augustus Caesar.

From childhood, Nostradamus' reading had abounded in such anecdotes as that; some historical, some mythical. In his

The Voyage of the Argonauts, Apollonius of Rhodes had woven into the story his own opinion of dreams. "Euphemus then remembered that he had had a dream in the night, and in deference to Hermes, god of dreams, he took pains to recall it".

Among many others who had had cause to believe in prophetic dreams had been such men as Alexander the Great, Daniel and Nebuchadnezzar. And even Plato, though he judged deliberate efforts to see into the future as mad, accepted that it would be unwise to ignore a dream.

For Nostradamus, the idea of using dreams as a means of obtaining precognition would have followed automatically from the opinions of so many people who had shaped western culture and influenced him from when he was old enough to read. And directed dreams would have furnished the considerable detail in which his prophecies are rich.

In his usual weblike manner, Nostradamus does supply hints that dreams are indeed his source of precognition. One of these occurs in his preface to the first edition of Les Prophéties, in the words, "Although by ambiguous opinions exceeding all natural reasons by Mahometical dreams..." That is a line which long made no sense to readers, yet had some purpose. It is of course a reference to Mahomet's experience near Mecca, in the cave on Mount Hira. There the Prophet received his call from God, relayed by the archangel Gabriel. Nostradamus would have understood that it was the bell-like quality of the 'voice', which had led to the conclusion that it was that of an angel. From this it would have followed that the Prophet may not have been in ordinary 'sleep' at the time, and so God's message not have been received in a common-or-garden dream. So Nostradamus' purpose in using the phrase 'Mahometical dreams' was to hint at the source of his own visions; even though a general recognition of this would have to await research into the workings of the brain and a reappraisal of the nature of 'time'.

Another such hint is contained in his preface to the second edition. There he refers to characters from the Bible, which contains many stories of visions, 'voices' and dreams. He specifically names Moses and Noah, Jacob whose vision is admitted to come in a dream, and Daniel who rose to prominence as an interpreter of dreams.

It is also relevant that dreams are a ready-made pathway to and from what is now called the unconscious mind, and that Nostradamus' precognition came by night. Though exactly how he obtained it cannot now be known for sure, the balance of probabilities very strongly suggests that it was in dreams of one sort or another. A trail leading to this conclusion had already been laid for us in one of his favourite sources, here in Homer's Iliad.

"For by Dreams the gods sent their messages to mortal men."

CHAPTER SIX

WHY HIS PROPHECIES ARE AMBIGUOUS

"He who does not know of whom to beware bewares of everyone."
(PRE-15TH CENTURY FRENCH PROVERB.)

Nostradamus intended Les Prophéties to be ambiguous. In the Epistle to Henry II with which he prefaces the second edition he warns that "Some may answer that the rhyme is as easy to understand as the sense is hard to get at".

He continues, "Therefore, O most human king, most of the prophetical stanzas are so difficult that there is no way to be found for the interpretation of them". He cannot have meant that to be taken literally, of course. Anything which would never be understood would not have been worth writing. So commonsense dictates that he meant one or both of two things. The first is that only those people able to unravel them were fit to receive the knowledge they contained. The second is that only in what was then the future, and with the benefit of the knowledge men would have accumulated in the interval, would they be understood.

NOT UPSETTING GOD

In this way he also disposes of any lingering hang-up he may have felt about upsetting God. For if He wished the future to remain unknown, ambiguity left the field open for Him to ensure that it did. It was a neat ploy in which: heads, the prophet won; and tails, God lost. And that Nostradamus was reluctant to risk annoying God is evident from the preface to the first edition, in which he says this. "I was willing for the common good to enlarge myself in dark and abstruse sentences, declaring the future events, chiefly the most urgent and those which I foresaw - whatever human changes happened - would not offend the heavens."

KEEP THEM GUESSING

It has been perhaps solely due to the ambiguity of Les Prophéties that it has never been out of print in over four hundred years, which is almost unique among books other than scriptures. That the ambiguities are the reason for this can be seen by comparison with what has happened to the predictions of people such as Cheiro.

The latter was an Englishman who was almost as well-known among the leading people of his day, both here and abroad, as Nostradamus had been in his. The accuracy of Cheiro's predictions was in many instances comparable to that of Nostradamus. But in his books Cheiro wrote in everyday English prose, not in cryptic verse. So it is not by chance that though Cheiro was still writing in the 1930s and did not die until 1939, already, few people other than astrologers have even heard of him.

Many of the masques and tableaux which the leisured classes of the sixteenth century put on for entertainment were enigmatic. Part of the audiences' pleasure derived from guessing what they symbolized. There was little if any tendency then, therefore, to condemn Nostradamus for ambiguity. And that he wrote in verse merely made his riddles easier to remember.

AMBIGUITY WAS TRADITIONAL

Ambiguity has accompanied prophecy from early times. One very practical reason for this was that if an unambiguous prediction proved wrong, the person who had made it would not only look a fool, but if he also had genuine premonitions, these too might be discredited by that one mistake. And if the prediction came true his information might have been said to have come from the Devil, which would put him on an even stickier wicket. And either way it might upset some powerful person. The answer to all these difficulties lay in ambiguity in the wording of the prediction, so that when necessary the prophet could claim that something else had been meant.

Ambiguity was a necessity rather than a choice for Nostradamus, living where and when he did. France in his time was particularly sensitive about anything smacking of beliefs other than those taught by the Church. And this was especially true of anything emanating from Languedoc and Provence. These were the areas in which ancient Manicheism had reappeared in the 12th. century as Catharism. That had been crushed by the Albigensian Crusade, but it had not been entirely wiped out, and nor had the brutal methods of its repression been forgotten. Yet in the 16th. century there was still no clear line between what was permissible and what was not. Francis I was easy-going, not allowing himself to be used as an instrument of the Church unless this coincided with the general good of the realm. By default, he allowed the measure of freedom of thought in which Nostradamus had grown up.

AMBIGUITY IN 16TH CENTURY FRANCE

Francis died in 1547. Henry II, who succeeded him, shifted his religious policy between opposing the politically destructive Reformation, and the need for a soft hand at home while he conducted a war against Spain. He kept the pot from boiling over by punishing heretics only if they left him little choice. It was up to them, when they spoke in public or published their opinions, to convey their meanings in acceptable ways.

Nostradamus could have been luckier in his timing. When he achieved his fame the war with Spain was over, but the threat to the state posed by the Reformation was not. During his reign Henry held back the thirty-six years of religious war with which France was to be stricken from 1562. He did this by switching to a firm line as and when he could. In 1551 this produced an edict establishing the death penalty for heresy and for failure to denounce heretics. That was followed in 1557, just two years after the first publication of Les Prophéties, by the Edict of Compiègne which extended the death penalty to anyone even secretly differing from Roman Catholic beliefs. Nostradamus was treading on very thin ice; and his use of ambiguity would have been fully justified for this down-to-earth reason alone.

AMBIGUITY IN THE CLASSICAL WORLD

But his personal safety aside, it would have been strange had Nostradamus, of all people, broken with tradition and not indulged in ambiguities. For the famous oracles of the Classical World, about which he was so well-read, used them almost all the time. Hence, "I now realise that he - Apollo - himself intends a prophet's revelations to be incomplete, so that humanity may miss some part of Heaven's design", says old Phineas in The Voyage of the Argonauts. That was certainly a subject on which Phineas was well qualified to express an opinion. He had once been a prophet himself, but had then "showed no reverence even for Zeus, whose sacred purposes he did not scruple to disclose in full". For which the god had punished him with blindness, and with a long old age in which to starve and to reflect on his lack of discretion. "My eyes are ruined and there is no cure", he warned his listeners. "I pray, instead, for death to take me soon".

Virgil's hero, Aeneas, seems not to have concerned himself about the reasons for them when he too met with ambiguities, even though he had paid in advance for some advice. This was his experience of an oracle

"Thus did the sibyl of Cumae chant from her shrine
Her dreadful enigmas, and shrouding the truth in dark places."

It was at Cumae that ambiguity had been taught to prophets by the gods themselves, and particularly clearly. Apollo, the god of prophecy, offered the sibyl of Cumae a year of life for each grain of sand she could hold in her hand. It was an offer which she hurriedly accepted. Too late she realised that she ought to have stipulated that she would not grow older during those years. In The Banquet of Trimalchio, in his novel

Satyricon, Petronius tells of the sibyl when she has shrivelled with age into a tiny wizened thing, on display in a bottle. Asked then what she wished for, miserably she replied, "I wish to die".

The Cumaean sibyl learned the hard way to look carefully at anything told by the god of prophecy. She was not alone in this. Failure to do so cost the life of Philip of Macedon, father of Alexander the Great. He had prepared a Greek invasion of Persia, and went to the Delphic oracle for the go-ahead. "The bull is garlanded. All is done. The sacrifice is ready", he was told. Had Philip studied that answer he might have recognised that the rite of 'sacrifice' directly preceded a war. What that prophecy had really warned him about was the completion of a conspiracy to murder him before preparations for the war were complete. A conspiracy which then successfully went ahead.

Croesus, a king of Lydia, also underrated the by then already established place of ambiguity in prophecies. He was wondering whether to invade the empire of the Medes and Persians. Having by a preliminary test-question satisfied himself that the oracle at Delphi really knew its business, he asked it about his chances against Persia. The oracle replied that should he ally himself with the strongest of the Greek states, he would destroy a great empire when he crossed the river Halys. The Halys was his border with Persia, so the invasion duly took place. Poor, careless Croesus! It had never crossed his mind that the empire to be destroyed might be his own. Yet later, when Cyrus the king of Persia allowed the chains to be taken off his prisoner, Croesus sent them in reproof to Delphi. Upon receiving them, the oracle blandly commented that Croesus would have been told which empire would be destroyed, had he bothered to ask.

In that instance the oracle's client had been a man so wealthy that we still use the phrase "as rich as Croesus". Having liked the big donation to temple funds that had accompanied Croesus' question, the oracle's reply had been worded in a way which invited a further question. But that is not the main point. Which is that neither Philip nor Croesus had their money's-worth, simply because they accepted predictions without carefully examining the wording.

Themistocles of Athens did not make that mistake. The 6th century BC Heraclitus, who was himself known as 'the Dark One' because his philosophy was expounded in cryptic phrases, had written that the Delphic oracle "Neither utters nor hides its meaning, but shows it by a sign". So when Themistocles, worried about the impending Persian invasion of Greece and what to do about it, went to Delphi, he knew he would have to examine the answer carefully. It came in these words.

> "Safe shall the wooden wall continue for thee and thy
> children.
> Yet shall a day arrive when ye shall meet him in battle.
> Holy Salamis, thou shalt destroy the offspring of women,
> While men scatter the seed, or when they gather the
> harvest."

Themistocles guessed that the 'seed' was the money in Athens, and the 'harvest' would be the result of how the defence budget was spent. Also working out that 'the wooden wall' did not refer to the city wall which had once been made of wood, but to ships, he spent the money on the navy. And his care about interpreting the prophecy correctly paid off. The Greek navy defeated the Persians,....and at Salamis!

Nostradamus, too, wanted to be understood only by men able and prepared to think. For everyone else, especially for those who would even believe what he said about using a tripod and bowl of water, - despite his having separated this from his prophecies by putting it into verses I 1 and 2, - bluntly he had this to say, in verse VI 100.

> "Qui legent hosce versus, maturè censunto,
> Profanum vulgus et inscium ne attrectato:
> Omnesque Astrologi, Blennis, Barbari procul sunto,
> Qui aliter facit, is rite sacer esto."

"Let those who read this verse, think about it carefully.
And idiots, ignoramuses, barbarians and foulmouths,
the common herd, keep away; and all astrologers far away.
And he who is different, let him use it with respect."

CHAPTER SEVEN

A MAN OF HIS TIME

"He is in a tavern for nothing, who does not drink."
(PRE-15TH CENTURY FRENCH SAYING.)

PUZZLES

Understanding Les Prophéties has already been compared in this book to the cracking of a cryptic crossword. It is a useful comparison. Let us pursue it here. Often, words in the cryptic clues themselves show something about the man who compiled the puzzle. For example, if he is a sailor, then nautical terms tend to appear among his clues; and for that same reason they can be expected among the solutions which we are seeking. There is nothing surprising about this. After all, seafaring matters have occupied his thoughts for years. So it is always a good start to find out what subjects the compiler is likely to know about. Then, when we have short-listed several words which fit the space and the clue, it is frequently the fact that one of these is, in our example, nautical, which finally identifies it as the right one. In other words, we begin by identifying the compiler's own specialized knowledge and interests, before using them against him in order to unlock his meanings.

All that, however, is of course no help unless one knows nautical terms oneself. So if we are to make use of this method in order to understand Les Prophéties, we do need to know as much as possible about Nostradamus' background; beyond when he was born and when he died, that he was French and a doctor. For if we knew only that much about him our interpretations of his prophecies would be almost as inaccurate as are weather forecasts from our Met. Office.

WHAT NOSTRADAMUS KNEW

When we speak of Nostradamus' background we mean all

those factors which, - assuming he was in this respect like other people, - influenced him, and produced his thoughts, his knowledge and his intentions. We have already seen most of the little that is known about his personal life. Fortunately, more is known about the age which contained the other things that moulded him. And these explain much more about Les Prophéties than hitherto seems to have been realised.

A glance through Les Prophéties shows that his interests included ancient, medieval and Renaissance astrology, geography, history, languages, literature and mythology. But the readers of this book should not despair! There will be no need for them to poke around among dusty tomes. This has been done for them already, and this book contains all the information on these subjects that is required. All that is left for readers to do is to separate those meanings which they themselves might otherwise have attributed to words, from those meanings which Nostradamus gave or would have considered giving to them.

PLACES THAT MOVE

Some place-names no longer convey quite what they did to the writers of Nostradamus' sources. This can be illustrated by referring to the dictionary forming Part Four of this book. For examples, as this dictionary will remind the reader, *AFFRIQUE, ASIE* and *GERMANIE* once covered significantly different areas from those we include in Africa, Asia and Germany today. This need for care with place-names becomes even clearer once we admit that we would have assumed that 'Iberia' must always have meant the Spanish and Portugese peninsula, and 'Albania' always to have referred to that country in the Balkans. For such assumptions would be wrong. In fact, in the ancient world, on the geography of which Nostradamus so often draws, an Iberia and an Albania were both between the Caucasus and Iran, in what is now Azerbaydzhan!

Locations based on mythology also require careful treatment. An example arises from the word 'Hyperboreans', (see BOREAS). What Herodotus, for example, actually records is this. "Above them" - the Issedones - "dwelt the Arimaspi, men with one eye; still further, the gold-gathering Griffins; and beyond these the Hyperboreans, who extended to the sea." 'Hyperborean' means 'Beyond the North Wind'. Hence the ancient Greeks accorded to *BOREAS* and *GRIFFON* the locations which Nostradamus gives them in verses II 99 and X 86. That is what matters. We must not care that modern scholarship suggests the ancient Greeks had probably got it wrong; that the Hyperboreans may originally have been the Chinese. Even that the Hyperboreans were never more than inhabitants of a fictitious land which, being located beyond the source of the North wind, had an ideal climate to which, in due course, credit for social ideals became attached; an early Shangri-la! Remember, they are 16th century 'facts' on which Les Prophéties is based,...not ours.

To assume that Nostradamus uses a place-name or any other word in the sense that automatically occurs to the modern reader is very often to be wrong,...as so many of his more sensation-mongering modern commentators insist on proving!

SOURCES FROM THE ANCIENT WORLD

Nostradamus widely uses stories told in books of histories and myths, in order to describe events to come. His references to *DACE* and *PANNONS,* to which we will return later, are examples of this. It is a method which allows him to supply considerable detail in as little as a single word. Though the stories which he selects resemble the events to come, this does not of course mean that the old story and the coming event will be identical. The one is, - as if in a lengthy simile, - 'like' the other; like enough for the resemblance to be hard to miss, and a sufficient guide to what will happen.

Unfortunately, in many instances more than one story has become associated with a single person, creature or place; and in some cases there is more than one version of the same basic story. But this complicates things more in theory than it does in practice. In fact, there is a reliable guide as to which version of a story Nostradamus is using. To begin with, it will appear in the literature of the ancient world, and specifically, from an author whose work or works Nostradamus uses in other instances. And, usually, it will also appear in Renaissance literature.

Nostradamus' sources from the Classical World include the drama of Aeschylus, the geographies of Pausanias and Strabo, the mythology of Hesiod and the histories of Homer, Thucydides and Xenophon, and the natural histories of Pliny the Elder. And perhaps above all Pliny the Younger whose *"Auguror ....historias tuas immortales futuras"* or "I prophesy that your histories will be immortal," confirmed Nostradamus' decision to tell about the future through parallels with the past.

AMMIANUS MARCELLINUS. (c330 - ? AD)

A Greek officer serving in the Roman army in Asia, Egypt, Greece and Rome, Ammianus was a lesser known historian. His work, the last history in Latin from the ancient world, probably came to Nostradamus' attention because it included an account of the great fire on the Palatine Hill in Rome. It was this blaze on 19 March, 363 AD in which the original books of prophecy purchased by Tarquin from the Cumaean sibyl at such expense, went up in flames. Once though that Ammianus had attracted Nostradamus' notice, he certainly held it. His account of the counter-claims on Rome's attention, posed by events in the Balkans and the Middle East, were far too useful a vehicle in which Nostradamus could predict their parallels today, for him to have passed up such an opportunity.

GAIUS JULIUS CAESAR. (c101 - 44 BC)

Caesar's written works are not particularly relevant to coming events. But he wrote with great clarity about things in which he he himself had been deeply involved. Though he seems not to have inspired many ideas in Nostradamus, as a source he was reliable, and one of his main stamping-grounds was the area in which Nostradamus spent most of his life.

PLUTARCH. (50 - c120 AD)

Where would many writers, Nostradamus among them, have been without Plutarch? Shakespeare, for one, might have been up a gumtree. This, for example, is what Shakespeare's Julius Caesar says of one of the conspirators.

"Let me have men about me that are fat,
Sleak-headed men and such as sleep a-nights.
Yond Cassius has a lean and hungry look,
He thinks too much: such men are dangerous.
Would he were fatter! But I fear him not."

Shakespeare had merely expanded Caesar's words here in Plutarch;

"It is not the fat, sleak-headed men I am afraid of, but the pale, lean ones".

And lifting ideas from Plutarch had started in Italy and caught on in France several centuries before this practice crossed the Channel to England. However, though both Rabelais and Nostradamus read him in the original Greek, their open attention to him was unpopular with the 16th century Church because Erasmus had compared his writing to the Bible.

Plutarch refers to such characters from mythology as Diana/*DIANE* and Hercules/*HERCLE;* also to Lusitania/*LUSITANIE* (see quatrain IX 49). And his habit of travelling great distances to Athens, just to obtain the right sourcebooks, let alone his actually being a priest at Delphi, had almost ensured his use by Nostradamus.

CORNELIUS TACITUS. (c55 - c120 AD)

Though Tacitus was sometimes careless about details, he was a close friend of Pliny the Younger and became a Roman senator, then consul, and then the governor of Asia/*ASIE*. He was therefore well-placed to write histories. In these he too mentions, for example, Hercules/*HERCLE,* and he explains beliefs about such gods as *MARS,* Mercury/*MERCURE* and *SOL* held by peoples then beyond the Roman sphere.

He was born in Gallia Narbonensis/*NARBON,* Nostradamus' own homeground, which might by itself have qualified him as a source for Les Prophéties. But that was certainly not the only reason. His account of what happened in Eastern Europe, which parallels so closely what Nostradamus predicts is to happen again, would also have been qualification enough in itself.

HESIOD. (8TH CENTURY BC)

Greek poetry, Hesiod's versions of myths have long and widely been accepted as the orthodox accounts. From Hesiod's description of Typhoeus/*TISON* it is not difficult to understand why Nostradamus uses references to this titan through which to warn against our institutionalising the terrorism which will exact the high cost he describes. Here is a part of Hesiod's description.

"Out of his shoulders came a hundred fearsome snake-heads with black tongues flickering, and the eyes in his strange heads flashed fire under the brows; and there were voices in all his fearsome heads, giving out every indescribable sound ....A thing past help would have come to pass that day, had the father of gods and men not taken sharp notice."

PUBLIUS OVIDIUS NASO. (43 BC - 18 AD)

Of all writers in the Classical World, Ovid has left the deepest mark on subsequent literature. Here, in Act 4, scene 2 of Love's Labour's Lost, Shakespeare says;

"Ovidius Naso was the man: and why, indeed, Naso, but for smelling out the odoriferous flowers of fancy, the jerks of invention."

That was very much Nostradamus' reason for using him. Ovid sparked ideas in Nostradamus as he did in Shakespeare. Ovid tells of Aeolus (see *ALUS*), of *BOREAS,* of the titaness

SELENE; and, in his Letter from Sappho to Phaon, also of Typhoeus/*TISON.*

This presentation of characters whom Nostradamus was to knit together in order to add extra levels to his meanings for them, was Ovid's passport to influence on Les Prophéties. So far as Nostradamus was concerned, Ovid had not needed to point out, as he did, that;

"I shall be on people's lips; in fame through all the ages - if poets' prophecies have any truth in them - I shall live."

PUBLIUS VIRGILIUS MARO. (70 - 19 BC)

Nostradamus certainly read Virgil. From the poet's death until the end of the last century, everyone who could read Latin did read Virgil. Although Nostradamus seldom uses Virgil as a direct source, this is in part only an impression we get. It comes of Virgil having drawn on Hesiod and Homer, and Nostradamus having done the same thing already for himself. However, we still read Les Prophéties with one eye on Virgil, because he retired to live at Cumae, and featured the sibyl there in his Aeneid. And also because, if only on the strength of his Fourth Eclogue, in his own lifetime Virgil was looked on as a seer himself.

CHAPTER EIGHT

A RENAISSANCE MAN

*"O power of fantasy that steals our minds
from things outside, to leave us unaware,
although a thousand trumpets may blow loud -
what stirs you if the senses show you nothing?"*
(DANTE. PURGATORY C.17, V. 5 & 6)

The Renaissance was the period of re-discovery of the art and literature of the Classical World. It began in Italy in the 14th. century. The early Renaissance writers who had the most impact on Nostradamus can be seen to have been Dante and Petrarch.

DANTE ALIGHIERI. (1265 - 1321)

There are similarities between the lives of Dante and Nostradamus. Both were well read, had sharp intellects and looked to the scriptures and to ancient literature for their inspirations. Both of them visited Paris, travelled widely in Italy and had to go walkabout when they had upset their respective establishments. Both lost young wives, - Dante when he was only twenty-five. They both experimented with new literary techniques, - Dante, in his *La Vita Nuova*. Both were influenced by the linguistic traditions of Provençal. Nostradamus' use of the latter's unstylised form is parallel to Dante's *De Vulgari Eloquentia,* 'On the Vernacular Language', in which he argues for the replacement of Latin by Italian regional dialects.

Like Nostradamus, Dante drew widely on classical literature. So widely that his definitions of sins in Inferno come almost straight from Cicero's On Duties, and his whole theme of Divine Comedy mirrors The Dream of Scipio.

Dante, also, made much literary use of astrology, as here in Canto 29, verses 1 and 2 of his Paradise.

"When the twin children of Latona share
the belt of the horizon and are crowned
one by the Ram, the other by the scales".

Both men use similar forms of symbolism, as where Dante alludes to the Roman Empire as 'The eagle that shed feathers'. Even Nostradamus' open contempt for stupid people is comparable to Dante's theme in his *De Monarchia*, 'On Monarchy'. The latter is that mens' goal in life should be to acquire all the knowledge of which they are capable. And in both men this attitude is closely connected to their concern about the future of humanity. In Dante's case this runs throughout The Divine Comedy; and in that of Nostradamus it is the sole thread in Les Prophéties.

Nostradamus is quick to seize on word-plays and ideas suggested by Dante. For example, in Dante's Paradise 'the monster Typhoeus' figures; and here in his Purgatory, in;

"God's emissary, born to kill the giant
and the usurping whore with whom he sins",
is what led Nostradamus to couch his warnings to modern Europe in the words which he uses.

It is not difficult to spot in Dante most of the many passages which sparked off ideas in Nostradamus. Here, in Purgatory c.20, v.17, is another example, this one reflected in Nostradamus' quatrain IX 20 (see Chapter Twenty).

"On earth beyond I was called Hugh Capet;
from me have sprung the Louises and Philips,
rulers of France up to the present day."

Indeed, it is not a great exaggeration to say that one would be hard put to find many words in Les Prophéties which Dante had not already used, and usually with exactly the same meanings.

Francesco Petrarca. (1304 - 1374)
Like that of Dante, Petrarch's life contained much to arouse feelings of fellowship in Nostradamus. In 1312 Petrarch's

family came to live at *AVIGNON*. In his boyhood Petrarch so liked this area, which was later to fire the imagination of Nostradamus, that in 1337 he bought a property near *SORGUES*. His father sent Petrarch to study law at Montpellier, where Nostradamus was to study medicine. And the Black Death, which Nostradamus was to treat and to which he lost his first wife and children, for years kept Petrarch on the move avoiding it, and, in 1348, killed his patron.

The analytical minds of both men led them to reject medical practices of their times. Nostradamus' disagreement with the bleeding of sick people matches Petrarch's attack on medical methods in his *Invectiva Contre Medicum*. In their respective publications, Nostradamus' secondary use of the word *BABYLON*, to mean a fallen existence, catches exactly Petrarch's description of the corrupt papal court at *AVIGNON* as an "earthly Babylon".

Petrarch's poem Africa (see *AFFRIQUE)* is about the conqueror of Hannibal/*ANNIBAL*. And much else in Petrarch has echoes in Nostradamus.

RENAISSANCE ENGLISH LITERATURE

Although Roger Bacon had gone to Paris in the 13th century, to teach among his intellectual peers, and Calais remained English until 1558, cross-Channel traffic in ideas was almost all one-way; from there to here. The fact that the Renaissance spread westward, and did not flower in Britain until a century after it had done so in France, accounts for this. It also accounts for the fact that, despite Nostradamus' interest in future events in Britain, which is to be seen in Les Prophéties, there are few signs that he was even vaguely conversant with English literature.

However, it is worth our taking a look at 16th century and earlier English literature, particularly at its use of astrological references and symbolism. These will show us the styles going out of use in France; and do so in examples familiar to us.

GEOFFREY CHAUCER. (c1343 - 1400)

Chaucer was already familiar with Ovid, and used astrological references to convey such things as times of year or day; and occasionally in making actual predictions.

ROBERT COPLAND. (1508 - 1547)

Copland, in his The High Way to the Spital House, here feels that it is still necessary to explain to his readers what a particular astrological reference means.

"To write of Sol in his exaltation,
Of his solstice or declination,
Or in what sign, planet or degree,
As he in course is used for to be;
Scorpio, Pisces, or Sagittary;....
It were but lost for blockish braines dull;
But plainly to say, even as the time was,
About a fortnight after Hallowmass."

Although Nostradamus positively wanted his readers to have to work in order to understand his references, rather than felt any need to explain them, he would have liked Copland's "blockish braines dull". It expresses the opinion which he himself held of many people, and even more bluntly than does his own quatrain VI 100.

EDMUND SPENSER. (c1552 - 1599)

Spenser studied history, Latin literature, philosophy, rhetoric and science. He spoke French, Italian and Latin; wrote on Plutarch and translated French poetry into English. He raised 16th century English literature by introducing into it ideas from Italy and France. His major work, The Faerie Queene, is packed with the astrological references, mythology and symbolism in which Les Prophéties abounds.

Here is an excerpt from it.

"Vpon a Bull he rode, the same which led
Europa floting through th'Argolick fluds:...
And after her, came iolly Iune, arrayed."

And here is another.

"Next was Nouember, he full grosse and fat,....
For it a dreadful Centaure was in sight,
The seed of Saturne, and fair Nais, Chiron hight."

MODERN ENGLISH COMMENTATORS ON NOSTRADAMUS

In making predictions and then cloaking them from casual
eyes, Nostradamus inevitably invites hostility from readers who
want to know what he predicts, but don't want to match his
labours with their own. While accepting his purpose, they say he
broke too many rules. But the reality is that his purpose
necessitated the means he used. The mere translation of names,
let alone ideas, originating in one language, into verse in another
language, has always been difficult. Pliny the Younger had
recognised this two thousand years ago, as can be seen from his
letter to Caninius Rufus.

"It is an excellent idea of yours to write about the Dacian
war. ....Another problem arises out of the barbaric names,
especially that of the king himself, when the uncouth sounds will
not fit into Greek verse; but every difficulty can be reduced by
skill and application even if it cannot be entirely resolved.
Besides, if Homer is permitted to contract, lengthen and modify
the flexible syllables of the Greek language to suit the even flow
of his verse, why should you be denied a similar licence,
especially when it is a necessity and no affectation?"

That was the question which Nostradamus had had to ask
himself. And his critics would have had a field-day long ago had
he not done as Pliny advised and Homer did.

We have not yet discussed literature from French
Renaissance writers. Yet it may already be dawning on the
reader of this book that much of the difficulty encountered in

understanding Les Prophéties stems from an awesome lack of general knowledge, ...even about our own literature. It would be unkind to say, straight out, that those commentators on Nostradamus who label him a crank of sorts, and criticise his style of writing as being, they allege, strange even for his own time, - with the obvious implication that such a nut could know little about much, let alone the future, - do so to hide the fact that they know so little about the past. Such a suggestion as that would place them in one of the categories Nostradamus refers to in his quatrain VI 100. And to do that, as we have said, would be impolite.

Of course they have not been the blind leading the blind!

CHAPTER NINE

THE FRANCE IN WHICH NOSTRODAMUS WROTE

"It is better to drink from the fountain than from the stream."
(PRE-15TH CENTURY FRENCH SAYING.)

Had Nostradamus lived in some other century or land, he might well not have had that acclaim in his own time without which he would not have been heard of in ours. Chance, if not some trick of the gods, had prepared the ground for him in 16th century France. Then, and there, to make the most of his talent for precognition he merely had to exploit the existing situation. We have already touched on some of the relevant circumstances. Now we will review those and look at others.

THE REFORMATION

Threatening as it did the stability of the political state, the Reformation united Crown and Church against anything which might cloak heresy. But by concentrating attention on those who would reform the Church, it actually diverted hostility away from those who, like Nostradamus, were merely free-thinkers with no political or religious axes to grind.

PRINTING

Gutenberg had perfected a printing-press with moveable type in about 1440. Thirty years later there was still only one such in France, in Paris. But by 1500, three years before Nostradamus was born, there were more than two dozen in the country. Indeed, one historian suggests that there were fifty printers' shops in Lyons alone. We are interested in printing at Lyons because that is where Les Prophéties first went into print.

Nostradamus' choice of Lyons as the place to have his

publishing done was wise. The city had just the right pedigree. It had been there that, under Charlemagne, the Englishman Alcuin had set up his official school for scribes; and in the 16th century the publications from there were still regarded as reliable and authoritative; or to use a modern phrase, 'up-market'.

Dramatically reducing the cost of books, printing gave an enormous boost to literacy and to the spread of new ideas. Overnight, as it were, the barrier between the very few who could afford a book, while these had been laboriously copied out with a pen, and everyone else, disappeared. No longer was thought stimulated only by the Sunday sermon or wandering story-tellers. Ordinary people could now read the scriptures for themselves. The classics and books on all manner of subjects were suddenly available and read.

A mania for printed matter developed, and the sheer volume of publications made censorship difficult and patchy. Previously, the Church had controlled much of what was written, because the copying had largely been done in monasteries. Now it was different. Printing spread like fire, and gave the Reformation much of its success. It certainly did the same for Les Prophéties de Michel Nostradamus.

SOCIAL CLIMBING

As everywhere, the upper class in France had always had at least a limited access to literature. Except through taking holy orders, the lower class had not. And that had been largely that, regardless of an individual's aspirations. But the 16th century witnessed a major change which was not entirely due to the introduction of printing. Between 1470 and 1560 the population of France increased by a third. Traditional ways of passing-on land produced uneconomically small holdings. Some farmers went out of business and were bought-out by their neighbours who were soon able to employ others to do the work. Thus an increasing number of landowners had the money and leisure with which to broaden their lives. They had joined a middle class, the *bourgeoisie*.

In the *bourgeoisie* already were professional people, administrators of all sorts, doctors, judges, lawyers, many priests, ship-owners and teachers; and also, among those who served them, the auctioneers, bailiffs, beadles and hosts of clerks. In their class too were many of those in trades, the apothecaries and more successful shopkeepers of every sort, skilled artisans and their guild-masters, gold and silversmiths and others. All that was necessary to attain entry to their class was enough money to avoid manual labour.

But that was by no means where it all ended. There was still an endless treadmill of social climbing to be done, within the *bourgeoisie,* and, just conceivably, out of it upwards. People became very sensitive to how their neighbours viewed them. Which depended on how they spent their money. At first it was on tapestries, carved furniture, and glass in their windows. But something else soon proved much more effective. This was the book. The mere possession of a book, carefully placed where anyone entering the reception room could not fall to see it, was only the start. Next, in case anyone asked what it was about, it was read. It was also loaned to friends, and to anyone who needed to be favourably impressed; and theirs in turn were borrowed.

Things grew from there. A genuine interest in literature developed, and books began to be borrowed or loaned so that variations between editions could be compared. Other stages followed. Though often still motivated by one-up-manship, people aired their new-found knowledge by quoting from their books; and eventually bought or borrowed source-books to find out what references to them meant. Amassing facts was in due course replaced by the sharing of discoveries, and then by literary criticism. The more that a book provoked thought and discussion, the better it was received. Solving cryptograms and arguing about the meanings of complicated word-plays became a national pastime. It was a situation which we today, having discarded much of our culture in favour of tv soaps and bingo, find hard to imagine. Nevertheless, it is small wonder that Les

Prophéties, written in the style it is, took 16th century France by storm.

16TH CENTURY FRENCH LITERATURE

Literary effects of the Renaissance in France accelerated early in the 16th century. Robert Estiennes' translations of Plato and Xenophon, - naturally, published at Lyons, - appeared even before the troops began returning in 1515 from the wars in Italy with tales and looted examples of the cultural wonders there. Because these influences were foreign, and too intellectually advanced, to appeal to the masses, they at first met with some rejection. But very quickly indeed French writers put that right. Soon available were French translations including Amyot's of Plutarch, Budés' of Thucydides, and Dolet's Commentaries on Cicero.

The intellectual ferment produced was fuelled by the Estiennes' Greek and Latin dictionaries, and allowed the slightly subversive tones of French writers such as Bodin, Montaigne and Rabelais to escape the notice they would have attracted a century earlier. It was not a case of 'anything goes', but it had become a time of literary experiment. This was a nearly ideal situation for Nostradamus. He could place the pagan figures of antiquity, already justified by their permitted importation from Italy, beside references to alchemy, - most treatises on which still appeared in Latin, - make use of his Greek because there were dictionaries about, incorporate the classical mythology for which Dante had prepared the country, and ground it all in French - which had recently replaced Latin for most purposes.

THE FIRST MARKET FOR LES PROPHÉTIES

Les Prophéties held some appeal for almost everyone. There were of course exceptions. At the bottom end of the intellectual range was the vulgar mass, illiterate and unable to comprehend anything above a ballad or a farce. At the top end were those who did not like Nostradamus' unsophisticated rhyming; who failed to realise that only the content was meant to matter; and also that the rough rhyming was intentional, to be attractive lower down the market.

Nostradamus' appeal among literate people was, nontheless, almost universal. He fed the new popular appetite for language and the written word. People with scarcely any idea as to what his verses meant, loved the style in which they were written.

And the more we see of Nostradamus' contemporaries, the easier it continues to be to understand their favourable reactions to the way in which he wrote. Comparison with other French writers of his day shows that his attitudes towards society, and his awareness of what would stimulate his readers, were by no means unshared.

FRANÇOIS RABELAIS. (c1494 - c1554)

Rabelais travelled to Italy, and spent time at Lyons. He took holy orders and studied archaeology, astrology, languages and law. Like Nostradamus, he took a doctorate at Montpellier university, where he too lectured on medicine before practising it. Until 1550 he, also, produced a series of almanacs. Rabelais' approach to the future, however, was wholly different from that of Nostradamus; for his Pantagureline Prognostication was intended to be taken lightly, being suited, in his own words, to "any coming year".

Between 1532 and 1552 the four books of his Gargantua and Pantagruel appeared. They comprise one of the all-time great works of European literature. A fifth book was published in 1562, after his death, but this was probably a forgery, - a penalty of success from which Nostradamus also suffers.

The range of languages employed by Rabelais is even wider than that of Nostradamus. It includes Arabic, Basque, Greek, Latin, Hebrew and almost every French dialect. There is no reason to suppose that Nostradamus and Rabelais ever met. But had Rabelais set out to justify Nostradamus' style of expression, and explain aspirations common in the 16th century to later generations, so that Nostradamus' style would not be misunderstood, he could not have done so better than he did. Here is a passage in a letter from Gargantua to his son Pantagruel.

"Now it is, that the minds of men are qualified with all manner of discipline and the old sciences revived, which for many ages were extinct. Now it is, that the learned languages are to their pristine purity restored, viz., Greek, without which a man may be ashamed to account himself a scholar, Hebrew, Arabic, Chaldaean, and Latin. Printing likewise is now in use, so elegant and so correct, that better cannot be imagined. ....All the world is full of knowing men".

Gargantua's letter goes on to recommend attention to Quintilian, Plato and Cicero, and to cosmography. And it continues;

"(Of) geography, arithmetic and music, I gave thee some taste when thou wert yet little, and not above five or six years old. Proceed further in them, and learn the remainder if thou canst. As for astronomy, study all the rules thereof. Let pass, nevertheless, the divining and judicial astrology, and the art of Lullius, as being nothing else but plain abuses and vanities".

PRECAUTIONS IN 16TH CENTURY FRANCE

Whereas Nostradamus, having found that voicing contempt for established notions on medical practices merely made trouble for him, had reacted by going away and quietly putting his own ideas into effect, Rabelais would not at first shut up. Persistently he tested how far he would be allowed to go. He took on the medical establishment in print, choosing its heart, the Sorbonne, as his target. Like Nostradamus, he counted on the king for protection. But eventually accepted what Nostradamus had been quicker to realise, that even royal favour had its limits. His attack on doctors, in his second edition on the subject, was a much watered down version of his first. The 16th century saw new ideas avidly accepted; but not when they too openly challenged the old ones.

CRYPTOGRAMS

Like Nostradamus, where it served a useful purpose to insert a cryptogram, Rabelais did so. In his criticism of the staff of the Sorbonne he referred to them as *'Nasiborsans'*, *'Sorbonigenes'*, and *'Sorbonagres'*. And he published Gargantua and Pantagruel under the pseudonym *'Alcofribas Nasier'*.

Many modern commentators on Nostradamus have failed even to recognise many of his cryptograms, let alone managed to decipher them. Others have condemned him even for using them. But as we have now seen, they were employed by the most talented and enduring of 16th century French writers. It would have been pointless for Nostradamus, of all men, not to have made full use of them.

CHAPTER TEN

MORE ABOUT THE SIXTEENTH CENTURY

"He who needs fire will seek it with his fingers."
(SAYING IN OLD PROVENCE.)

The wish to enjoy life is older than mankind. But a suspicion that life might have some purpose beyond enjoying earthly experiences was more pervasive in the 16th century than it is today. People of all classes accepted the teaching of the Church, or sought for hints as to what that purpose might be. They felt that there were more things at work in the world than they understood. It is that outlook which we now refer to as their 'superstition'. And it is a mistake to try to judge what they did, or wrote, without taking that into account. Witchcraft, for example, did much to produce royal patronage for Nostradamus.

In 1533 Catherine de Medici, from Italy, married Henry, then Duke of Orleans and second son of the king of France. But when, in 1547, Henry ascended the throne, the pair had all the responsibilities of monarchy descend upon them. One of these was to produce an heir. Time passed, and still no child was born. As pressure on the royal couple increased, they tried yet more prayer and further pilgrimages to shrines to Our Lady of Conception. None of these worked, and for ten years Catherine remained barren.

Eventually, in desperation, Catherine turned to astrologers, whose methods included witchcraft. She persuaded Henry to join her in nocturnal rites which involved the sacrifice of hens and the mixing of their blood with the semen of bulls. Almost immediately, she became pregnant; and on 19 January, 1544, eleven years before Les Prophéties first appeared, her first child was born. From then on, the royal faith in astrologers, in

Catherine at least, continued to be reinforced. For she and Henry went on to breed like a pair of rabbits, until they had had ten children.

Nostradamus himself may or may not have believed in astrology. It did not matter. It was enough that Catherine did so, and that Nostradamus was said to be an astrologer.

THE STUFF OF MYTHS

When, round their fires at night, pre-historic men had finished recounting the details of that day's hunt, the story-tellers took over. Some of their tales have endured, and have come down to us in what we call myths. Like the best fiction today, these were based on facts, such as the rumblings of volcanoes, for which the tales would account. Myths are referred to too often in Les Prophéties, and in the literature on which Nostradamus drew, for his readers to ignore them. It is also important that we recognise the power which anything that is unexplained holds over the human imagination. For the latter, in itself, explains why Nostradamus introduces myths so frequently. If we fail to recognise these factors, there is much in Les Prophéties which will remain above our heads.

It has never taken much to fire the imagination ....often to thoughts of giants. On Staffa in the Hebrides, and in Antrim in Ulster, natural columns of basalt became Fingal's Cave and the Giants' Causeway. And here, in his Aeneid, Virgil's Hercules hunts the monster Cacus to his lair in a volcano where;

"A vision as if earth were rent asunder
To open Hell, and lay bare to the sun
The shadow world where gods go gingerly,....
The monster sought his only means of refuge,
Smoke billowed from his jaws - I swear to you -
To blind the hunter's eyes, and make his den
As black as pitch. Night lay upon the cavern,
And here and there a sullen tongue of flame."

In his books on natural history, Pliny the Elder says of some fossilised sharks' teeth which someone had found, that they "groweth not upon the ground, but in the eclipse of the moon falleth from heaven".

In the 14th century Boccaccio, - a friend of Petrarch and biographer of Dante, - identified the teeth of some extinct animal, then on display in a church at Trapani in Sicily, as those of a giant. He calculated the height of the titan to have been two hundred cubits, about three hundred feet.

But in our approach to Nostradamus we will be the losers if we denigrate our ancestors in any way. As well as such examples of mistakes they made, there are other facts to be born in mind. Until the last century we still disbelieved Homer's tale of Troy. Well into the second half of this century we still harboured the thought that there might be life on Venus and the Moon, and civilisation on Mars! Embarrassing? Yes, but true! And one other thing. Whatever harm they did to our common habitat, while building what we have inherited, they did in ignorance. We are wrecking that inheritance in full knowledge of what we are doing. If there is a dunce's cap to be worn, let us give thought to who it fits. Let us also, regarding Nostradamus in particular, ask ourselves why we are so anxious to understand what he says? It is certainly not out of love for 16th century French literature!

RELICS OF THE PAST

Rabelais' Gargantua and Pantagruel contains reflections of his interest in archaeology. This one is in a letter from Gargantua to his son.

"Here I must not forget to set down unto you a riddle, which was found under the ground, as they were laying the foundation of the abbey, engraven in a copper plate, and it was thus as followeth."

Gargantua's letter then continues with 'A Prophetical Riddle'. Unlike Nostradamus, however, Rabelais was only story-telling. But in that same period the Renaissance also kindled in Nostradamus an awareness that the relics of the past, which he too saw round him, could be used to carry predictions.

As we will see, he makes such a use of the names of the places he had travelled through, and of legends attached to these. Yet what we most expect to find in Les Prophéties are references to things in or near St. Rémy, where he had passed his formative years, and his lifelong absorption in mythology and the ancient world had its origins. For this is the countryside that, as an impressionable adolescent, he had roamed, with his grandfathers' teachings in his ears. What then had he seen, and Les Prophéties show that he had remembered?

Local references include those to the river DURANCE and to the Lubéron mountains (see LEBRON). One of the many others concerns that strange desert known as the Crau. It is a landscape of stones deposited there by the river DURANCE as it altered its course through the ages. It had fired human imaginations before Strabo recorded the myth which had grown round it. This tells that JUPITER had supplied the stones to Hercules/HERCLE for use as ammunition against the Ligurians when the hero had run out of arrows. Stones large or small were weapons of war long before David's fight with Goliath, as can be seen here in Hesiod's description of battle between gods and giants, given in his Theogony.

"Three hundred rocks from their stalwart hands they discharged in a volley, darkening the Titans' sky with missiles."

But here at Crau, in this myth about Hercules, can be seen one explanation for Nostradamus's alluding to missiles as PIERRE and PIERREUSE.

In the St. Rémy area there were also man-made relics of times past sufficient to make the boy's lessons come alive. At the northern end of the town itself was a triumphal arch commemorating victories of Julius Caesar, and a memorial to two grandsons of Augustus Caesar. The Domitian Way had passed close by, and a mile from St. Rémy had been the Roman town of Glanum. The latter was not fully excavated until the

20th century; but for several centuries and perhaps ever since Glanum was destroyed by barbarians in the 3rd century, relics of it, along with those from the old St. Rémy-de-Provence close to the ancient site, had been picked up. The Nostradamus whom we are beginning to know, would, we can be sure, have done his share of the probing round.

PART TWO

THE RIDDLES

"The dream of gods came.
Divine what that meant!"
(ATLAMAL in GROENLENZKO. VERSE 21. THE POETIC EDDA.)

CHAPTER ELEVEN

GETTING ONTO
THE RIGHT WAVELENGTH

"How can you speak the Tuscan tongue?"
(DANTE. PURGATORY C.16, V.46.)

In Nostradamus' day professional interpreters of prophecies like his made a living by going round the country with explanations, for those who could not work these out for themselves. While access to books containing the necessary background information, and even literacy, were rare, such interpreters filled a cultural gap. They continued to do so when enlargement of the *bourgeoisie* reduced their audiences. But when the Industrial Revolution distracted men from thoughts about much else than worldly wealth, the interpreters' profession died out. The mystique surrounding it though, did not.

Understanding cryptically worded predictions is a subject still beset by a belief that some special skill or knack is required; something beyond common sense and literacy. That, however, as is about to be shown, is not so. All that is required is a taste for probing, and a little care. There are, however, particular things to be kept in mind when approaching any subject. Here, it is that whereas, for example, cricket can be enjoyed by those who do not know a back-foot drive from a leg glance, and music by those who do not know a semiquaver from a crotchet, with Nostradamus no words can be ignored.

Getting the feel of how Nostradamus uses words, getting on his wavelength, is a gradual process. All attempts at short-cuts prove facile. The necessary knowledge has to be accumulated layer by layer. However, this does become much easier as one goes along until, surprisingly soon, everything falls into place. The earliest stage, which otherwise tends to include some bafflement and frustration, can be avoided though, if from the start one's attention has been drawn to certain points. This chapter deals with some of these.

A flip through any dictionary reveals that most words can have several different meanings, in addition to thelr strict usage and their special meanings in metaphor and symbolism. 'Blood', for example. In verse II 89 there is a "Man of blood". If this is as in 'of flesh and blood', it could be any man. Or it could mean that he is well-born, or vigorous. Or he may even be murderous. By itself the word 'blood' does not tell which. And as an adverb it can be even more indefinite. When an old lady forces herself to say "bloody" she is almost certainly describing something covered in blood. But in general use it has wider applications. Most men use it non-specifically, either for emphasis, to express disapproval, or for a macho image. And the labourer uses it as a password among his mates. So what a word means, even when it is not being used symbolically, can depend on no more than who uses it.

We have to judge how Nostradamus meant his words quite largely from his experiences in life, and how these affected him. Keeping this in mind will keep us on his wavelength.

His Languages

From Nostradamus' classical education the reader can expect a wide use of Greek and Latin words, grammar and literary references. From the presence behind the scenes of the Inquisition, and Nostradamus' consequent movements, at least a small number of German and Italian words are to be expected, as is an otherwise surprising absence of Hebrew. While to his visitors from England, due to the popularity of his writings here, are owed the few words of English which appear in some editions.

His Provençal or Langue d'oc, the Old French of southern France, and a few words of Catalan from adjacent Spain, are not, however, the only legacy from his living where he did. (See map, Appendix Two). Local place-names frequently appear in verses in which they clearly do not fit their contexts. The explanation for this is that his passing often through those towns and villages, hearing their local folklore, triggered ideas for uses of their names as vehicles for other meanings. An example of this occurs in verse VIII 46. In this, *Tarasc* is an abbreviation of Tarascon, a town in southern France. In local legend the *Tarasca* or *Tarasque* was an amphibious monster which haunted the river Rhone round there. It will occasion little surprise that that verse is one of many concerning terrorism in the twentieth century.

Before we leave the subject of languages used by Nostradamus, there is something else worth mentioning. This is that one could scarcely expect to get inside anyone, let alone Nostradamus, unless prepared to take note of more than just those factors which he had consciously contrived. We know, from our own experiences in life, that many things beyond his control and due to chance must also have played their parts. One of these is the fact that he came from the South of France. This ensured that he was familiar with the history and linguistic variations of Provençal. In the 12th century the South of France was not united under the king of France. Its separate regions were ruled by noble families. Their small courts were toured by troubadours who produced a refined form of Provençal. This then changed over the years less than did Latin, and so became an 'in' means of communication between cultured people, even beyond France. It thus came to differ widely from the Provençal of the masses; and the two forms presented Nostradamus with a fountain of words the meanings of which varied. It was an unsought gift which he did not look in the mouth.

HIS NOMINAL SOURCES

Nostradamus openly confirms much of what the reader already expects. In his Epistle to Henry II, prefacing the second edition of Les Prophéties, he says that his source books include the "Sacred Scriptures", the "Punic Chronicle of Joel" and the "Life of Lycurgus" by Plutarch. The truth of this is limited. He does mean that he has drawn upon the Bible and Plutarch. But no more than that. The list of names which he gives, including Abraham, Adam, David, Isaac, Jacob, Moses, Noah and Solomon, is almost entirely irrelevant. It does not draw attention to those parts of the Bible which he uses most. Far from it. His actual biblical references are almost all drawn from other parts of both testaments, and notably from Revelation. Abraham and company are named in order to exaggerate his use of holy scriptures, to disarm the Inquisition. But the same preface does genuinely confirm other things. For "the Arabians", "the Kings of Persia", and "the Saracens" are associated with many of his as yet unfulfilled predictions. He has, however, and typically, had a second purpose in giving away so much useful information. For it is also a smokescreen concealing the fact that he omits to mention any of the other principal sources of his literary references such as The Histories, by Herodotus.

HIS MONARCHISM

Nostradamus' monarchism, which is displayed in his attention not just to the French but also the British royal house, is attributable to his patronage by Catherine de Medici and her family. There is no reason to doubt its sincerity. In the 16th century, however, monarchism had broader implications than it does today. Then, when a sovereign had so recently been almost synonymous with the state, and vice versa, there was little to separate monarchism from patriotism. That though he was undoubtedly a monarchist, he was also an ardent patriot, is evident from the verses in which he bemoans the replacement of patriotism with greed, and with short-sighted policies which will injure modern France.

HIS SOCIAL OUTLOOK

Clearer still is his intellectual snobbery, already displayed in verse VI 100 above. This was probably an inevitable consequence of precognition, of seeing his and others' progeny so rapidly destroying that which they depend on for a future for their genes. Nostradamus' impatience with his species reflects that of Heraclitus, the obscureness of whose pronouncements his own resemble, and with which he would have been familiar. For Heraclitus wrote that "One man is worth ten thousand, if he is first rate", which was a sentiment that could scarcely have failed to find an echo in an enlightened man who had been assured by the supposed intellectuals of his day that the sun goes round the earth.

There also seems to have been another reason for Nostradamus' social outlook. Surviving records about the gouty old doctor suggest that his neighbours contributed to his impatience. Three years before the first edition of Les Prophéties was published he had written that, "Here where I live I carry on my work among brute beasts, barbarous people, deadly enemies of learning and letters". And those words, *bêtes brutes,* he uses again, in verse I 64. He felt so strongly about his neighbours that he even asked that when he died he should be buried upright, so they could not walk over his remains. Certainly, any sign of respect for the common herd is absent from his writings. One suspects he fully intended his verses to be over the heads of those for whom he expressed such contempt, and probably over those of their like in later generations.

HIS USE OF VERSE

In Les Prophéties, Nostradamus refers to himself as an oracle, and of course knew that in the Classical World oracles often put their predictions into verse. From what we know about him already, it would be expected that he should do the same. But he would not have done so merely because others had done it. All did it for the same reason. Which was that verse can be a shorthand. Using the devices available to him through the grammar of poetry, he would not need laboriously to spell out every word. For in a few lines the poet is able to paint mental pictures which it takes a paragraph of prose to describe.

Verse also conveys more subtle shades of meaning than can prose, and is more easily remembered. It is, too, a literary form which suggests origins in the lofty and cultured minds expected of muses and mediums for gods, including the god of prophecy. But, above all, cryptic verses full of puns and other literary devices gave bright minds in the 16th century something more extending than the price of corn to think about. They served much the same purpose as does The Times crossword today.

HIS ASTROLOGY

Nostradamus' use of symbolism had its beginnings in the astrology learned from his grandfathers. The subject then embraced what is now termed astronomy, and was a routine part of the practice of medicine. Indeed, Pope Leo X had recently founded a chair of astrology in Rome. It was what Nostradamus began to develop into the homeopathic medicine which Sarazin mistook for witchcraft. But aside from its value as a storehouse of symbols, it features so often in Les Prophéties because his 16th century readers expected it to be there. Its reception was much like that to be had nowdays from claiming that something has a scientific basis. We ourselves do not have to believe in astrology, or condemn it. In dealing with Les Prophéties it suffices for us to recognise that in his own time Nostradamus was looked on as an astrologer, and profitted by encouraging belief that this was so.

THE NOSTRADAMUS TOUCH

It is the use of references to mythology, gleaned from his classical reading, however, which really shows 'the Nostradamus touch'. For as the waste bin containing early man's discarded probings for truths, myths themselves contain prophecies.

CHAPTER TWELVE

WE ALL SPEAK NOSTRADAMIAN ALREADY

"Dogs bark at those they do not recognise."

Among the standard excuses given for not understanding Nostradamus' predictions are that he uses French words which some Frenchmen have never heard, and half a dozen other languages, with the grammars of all these mixed. And that all this is overlaid with literary devices, phrases which do not make sense, and symbolism. These accusations are true. The trouble about using them as excuses though, is that we ourselves do these things. We do them all the time, and think nothing of it.

LANGUAGES DEVELOP

Nostradamus uses some Langue d'oc, a dialect which has never been spoken all over France. But even today there are English words which are still confined to local usage. Banting, for example. In part of the North of England that means 'slimming'. Mush is another example. In Hampshire that word means a 'man'. Beyond those localities, however, few people have heard either word. A fact which, though, does not make their use wrong. Merely inconvenient, if the dialect happens not to be one's own.

The French language, like most other living ones, adapts to needs. For one reason and another words go out of use; and others, often at first referred to as 'jargon', come into use. The terms they replace are always apt to cause a hiccup, regardless in which writer's work they appear. Readers of Shakespeare come across such words; but do not let this interfere with their enjoyment or their understanding of the Bard.

As to the non-French words in Les Prophéties, there are

hundreds of foreign words and phrases in common use with English. Indeed, many of these are preferred to their English equivalents. *Au pair, esprit de corps, fait accompli, genre* and *nouveau riche* are among French ones. And *alter ego, modus operandi, per annum, per cent/um, status quo, tempus fugit* and *terra firma* are among the Latin. Though less often, we similarly use words from other languages too. And all these, far from creating doubts about what is meant, make meanings clearer.

Because much French, like much English, is based on imported words, there is only a fine line between those of foreign origin and those which are still foreign words. As a result, as the latter cross that line into the new language, the grammar which accompanies them is often a matter of choice rather than of right and wrong.

The literary device which Nostradamus uses more often than any other is the anagram. This is a word or phrase constructed by rearranging the letters of another word or phrase. Strictly speaking, all and only the letters in the one are used for the other. And more often than not, it has to be admitted, this is a rule to which Nostradamus does not rigidly adhere. But anyone familiar with riddles and cryptic crosswords knows that other people often do not stick to it either. However, to avoid confusion below, the looser form will be referred to as a 'cryptogram'.

Because most words have a range of meanings, when they are spoken the listener is helped to understand what each means in that instance by the pauses between them. When they are written, the same thing is achieved by punctuation marks. To omit or to change the position of the marks is to change the meaning of the sentence. This was the point made by the old riddle which said that, "King Charles walked and talked half an hour after his head was cut off". Hence our care to put punctuation marks in the right places. But hence, also, punctuation marks being among the most effective tools in any cryptic writer's box of tricks, and his putting them in the wrong places to catch out the unwary.

Occasionally, Nostradamus uses ploys less familiar than those mentioned. One such is the running-together of two or more words to make another. Though sometimes, as with *Marnegro* in verse V 27, where he uses the Latin *mare* = 'sea' and *negro* = 'black man', and also the Italian *mare* = 'sea' and *negro* = 'black', the reader may wonder why he did so as it clearly conveys the Black Sea in one word or two. A more interesting example is *Tardeigne* in verse VIII 49. This word, from *tard* = 'late', and *deigner faire* = 'to deign to do', means 'to do too late'.

He splits words also, though more rarely. *D'eux* is an example of this in which, by having it recognised here as no more than a flourish, he invites the reader to assume that this is always all that split words will be. Whereas, as with *par dons* in verse III 95 for example, he is doing something entirely different. Which incidentally, serves also as as example of his placing something intended to mislead, as he so often places his clues also, in different verses from those which they affect.

As we have seen above with *Tardeigne,* with Nostradamus a capital letter does not always indicate a proper noun or the beginning of a sentence. Like most other literary tricks, however, the effectiveness of this depends on its being unexpected. Once a reader's attention has been drawn to it, it is a ploy which should never work again.

But though Nostradamus plays with grammar, he does not invent his own rules and expect us to know them. He plays by our rules. He just knows our rulebook....cover to cover. Here are more instances.

Into *faulx, huille, mittre, pourceau, rhege, simulachres, Thunis* and *Timbre* he has inserted extra letters. This is known in grammar as 'epenthesis'. From inside *beuf, rogie* and *Sagitaire* he has omitted letters. That is known as 'syncope'. He starts *hurne* with an extra letter, in what is called 'prosthesis'. While from *Adrie, Alus* and *Annibal* he leaves out their first letters, which is 'apheraesis'. From such as *Agath, cap, mercu* and *Tarasc* he has omitted the last letters, in what is styled 'apocope'. So slight a shuffling of letters as occurs in *scepter* can scarcely be described as an anagram, but it is what is called 'metathesis'. And so on. Those examples are no more than the tip of an iceberg. But each item falls into a grammatical category which was not invented merely to cope with Nostradamus. They were introduced to grammar to meet a much wider need. All the word-plays involved are long established features of literature. And if his readers are not already familiar with them, it is only fair to point out that that is in no way the fault of Nostradamus.

The closest thing to a key to words in Les Prophéties, as everywhere else, lies in their contexts. For, as with everyday conversation, the best guides to what a word means are the words which qualify it. In Nostradamus' hands, however, a context is more important than usual. This is because, to make his meanings completely clear to readers who are willing to persist in working them out, he envelopes the meanings in layers of mutual confirmation. And unless and until these further layers have been identified, any interpretation remains uncertain.

Degrees of certainty are not all that the layers of meaning mentioned above impart. Like rhyme, they are also a form of shorthand. For in most instances they add as much to the meaning as would a string of adjectives. So an interpretation which is correct is often also rich in detail.

As we have seen, in verse VI 100 Nostradamus admits his predictions need careful scrutiny. Where there was to be no such study, he intended there should be little understanding. And study involves attention to more than one edition of Les Prophéties. For this leads the student to the discrepancies between editions. An unknowable proportion of these were doubtless due to printers' errors. Not all, however. Verses VIII 2 and VIII 77 contain an example of one exception. *Grêle* appears in various editions also as *grêler, gresle, gresler* and *guerre*. On statistical grounds alone it is unlikely that any one word would be subject to so many variations all due to chance and printers' errors. It is reasonably certain, therefore, that these variations of *grêle* are deliberate; intended to clarify and add to its meaning.

Because *grêle* means 'hail', and it is unlikely that hail would be sufficiently important at any moment in history to warrant a mention in a compressed account of an event, it is not meant to be accepted literally. Which is where the edition-variations and also Nostradamus' liberties with accents come in. *Grêlé* means 'pockmarked', that is, 'marked by disease'. So we now have disease which falls like hail. And *guerre,* meaning 'war', completes the explanation; for modern defence planning assumes that biological agents will be sown from the air. In these instances, therefore, *grêle* refers to a biological weapon; an interpretation fully supported by its contexts.

As much as is illustrated above in relation to the word *grêle* could not have been said in one short word without recourse to those variations between editions. And study confined to any single edition may always, therefore, leave some part of a word's meaning unsolved.

REVELATION AND CHERNOBYL

Grêle, just discussed, has much in common with *TARRACONNE* in verse VII 22. Tarragon is wormwood, which is a bitter herb. What Nostradamus means by it can be seen here in Revelation VIII 10 and 11.

"And there fell from heaven a great star, burning as a torch, and it fell upon a third part of the rivers, and upon the fountains of the waters; and the name of the star is called Wormwood: and the third part of the waters became wormwood; and many men died of the waters, because they were made bitter."

It is interesting that the wormwood plant *artemisia dracunculus* is a native of eastern Europe and southern Russia; and that 'wormwood' is in Russian, *Chernobyl!* And in that we have no reason to suppose that Nostradamus knew any Russian words, this Russian link suggests that Les Prophéties was written with more help from his unconscious mind than even he himself realised.

INTERCHANGEABLE LETTERS

Les Prophéties was written at two levels. Its upper level can be understood reasonably completely by means of this book. Underlying that one, however, is a deeper level which it is not essential to understand because its purpose is only to confirm meanings which should already have been arrived at. This lower level employs methods of communication such as the medieval Jewish code the Gematria. It also makes use of the routes through which the European alphabets have developed. Latin, for example, drew on the Greek and Etruscan alphabets, as these did on the Phoenician, and so on.

The origins of modern European alphabets is a subject for study in itself, and so is unsuitable for inclusion here. But because Nostradamus does not, or cannot, avoid some overflowing from one level to the other, we do need to remind ourselves, briefly, of the more recent developments of the alphabet.

These developments have included some interchangeability between letters. Sanctioned by this, Nostradamus substitutes letters for other ones himself, beyond doing so in cryptograms. Usually, as in the examples below, it is clear where he has done so. Where he is writing at his deeper level, these substitutions are not usually as obvious. Yet even there he is like a cricketer, he 'plays the game' with us. There are definite precedents for all he does. All we have to do is know them also.

C, G, K AND Q

The Etruscans used C for G, K and Q sounds. The Romans replaced K with C; and added a bar to C to make G. In verse IX 83, for example, _VOQUERA,_ as a variant of _VOGUERA,_ reflects Nostradamus' travels through Tuscany.

U AND V

U was at first a writing-variation of V. Until the 10th century there was no general rule about which to use where. But then V began to be used at the beginnings of words, and U in the middles and at the ends. Nostradamus' variations of *CAPTIVE/CAPTIF* in the forms of *CAPTIFE* and *CAPTIFUE* puts this confusion to use. Then, during Nostradamus' lifetime, continental printers began using U for vowels and V for consonants. V remained in use for all capital forms of U and V, though, for another hundred years. In verse IV 20 Nostradamus reflects this transition with *VBERTE* as a variant of *UBERTÉ.*

The history of the letter V gives us a chance to glimpse Nostradamus' second and deeper level of expression, because it provides an example. This letter being the Roman numeral for '5', and 'E' being the fifth letter of the alphabet, opened for him possibilities of which he avails himself. But then, so too do our poets,.... in their case perhaps on the basis that one can easily have too many 5s! Hence one is dropped from such words as 'e'en', 'e'er' and 'o'er'. For Nostradamus, though, the relationship of V to 5 and thus to E has a wider range of uses.

W

Norman scribes had difficulty in writing one of the English sounds. At first they tried a double V, but this still got confused with the French V. Next they tried a double U. After the Conquest the latter was replaced by W, a letter which still remains almost unused in French.

I, J AND Y

J, - then pronounced like Y, - emerged as a consonant form of I, and became a separate letter only in the Middle Ages. It did not sever all its connections with I until the 14th. century. The interchangeability of I and J in Les Prophéties can be seen in *IOUË* and *JOVE,* in *IUPITER* and *JUPITER,* and in *IEUX* and *JEUX.*

The historical association of I with Y is used by Nostradamus in such variations as *NÎMES* and *NYMES* in verse V 59, *MARI* and *MARY* in verse IX 34, *OISEAU* and *OYSEAU* in verse V 81, *TRAHI* and *TRAHY* in verse V 47, and *IREZ* and *YRES* in verse VII 22.

CHAPTER THIRTEEN

PHRASES WHICH DO NOT MAKE SENSE

*"Reader, if ever you have found yourself
caught in a mountain fog, trying to see
your way through it, as sightless as a mole".*
(DANTE. PURGATORY C.17, V.1.)

FIGURES OF SPEECH

Nostradamus does say things which, strictly speaking, do not make sense. However, those who live in glass houses should not throw stones. Which should preclude most of the carping at Nostradamus. Unless, of course, people small enough to fit into frying pans have indeed been known to jump out of them and into fires. Though, with their heads in the clouds and their feet on the ground, noses to the grindstone, shoulders to the wheel, backs to the wall, ears to the ground, keeping their hands in, with a finger in every pie, while they stick their necks out, putting a foot in it and having one in the grave, those fires might be a relatively comfortable option. Not least because, should one get bats in the belfry, one would need a psychiatrist and not a zoologist.

Taken literally, such phrases do not make sense. But they are not of course supposed to be taken literally. They make sense in another way,...figuratively. Figurative speech is a constantly used and almost essential part of language. Were we to stop using it we would sound pedantic and take much longer to say what we mean.

As can be seen from Luke XII 34, "For where your treasure is, there will your heart be also", - which was not a recommendation for a transplant, - figures of speech are of ancient origin. They appear throughout most forms of literature, in verse no less than prose. Hence, for example, Marlowe's

Helen whose face "Launched a thousand ships and burned the topless towers of Ilium" was not used to knock out the wedges down the slipway, nor as firewood in Troy. And even the towers of Ilium, though high, were not topless or even roofless.

No objections are raised to these discrepancies between what is actually said and what is meant. This is because they say so much, so concisely and so memorably. In fact we admire this sort of expression so much that we copy it. As result, people who like or work well with each other 'get on like a house on fire', without a house or a fire.

Irrelevant to their strict meanings, and foolish such phrases may sound. But everyone uses them. Then condemn Nostradamus for doing the same thing. Yet his figures of speech are not nearly as way out and absurd as those cited above.

'BROTHERS'

In his predictions the 'brothers', who are mentioned in six verses, have usually been accepted in the literal sense of the word. When, as a consequence, actual brothers have risen to prominence, Nostradamus' references have tended to be associated with them. The Kennedy brothers in the United States became subjects of this vogue. And Nostradamus' Epistle to Henry II does speak of "the three brothers". However, that reference continues, "And there shall be such great noise and warlike tumult that all the East shall quake for fear of these two brothers of the North who are not yet brothers": Let us look at that again. "Who are not yet brothers". From Nostradamus, no heavier hint than that, that 'brothers' is not to be taken literally, could be expected. Yet others are given. One appears in verse VIII 97, - which, in the final order in which all his predictions are intended to be read, follows a linked verse about 'brothers'. The hint concerned is contained in *"Les trois beaux enfants"*. For many children are indeed beautiful. But in a book of potted future history such a detail has no place. If, therefore, that phrase has another connotation, the latter is more likely to be correct. And this one has. In *beaux freres* = 'stepbrothers', *beaux* does not signify beauty. It shows that the children who are referred to are not actually brothers. Another, yet heavier, hint appears in verse IV 96. In this the island of Britain is said to be a brother. Which obviously cannot be accepted literally.

In the 16th century the concept of a non-literal brotherhood between men was already widespread. Shakespeare, who was almost contemporary with Nostradamus, put it into the mouth of Beatrice in Much Ado About Nothing. "No, uncle, I'll none," she says. "Adam's sons are my brethren; and, truly, I hold it was a sin to match in my kindred."

And in the eyes of Shakespeare's Henry V, men could become his brothers simply by their actions.

"Crispin Crispian shall ne'er go by,
From this day to the ending of the world,
But we in it shall be remembered,
We few, we happy few, we band of brothers;
For he today that sheds his blood with me
Shall be my brother."

Even the Western concept of 'brothers in Christ' has a parallel in the East, in one of Islamic brotherhood. This goes back at least a thousand years and appears in such as Ikhwan al-Safa, the 'Brothers of Purity' at Basra, in the 12th century Naqshbandi brotherhood, its Baghdad-based contemporary the Qadiriya, and in the Ikhwan al Muslimin or 'Moslem Brotherhood' in Egypt. In casual conversation too, 'brother officer', 'brother Englishman' and 'brother Arab' are phrases in common use unconnected with close blood relationships. As with so much else, therefore, only by its context can a use of the word 'brother' be recognised as literal or figurative.

PADDING

The one thing in Les Prophéties which it is always difficult to be sure about is that every layer of meaning has been recognised, so tightly are these superimposed one on another, even within single words. But even this does have its good side. It removes all need to look for padding, of which there is none. Anything which does not make literal sense, does so as a figure of speech.

COMMON SENSE

Of all the tools available to those who would like to read the future in Les Prophéties, common sense is the best. It is particularly useful when dealing with words or phrases which, while making literal sense, do not sit comfortably in a book about historical events. One example of such a word is 'rain'. It could indeed be said to have altered the otherwise likely outcome of the Battle of Waterloo, and to have been significant at other times also. But in the pageant of four hundred years, the proportion of occasions when this was so was very small; and there is no reason to suppose that Nostradamus selected such moments for attention. It is common sense, therefore, to proceed from the premise that 'rain' should not automatically be accepted in its literal sense. Instead, it may mean something else; something which descends like rain. What that is, will be found in the context of that or a related verse. Similarly, just as Les Prophéties is not a book on the weather, nor is it about zoology. Yet in it there is reference to 'serpents', despite the rarity in European affairs of instances in which these have been influenced in any way by snakes. So, again, one proceeds from the premise that something else is meant. And other ill-fitting words, not necessarily about the weather or animals, should be accorded the same treatment.

CHAPTER FOURTEEN

HIS SYMBOLS AND GRAMMAR

"Where there no wood is, there the fire goeth out."
(PROVERBS XXVI, 20.)

NOSTRADAMUS' SYMBOLS

As the device used by the unconscious mind to express itself in dreams, the idea of using the symbol in his writings would have had a strong appeal to Nostradamus.

A symbol is something which represents something else. Unlike a metaphor or a simile, which each use several words, a symbol does the job in one. Indeed, trademarks, other badges, flags and roadsigns are all evidence that even a single word is not essential. All that is necessary is that the meaning of the symbol can be recognised. Colours are often symbolic; red of rage or danger, white of fear or purity, and yellow of cowardice. Green, traditionally indicating naivety, is now also becoming a symbol of environment-awareness. As with a metaphor, the value of a symbol lies in its power to say a lot, ...without literally saying much or anything.

Symbols are a feature of most literature. It is scarcely an exaggeration to describe Les Prophéties as being, in some places, a mass of symbols with only enough other words to hold them apart. A difficulty with symbols is that, as with red, white and green above, they can symbolize more than one thing. And as we have already seen, and will often see again, many of the symbols in Les Prophéties are not exceptions to this. Nostradamus chooses them for just that reason. So, as we have also seen already, we must judge his meanings from those hallowed by the writers of ancient and Renaissance literature. Recognising the right ones from among the resulting short-lists seldom presents problems. But there are a few exceptions to this.

SULPHUR

There is a Zen saying that, "The instant you speak about a thing you miss the mark". The word *soufre* or 'sulphur', occurring in verses IV 23 and X 49, might easily be an example. Of course we all know what sulphur is, and what its chemical attributes are. But let us test our confidence - if any - that we already understand all that Nostradamus means by 'sulphur', by source-checking in, for example, Revelation, in which sulphur is referred to as 'brimstone'. Chapter XIX, verse 20 reads;

"And the beast was taken, and with him the false prophet ....they twain were cast alive into the lake of fire that burneth with brimstone".

Revelation XX, 10 maintains that theme with;

"And the devil that deceived them was cast into the lake of fire and brimstone, where are also the beast and the false prophet; and they shall be tormented day and night for ever and ever".

When the list of those qualifying for a very hot bath has been broadened to embrace heathens, murderers, sex-offenders and liars, Revelation XXI, 8 reads; "Their part shall be in the lake that burneth with fire and brimstone; which is the second death".

These returns in Revelation to the same theme and the same word almost demanded Nostradamus' attention, and then his own use of their meaning. Superficially, the subject is punishment. The 'second death' is physical death. The first led up to it, and what that comprises is told in the list of offences. The repetition of 'false prophet', followed by 'liars', is an oblique reference to leaders. The victims of the 'sulphur' in Les Prophéties have been both misled and badly led. This interpretation is fully supported throughout Nostradamus' verses about the 20th century. As St. Thomas Aquinas wrote, back in the 13th century, precognition can sometimes be no more than judging from the present, in which future events are already "as in their causes sleeping". But have we the whole meaning of Nostradamus' 'sulphur' now? Becoming sure of that can be as tricky as picking up a blob of mercury while wearing boxing gloves. That Zen saying must always be born in mind!

TRADITIONAL SYMBOLS

Some symbols pre-date history, and many have conveyed the same meanings so widely and for so long that they are termed 'traditional'. To his study of alchemy, astrology and classical literature is owed Nostradamus' fondness for these traditional symbols in particular. They include the serpent, already mentioned, and also the sword, the cross, the comet, certain colours, blood and 'the deluge'.

Of these examples the comet is of especial interest. Traditionally, it is a portender of wars, plagues, famines and the births or deaths of great men. These are meanings which can be traced back to the Chaldean and ancient Egyptian belief that the appearance of a comet preceded some great event. Seneca suggested that a comet had been connected with Noah's flood; and the Star of Bethlehem was said to have been a comet. And comets do happen to have preceded events which include the fall of Jerusalem in 70 AD, the death of Attila in 451 AD and the Battle of Hastings in 1066, keeping the belief alive. In verse II 62 Nostradamus does use the word *comète*. In other verses, however, for examples, II 43 in which there is a "bearded star", and II 46 in which, "In the sky will be seen fire with long sparks", to the extent that these are references to tangible objects, these descriptions might equally apply to meteors. But while it is possible that one or more of the events which Nostradamus chose to describe in Les Prophéties should have coincided with noteworthy comets or meteors, unless he went out of his way to select such events, that does not satisfactorily account for so many heavenly accompaniments.

The explanation is typically Nostradamian. The pre-existing belief that an actual comet marks an important event presented him with a way of showing, simply by adding a comet to an account of an event which was not necessarily really accompanied by one, that he, Nostradamus, judged that event to be important. The actions in the verses in which comets are mentioned sound quite ordinary. That their effects will prove far-reaching we could not have guessed, without Nostradamus' additions of 'comets' to tell us so.

Fortunately, the instances in which Nostradamus seems deliberately to set out to outdo most other writers in subtlety, as different from merely the amount of his symbolism, are rare. As mentioned in Chapter Twelve, he obviously could have, yet does not, employ a coded language of his own construction, - other than as a back-up for what should already have been understood. And where Nostradamus uses traditional symbols, he certainly should have been understood. For these are words which echo in deep levels of all our minds. Receiving them correctly should be like the re-kindling of a fire with wood that is still warm.

OTHER FIGURES OF SPEECH

His figures of speech fit into the usual rules of grammar taught in schoolrooms and classified in such further terms as follow.

In verse IV 95 _vestales_ is a reference to vestal virgins who, from the Latin _vestalis_ = 'pure', were priestesses who kept alight the fire sacred to Vesta the goddess of the hearth. Here, representing religious fanaticism, this is therefore a euphemism, which is an agreeable description of a disagreeable thing.

In Chapter Twelve, the composite words _Marnegro_ and _Tardeigne_ were met with from verses V 27 and VIII 49. _Tempiera_ in verse X 66 is a hybrid word. That is, a composite one for which the parts are drawn from more than one language. Coming from the Latin _tempi_ = 'times' and _ère_ = 'era', together with _piera_ which is a cryptogram of the French _pierre_ = 'stone', this refers to 'the times of the stones', a phrase which in this place links the accompanying action with that of particular other verses.

Argent = 'silver', and when accompanied by _or_ = 'gold', it represents wealth. Headgear symbolizes its wearer's thoughts. So _Fez in_ verse VI 80, being a cap worn in Moslem lands, stands for religious motives there. And the city of Fez in Morocco being a principal Moslem religious centre, *Fez* further represents Islamic zeal. In verse II 5, in which it is described as 'iron', *poisson,* rather than being merely a fish, can scarcely be anything other than a submarine or, as in naval slang, a torpedo. And in verse VI 44 *truie,* literally 'a sow', a pig, by common usage stands for 'greed'. There, those words are used metaphorically.

A metonymy is where a person or thing is not named directly, but through some associated thing. Thus, as it occurs in verses I 32, I 62, V 14, and V 48, and being literally a staff representing sovereignty, *sceptre* stands for power or rule.

It is a personification when an abstract thing is presented as an imaginary person. Mars, the Roman god of war, has, especially in literature, become its personification. Similarly, in verses IX 55 and IX 73, Mercury, as the Messenger of the Gods and therefore concerned in the presentation of opposed cases, is a personification of mediation. And in verse IV 23, *Hercle* or Hercules personifies great strength. From the story in Genesis XI about mankind's attempt to co-operate with each other in the building of the Tower of Babel, and the chaos in which that project ended, *Babel,* named in verse II 30, has become the prototype of confusion.

Puns

Words which suggest two meanings at the same time are classified as puns. So useful were these to Nostradamus that solving his cryptic verses completely, becomes largely a matter of hunting for puns. This is because the two or more meanings his words can have, are, usually all of them, among what he wants those single words to express. For Nostradamus the pun serves to extend a meaning; while for the reader it confirms, or not, whether an interpretation is correct. In verse III *13 Arche* is a pun, and a multiple pun at that. From the Latin *arx* = 'a box' comes the Ark of the Covenant which, when captured by the Philistines, caused plagues in every city into which it was taken. While from Noah's ship or 'ark' comes 'survival' as the meaning accorded to the Ark by the early Christian Church. Which, however, merely confirmed the ancient Greek belief that the sky would fall down were it not for the arch that it forms. Which is in turn a belief carried on in the architectural triumphal arch which also helps support that larger arch of the sky. And the several verses of Les Prophéties which concern a desperate hunt across Europe for a terrorist gang, following a particularly nauseating megatrocity, - which read like pages from a Frederick Forsyth novel, - though they are as concise as all his other verses, all only spell out the hope caught in that single punning word *arche*.

Adust in verse IV 67 puns more simply in that the otherwise dry dust from the Latin *adustus* = 'scorched', 'charred', becomes also liquid droplets from the Low German *dunst* = 'vapour'. A very similar example is contained in verses II 1 and X 86. In these, *gélee* = 'frost', and from the Latin *gelare* = 'to freeze', there is a pun with the edition-variation *gellee* from the Old French *gelee* = 'jelly', to indicate that this is a liquid in solid form. But the pun in which Nostradamus' personal feelings were probably most deeply involved, because he is speaking of his own infant son, occurs in verse X 21. In this, *bagues* = 'treasure' and also 'methods'; indicating the value he sets on use of the methods he describes in the verse. And the verse itself is a very apt setting for the most subtle word-play because it is almost the only one which deals with two different and entirely self-contained subjects, every word in it playing its part in each.

A synecdoche is where a part of something represents the whole, or vice versa. It is a kind of metonymy. One example occurs in verse IV 67 in which *trejection* = 'trajectory', - the path of a flying missile, - represents the meteor or flying missile itself. Another occurs in verse V 62 in which *tridental,* by pertaining to a trident, - traditionally held by Poseidon the Greek sea god and Neptune his Roman counterpart, and which represents in turn the thunderbolt it is in their power to wield, - stands also for all else that they represent.

SUMMARY

To summarise, whether Nostradamus is employing idiom or stricter grammar, the connotations are often to be found in word-plays, all of them in forms with which the average reader is familiar. This is done by recognising which of its potential range of meanings should be accorded to each word in that instance. Which means, according to its context. And even this is a process in constant use by everyone. For we are all accustomed to having to judge, for example each time the word 'green' is used, whether it stands for naivety, inexperience, jealously, environment-friendliness, an instruction 'to go', or imminent vomiting.

Certainly, nothing in Les Prophéties is as difficult as would be, for example, understanding without prior knowledge who killed who in *Brutus Caesarem occidit,* 'Brutus Caesar killed'. Which is a familiar riddle, that Nostradamus did not compose.

CHAPTER FIFTEEN

HIS ANALOGIES

"What is the cause of this? Please make it clear
that I may teach the truth to other men;
some see it in the stars, some on the earth.
(DANTE. PURGATORY C.16, V.21.)

Anyone could invent a system of writing in which words arbitrarily represent things with which they are in no normal way connected. Such a system would be almost impenetrable by anything other than chance. But, making no headway, its would-be readers would soon tire of trying to decipher it. Hence cryptic writings, other than codes, have connections between their words and meanings which are not merely arbitrary. Due to Nostradamus' liking for multiple meanings, it sometimes cannot be more than a matter of opinion as to into which grammatical classification his words fall. But as we have seen already, they do so into familiar terms.

When, in everyday speech, the connection between word and meaning, the symbolism, is so clear that it needs no explanation, it is usually in the form of a metaphor. But when the speaker wants to convey a parallel which may not be obvious to his audience, he does so in the form of a simile; that is, he draws attention to the parallel by saying one thing is 'like' another.

In practice though, these alternatives are only open when the message is fairly short and simple. For example, 'He was a bullet from a gun', or, 'he was like a bullet from a gun'. Both mean that someone moved suddenly, fast, and perhaps with force. This is understood because speed and impetus are well-known characteristics of a bullet. But the longer the message, the more difficult it becomes to convey without spelling it out. If, therefore, the message is to be cryptic, more complex symbolism has to be used.

ANALOGOUS PERSONS

For this reason Nostradamus sometimes names persons whose actions parallel the events he is cryptically describing. He takes most of these names from Herodotus' The Histories. This is because coming as they do from the first European historian, he knows that these books will survive unchanged for as long as a European culture exists. And because The Histories are lengthy, and tell about the area he is dealing with, he is able to find in them events analogous to those he wants to describe. For example, in verse X 21 he speaks of the Magi, to read more about whom in Western literature the works of Herodotus are the most obvious source. Finally, to further ensure that The Histories will not be overlooked by students of Les Prophéties, he lays a trail to them. He does this by introducing many references from the same work, in addition to 'Magi', such as *ARAXES* in verse III 31, which he does not need or even use for analogies. So he has done his best. He has led the horses to water. And as far as he is concerned they can now drink if they have the common sense to do so.

MABUS

One of these analogies from Herodotus concerns *MABUS* in verse II 62. The relevant passages are contained in Book Three of The Histories. In brief, two brothers who are Magi, or priests, persuade King Cambyses of Persia to have his brother Smerdis murdered. Then, when Cambyses is out of the country, they seize power themselves, the Magus Smerdis, who happens to physically resemble his dead royal namesake, impersonating him. Guilt about his brother's murder, and knowledge that he must make this public in order to recover his throne, prove too much for Cambyses, and he dies. This leaves the Magi usurpers ruling Persia. However, a handful of Persian nobles know that the dead king's brother was murdered. They decide to assassinate the impostor. Darius is the leader of this plot, and his most forceful supporter is Gobryas Megabyzus. The seven conspirators bluff their way past the palace guards. While the other five keep the palace staff at bay, Darius and Megabyzus force their way into the throne room. The two Magi snatch weapons from the walls and defend themselves. One of them escapes into an adjoining and unlighted room. Darius and Megabyzus follow. Soon Megabyzus is wrestling in the darkness with the Magus, and calling on Darius to use his knife.

"I dare not strike, for fear of killing you", Darius protests.

To which Megabyzus replies, "Fear nothing. Spit both of us at once if need be."

Darius strikes, and kills the Magus. When news of what has happened spreads, all Magi who can be found are slaughtered. And Darius, backed by Megabyzus although the latter does not believe in monarchy, is made king.

As will have been noticed, *MABUS* is a cryptogram of *Megabyzus,* which also contains the letters which spell 'Magus'.

RAYPOZ

Another extended analogy concerns *RAYPOZ* in verse IX 44. This is a cryptogram of Gobryas Zopyrus. He is the son of the Gobryas Megabyzus who helped put Darius on the throne. His story, also told in Book Three of The Histories, goes like this.

Babylon, then part of the Persian empire, is in revolt. Darius' siege of the city has lasted a year and seven months. The Persians are disheartened. From the walls a defiant defender shouts,

"What are you sitting there for, men of Persia? Why don't you go away? Oh yes, you will capture our city ....when mules have foals".

A month later one of Zopyrus' mules does foal. Astounded by this phenomenon, but determined to make personal use of so clear a signal that the city is fated to fall, Zopyrus swears his servants to secrecy. He then cuts off his own ears and nose, shaves his head like a criminal's, and raises weals on himself with a whip. Next, he presents himself in this condition to a horrified Darius, to whom he explains his plan. That done, he easily gets himself accepted into the city as a deserter from the besieging army. And as a noble who has been so maltreated by his king, particularly as one skilled in war and familiar with the enemy's dispositions, he is soon entrusted by the Babylonians with a military command. When he has risen to be their General-in-Chief and Guardian of the Wall, he opens the city gates to the Persians. Afterwards, Zopyrus is well rewarded by Darius.

The full connotations of both these analogies only become clear, of course, when seen in the contexts supplied in their verses. That *RAYPOZ* is the more important of the two is already suggested by its appearance in capital letters. It is the more important from Nostradamus' point of view in that it serves a second purpose. This is that Zopyrus' story draws attention to the benefits to be derived from acting on a prediction.

MABUS and *RAYPOZ* involve analogies which are very simple to understand, in that Megabyzus and Zopyrus each had an outstanding event in their lives, with which they will always be associated. The subjects of some of Nostradamus' analogies have more than one, and this makes it less clear which events are referred to.

HEROD

Herod is an example. He is referred to in verse V 14, in the cryptogram *HERODDE*. He was an Arab who was a king of the Jews. He was an ally of Rome, and its puppet. He was president of the Olympic Games. He was also the slaughterer of 'the innocents', and of many of his own relatives. On his deathbed he had the leaders of the Jewish nation confined in the hippodrome at Jericho, and left instructions that when he died they should be slain. The full connotation of his name involves these several threads.

PLACE-NAMES AS ANALOGIES

As we have seen, when used as analogies the names of

some persons are like symbols in that they say a lot in a single word. In several instances, by using the names of places as analogies, Nostradamus manages to squeeze even more meaning than that out of a word.

The place-name analogies work like this. Some places which were associated with a particular set of events in the past, are going to be connected with a similar set of events in the future. Naturally, the future ones will not exactly duplicate the past ones. But they will be sufficiently alike for us, when the earlier ones have been repeated, to recognlse that we had been forewarned.

However, Nostradamus names numerous places, and uses very few of these as analogies. We have to find which ones. Unavoidably, this involves sifting all the place-names in Les Prophéties. We can begin by discarding any such as *VARENNES* because that appears in IX 20 for a specific reason which we will come to in due course. We also discard any such as *PARIS,* because further use of it would so overload it with meanings that it would not convey any of them. This leaves us with a short-list to be sifted further. Now, though, we can look for positive clues, using our growing familiarity with Nostradamus. We know he is addicted to making his 'idiots' feel uncomfortable for having missed things which others see. Teasing us, he is going to flap his coat-tails right under our noses. So these particular place-names are going to invite attention. They are going to shout loudly that they are different from the others, and have something in common with each other.

What they have in common should occasion little surprise. It is that the histories of these places, though well-recorded, are little-known beyond their borders, so some work will be involved in learning them. This obligation on his readers to do some work, to match his own, is, after all, one of Nostradamus' fingerprints, and is found to a lesser extent throughout Les Prophéties. It does more than cloak his meanings and make them fun to work out. It is also intended to sort out wheat from chaff among those who try to do so.

And as we of course expected to find, at least part of the relevant history of places which he uses as analogies appear in the works of his favourite authors.

This simple sifting process having produced the goods, we can now examine three examples. At least, superficially these are three. In fact, they are one. The places concerned are next door to each other; Nostradamus uses the three names to vary his vocabulary and spice up his clues. It will not be necessary for the reader of this book to find the relevant information about these places for himself. That job has been done for him. Here is the geography and a selected history of each place.

DACIA

Dacia figures in Ammianus, Caesar and Tacitus. It appears in verse VI 7 as *'DACE'*.

Dacia was in the southern part of East Central Europe. The tribal lands of the Dacians lay along the Danube, mostly North of the river and in what is now Rumania. As the Dacians were pushed westwards by tribes migrating from the Steppes, they met the eastward movement of Roman armies. In 107 AD, after five years of warring with the Dacians, Trajan annexed Dacia to the Roman Empire as an Imperial province. Pressure from the East later shifted the province southward, and it eventually consisted of part of what is now Hungary, southern central Yugoslavia, North West Bulgaria and the northern tip of Albania. Its western neighbour was then the Roman province of Illyricum (see *PANNONS*).

In the mid-3rd century the original Dacia North of the Danube was lost by the Romans to Germanic tribes; and later invaded by Mongols and Slavs. In the 11th century it passed under the Hungarian crown; and though invaded by Mongols and Turks in the 13th century, was still part of Hungary in Nostradamus' time. In the 17th century its possession passed to the Austrian Hapsburgs. But the name 'Rumania/Romania', and of its 'Romance' language originated with its Roman colonists.

DALMATIA

Dalmatia is mentioned by Caesar and others. In verse IX 60 it appears as *ALMATIE*.

Dalmatia, the tribal lands of the Dalmatae, lay in what is now Yugoslavia, along the Adriatic coast between the Gulf of Kotor and where Fiume now stands. Incorporated by the Romans into Illyrium/Illyricum in 33 BC, it became a separate province from Pannonia (see *PANNONS*) in 9 AD, following an Illyrian revolt. Among its tribes was the Parthini (see *PARTHE*).

It was overrun by Goths in the 5th century, and became part of the Byzantine Empire (see *BISANCE)* in the 6th. All except its coastal towns was settled by Slavs (see *ESCLAVONIE),* mainly Croats, in the 7th century. And by the 10th century it had separated into Croatia in the North and Serbia in the South. Its North and South became known as White and Red Croatia. From c1100, though still administered by a Croatian *BAN,* it passed under the Hungarian crown. In the 14th century it fell to the Ottoman Turks.

PANNONIA

Ammianus tells of Pannonia; as does Tacitus in both his Annals and his Agricola and Germania. These were Nostradamus' main sources for the early history of the area which he has selected for an analogy with events which are shortly to unfold. The area and its people the Pannonii are named as *'PANNONS'* in verses V 48 and VIII 15, and *'PANNONOISE'* in verse V 47.

Pannonia was the area of Eastern Europe between Epirus in the South, the Adriatic in the West, the Rhodope mountains in the East and the Danube in the North. It included what is now northern Greece, part of European Turkey, South East Bulgaria, Albania, Yugoslavia, Hungary and much of Austria.

That does not mean though that at any one time that entire region belonged to the Pannonii. The many ancient tribes living in the area had few fixed boundaries themselves; and because the Romans periodically created new provincial ones, no name was permanently applicable even to its parts. In their literature the Romans often lumped all the peoples of the area together as 'Illyrians', without specifying the tribes they were referring to. The main tribal groups of Illyricum were the Dalmatae (see *ALMATIE)* and Pannonii.

When Nostradamus writes of the Pannons or Pannonoise he refers to what the Pannonii, - or more accurately, the Illyrians, - did, and to their characteristics when judged from Roman literature. Velleius Patercullus, for example, thought them untrustworthy, their civilized appearance only superficial. And Ammianus speaks of "their cunning and versatility". And in his History of the Peloponnesian War, Thucydides had already recorded that Illyrian mercenaries employed by Sparta treacherously switched sides.

When the area was a part of the Roman Empire, disorders in Pannonia tended to spread; and as troops from elsewhere became involved, the disorders spread further, to as far away as modern France. And these distracted Western attention from threats growing in the Middle East.

Here are a few details which serve as examples of the effects on Roman Europe of involvement in Pannonia.

The Pannonian revolt of 6 AD had to be dealt with by troops from Germany. But it still simmered, and for 9 AD Tacitus records, "A desperate revolt against Roman rule in Illyricum and Pannonia". Next, in 14 AD, again in Tacitus, "Mutiny broke out in the Roman army in Pannonia". The latter followed the death of Augustus, when the army sensed weakness and division in the civil authority. And, "At just about this time, and for the same reason", continues Tacitus, "the regular brigades in Germany mutinied too. They were more numerous, and the outbreak was proportionately graver".

Western involvement in the Balkans continued to bring troubles with it until Rome abandoned the area to the Huns in 395 AD. Ammianus describes what are now called guerilla tactics, used in Pannonia shortly before the Roman departure.

"Illyricum was being overrun by the fury of our foes ....while we were away defending Italy and Gaul ....They did not pin their hopes on pitched battles ....but on their usual surprise attacks."

In the Middle Ages a threat to the concept of a united and peaceful Europe was still associated with Pannonia. For in the 9th century the Magyars, a nomadic tribe of mounted archers from the Steppes, swept across Europe. They reached down into Italy and across into South West France. After the Magyars were defeated at Lechfeld in 955 AD, they settled down on the Pannonian plain where they are now Hungarians. In that same period Slav tribes, mostly Serbs and Croats, introduced to the region a policy of planned resettlement and conversion of its inhabitants to Christianity.

The conqueror of the Magyars at Lechfeld, the Saxon Otto the Great, brother-in-law of King Athelstan of England, - went on to establish a Holy Roman Empire based on Germany and embodying the idea of a united Christian Europe. This 'all-Europe' historical dimension was not lost on Nostradamus. In it he also saw a linguistic parallel featuring a hybrid root. The first syllable of 'Pannons' and also of 'Pannonoise' is 'pan'; and *pan* = 'all' in Greek. Thus, as well as referring to the doings of the Pannonii, these names approach the same subject from a different angle, reinforcing Nostradamus' meaning of 'all-European' or 'people of Europe' as those who will be affected by 'Pannonia'.

ANALOGIES WHICH INFLUENCED WHICH EVENTS
NOSTRADAMUS WOULD PREDICT

Nostradamus liked to predict future events by naming persons or places associated with similar events in the past. He had become 'hooked' on analogies. This was probably inevitable, because from puns to synecdoches almost all his word-plays are necessarily also analogies in that they depend on partial correspondences between things which are otherwise different. But not all of these appear in easily spotted grammatical tricks or name-analogies such as those above.

To find the others, instead of searching his verses first, and then looking for his literary references, the reader begins to work the other way round. Keeping in mind all that one has learned about his tastes and methods, one reads his sources, looking for passages which had to have invited his attention and use of them. Then one goes back to his verses; frequently to be pleasantly surprised by how well one has come to know the man, and sometimes to find that doubts about meanings have been dispelled and that new connections between verses can be made.

There are of course far more events described in classical literature which could have influenced his choice of subjects for Les Prophéties than actually did so. So even one's short-list of items for further examination has to be limited to such as references to premonitions or statements which turn out to have been prophetic. And it helps to cheat a bit, by remembering what subjects one has already recognised in his quatrains.

Scipió's foreboding about what will follow the destruction of Carthage has both these qualifications.

This was its background. The First Punic War - between Rome and Carthage - ended in a draw. The return match, the Second Punic War, memorable for the crossing of the Alps by Hannibal/*ANNIBAL*, ended at Zama in 146 BC in a complete win for *ROME*. Carthage was finished as a military threat to the Roman Empire. But fifty years later, jealous of Carthaginian commercial success, Rome opened the Third Punic War. This mismatch ended with Carthage burned to the ground.

As the victors watched the city burning, Polybius remarked, "Isn't this a splendid sight?"

At these words Scipio Aemilianus the Roman commander wept.

"A splendid sight indeed Polybius," he replied. "And yet, I am in fear, I know not why, that some day the same order will be given to destroy my own country".

Les Prophéties explain in what way Scipio's hunch will be fulfilled. And this less-elementary means of connecting prophecy and literary reference prepares us for it.

Chapter Sixteen

HIS DATES

"'Master, those voices - are they shades I hear'? I asked.
And he to me, 'Yes, you are right'."
(Dante. Purgatory c.16, v.8.)

THE VALUES OF DATES

Dates in Les Prophéties have four values or uses. First, a date can finally identify a verse with an event. Secondly, when a year has been identified, other words in the verse tend to make much more sense. Thirdly, it is easier to react correctly to something, if when it is likely to happen is known before it does.

Fourthly, there are instances in which Nostradamus deals with an event because it resembles another and he will get credit for foretelling both. In these cases the date of the less noteworthy event ensures that the applicability of the verse to it will not be overlooked or ascribed to chance. It is to this fourth purpose that Nostradamus usually limits his use of the Gematria and the alphabet-based codes mentioned in Chapter Twelve. Here we are going to ignore dates in this fourth category; first because in most cases they merely cite a sample year in a period of several years during which something develops; and secondly because this way we can concentrate on dates of greater interest to us, and the reader will get maximum return for minimum effort.

Quantity of dates

Relatively few verses in Les Prophéties are self-contained. Most are linked with others by subjects common to them. So although not many dates are given, more verses are connected with dates than at first appears to be the case.

DATES IN VERSE-NUMBERS

The best-known date in Les Prophéties occurs in verse IX 49. This includes the line,

"Senat du Londres mettront à mort leur Roi,"

This translates as,

"The Parliament of London will put to death their king".

Charles I has been the only English king put to death by Parliament. He was beheaded on 30 January 1649. The year is the same as the number of the verse. And as the chances are 99 to 1 against both verse number and date being the same by chance, it is safe to conclude that it is his death which was predicted here. However, by now it will not have escaped the reader's notice that, for Nostradamus, this was a very uncharacteristically obvious clue. The explanation is contained in the placing of the clue outside the verse itself. In this way the verse, which has two separate and entirely different meanings, is not saddled with a date which fits only one of them.

Had Nostradamus used only one method for imparting dates, as with all his tricks once that was discovered most of the mystery which has kept his works alive would be gone. He therefore employs several dating methods.

DATING BY ASTROLOGY

As is to be expected from an at least nominal astrologer, one of these methods concerns stars, planets and comets. There are advantages to the use of astrology. First, conjunctions between heavenly bodies are frequently repeated. Successive generations of readers are thus kept on the edges of their seats by the possibility that the next appropriate conjunction will be the one referred to. Secondly, the mere possibility that this will prove to be the case distracts the careless reader from the other connotations which the words used carry. An example of this is contained in the first line of verse VIII 49. This reads,

"Satur au beauf iouë en l'eau, Mars en flèche".

Astrologically, this would be,

"Saturn in Taurus, Jupiter in Aquarius, Mars in Sagittarius", and might readily be taken for a date given in the form of this rare conjunction. But in fact it is not. *L'eau* = 'water' does represent Aquarius the zodiacal Water Carrier sign covering 21 January to 18 February. But it only does so to confirm the unconcealed "The sixth of February" in the next line. *Flèche,* literally 'an arrow', is a missile. *SATUR,* from 'satyr', means 'wanton'. *MARS* means 'war'. (For the remainder, see Dictionary in Part Four.)

This is an appropriate moment at which to serve up a reminder that verse VI 100, already looked at, implied that one should be reluctant to accept an explanation based on astrology where there is another one which is more likely.

OTHER SYSTEMS

Enthusiasm for working out Nostradamus' dates would soon fade were readers to find that only by the predicted thing happening could they know for certain when that would be. So in some places Nostradamus adopts systems which do allow the dates of events to be known in advance. Those dates which form parts of one of these systems are easily recognised as doing so because even before they are understood they do have the appearance of dates. And their being parts of a system, the cracking of one date in it leads quickly to the cracking of the others.

CREATION-BASED DATES

The subject of dates having brought us past verses numbered IX 49 and VIII 49, it is vintage Nostradamian that he introduces one of his principal systems in verse I 49. Here the third line begins,

"L'an mil sept cent", which is, "The year 1700".

Just as 1991 signifies this number of years from the nominal birth date of Christ, all similar systems have a 'year one'. This is usually the year of their introduction or of some significant event. In his Epistle to Henry II, Nostradamus suggests that his system starts from the date of that epistle, which was 14 March 1557. However, later in that same preface he says that Creation was his start-date. And many 16th century Christians would have agreed that that took place in 4004 BC, the date which is now associated with Bishop Ussher. Most of those scholars who did disagree, accepted another chronology, that of the 4th century bishop of Caesarea and foremost of early Church historians, Eusebius. Eusebius calculated the birth of Christ to have been 5200 years after Creation, and in his preface Nostradamus actually names Eusebius as being among his sources. However, agreement about the date of Creation remained rare. Josephus put it at 3952 BC, and the Venerable Bede at 3949 BC. And to add to this general - and in Nostradamus' case, deliberately contrived - confusion, yet lending strength to our suspicion that Eusebius does fit into the picture somewhere, is Nostradamus' respect for Dante. For the latter's line in his Purgatory,

"More than five thousand years in pain he yearned",

shows that at least he, Dante, was using Eusebius' arithmetic.

Puzzled? At this stage, you might well be. But do not worry. The explanation of the 'Eusebius connection' is coming later. At this stage it is enough to know that Nostradamus uses a Creation-based system once. Then, it is only to give an approximate date, whereas his other systems, - bar those based on the Gematria and alphabet codes, - are precise. But that one Creation-based date up his sleeve would be enough to satisfy the king, and might be enough for the Inquisition too, should they press him for an explanation. However, dates based on Creation or on the other main BC contender, the *Anno urbis conditae,* that of the foundation of Rome in 753 BC, shared a serious drawback. They gratuitously implied that important things happened before the birth of Jesus and of the Church. For Nostradamus to have used either of them widely would have been bad politics. And had he done so, he would scarcely have then destroyed the point of the system by openly giving away its key.

The Council of Nicaea

During the first three centuries AD, a combination of fertile minds in the early Church, and slow means of communication, had resulted in Christian dogma developing along different lines in different places. As a consequence of this, in those days Christianity included much Arianism, Gnosticism, Manichaeism and other beliefs which have since been rooted out as heresies.

That was the background against which Emperor Constantine I summoned three hundred bishops to the first ecumenical council, to get a single creed agreed upon. It met at Nicaea from 20 May to 25 July in the year 325 AD.

In deciding what was to be Christianity, and what was heresy, that of the Council of Nicaea became a key date in Church history. And in that it was this council which, by a vote, decided that Jesus was divine, it was also more signiflcant than the latter's date of birth, which is, in any case, uncertain. There are two strong suggestions and a final proof that 325 AD is Nostradamus' start-date in this system. The first suggestion comes with the fact that the Council of Nicaea was adjourned until 327 AD. This allows it to be used by Nostradamus with a two-year range either way. It also covers events which span more than one year, and preserves curiosity to the last moment. All these were factors of which Nostradamus could, and did, make good use. This now is where 'the Eusebius connection' comes in. The second suggestion, or hint, was inserted by Nostradamus into his Epistle to Henry II. There, as we have just seen, he names Eusebius. And he does this because Eusebius was deposed at the Council of Nicaea in 325, and re-admitted to fellowship when the council reconvened in 327. And not only did Eusebius' list of dates end at 325 AD. When, later in that century, his list was extended to 478 AD, this additional work was carried out by another Eusebius, Eusebious Hieronymus. The Eusebious thread is therefore hard to miss. Nicaea itself is mentioned by Ammianus.

The proof that 325 AD is the start-date of this system is quite simply that all the dates included in the system fit the events described in their verses. There could be no stronger proof than that.

This, briefly, is how this system works. In verse I 49, for example, we find '1700'. To this is added 325, the date of the Council of Nicaea, producing 2025. With this we turn to the Julian calendar, because that was the one in use in Nostradamus' time. Julius Caesar introduced it in 46 BC. And 2025 minus 45, - not 46, because there was no 'year zero', - gives 1980. And as will be seen below in Chapter Twenty-Five, the events described in verse I 49 are those which happened in 1980.

THE BIRTH OF CHRIST

It has already been mentioned that Nostradamus' Nicaean system gives him a two-year flexibility. In deliberately taking advantage of this, to cover events which take time to unfold and also series of events, Nostradamus does not go beyond accepted looseness with dates. '3 BC', for example, nominally means 'three years before Christ'. But this is inaccurate. Christ was born in 4 BC, if not earlier. So the year which followed that should be called '1 AD' and not '3 BC.'

Even the '4 BC' is no more than a best guess by scholars. In fact almost all that is known of the matter is what Matthew says.

"After Jesus was born in Bethlehem in Judea during the time of King Herod, Magi from the east came to Jerusalem and asked, 'Where is the one who has been born king of the Jews? We saw his star in the east' ....When they" - the Magi - "had gone, an angel of the Lord appeared to Joseph in a dream. 'Get up', he said, 'take the child and his mother and escape to Egypt' ....where he stayed until the death of Herod ....Herod gave orders to kill all the boys in Bethlehem and its vicinity who were two years old and under, in accordance with the time he had learned from the Magi".

Herod died in 4 BC, by which time Jesus was up to two years old; putting his date of birth as far back as 6 BC. But even this date depends on Herod having died within months of the slaughter of the innocents.

ASTROLOGY AND THE BIRTH OF CHRIST

There have been many attempts to establish Jesus' date of birth. Not all have been by theologians. Astrologers too have been in on the action. One astrologer arrives at 12 BC, because Mary and Joseph went to Bethlehem to register in a census: and in that year there was a census in Palestine, and Halley's comet could have been the Star of Bethlehem. Another astrologer arrives at 15 September, 7 BC, on the basis that *JUPITER* which in ancient astrology was associated with kings, rose at sunset on that day; while Palestine was associated with the zodiacal *PISCES,* leading to the adoption of a fish as an emblem by the early Church. A third astrological theory agrees with the latter as to the year, but arrives at 17 September. This third one is based on the sun having been in the constellation of Virgo that day, accounting for the belief that Jesus was the son of a virgin. But the truth is that we do not know the date of Christ's birth.

A RESULT OF CHRIST'S BIRTH-DATE BEING UNKNOWN

The discrepancy between the likely actual birth date of Christ and the BC/AD system nominally based on it did not go unnoticed by Nostradamus. So, in addition to the two years furnished by the adjournment of the Council of Nicaea, our own dating system supplies six or more years latitude, giving him a legitimate range of almost ten years with which to cover events which take that long to unfold. But he exploits this right only occasionally. He does so for example, in verse VI 2, in which he omits the step concerning the Julian calendar.

CHAPTER SEVENTEEN

THE UNSCRAMBLING PROCEDURE

"Homo non proprie humanus sed superhumanus est."
"To be properly human you must go beyond the merely human."

Fortunately, that saying exaggerates our situation more than somewhat. But it is apt insofar as it warns that there is work to be done if we are going to lever all Nostradamus' meaning from his verses.

When Nostradamus had finished writing what he intended to say on each subject, in one or more quatrains, he scrambled the lines and verses. His scrambling consisted of lifting words or phrases from their original places and exchanging them with words or phrases from another line or verse. This was followed by any necessary adjustments to the rhyme and scanning. Occasionally, this procedure extended to exchanging words or phrases between the subject he was working on and verses which he had written already on other subjects. All that done, he shuffled the verses out of any form of order. We can be sure that this is how he composed because it is not credible that he had the finished work in detail in his head before he began writing Les Prophéties.

Due to their having been scrambled in this way, many of the verses are not self-contained, and cannot be fully understood without reference to other verses. This does not, however, mean that all of Les Prophéties' almost one thousand verses have to be examined simultaneously. In practice there is a short-cut which allows the reader to work systematically; yet with smaller, more manageable groups of verses. This consists of dividing all his verses into historical categories.

HIS FIRST HISTORICAL CATEGORY

The first category includes all verses which deal with

Nostradamus' own time and the immediately following decades. That was the period in which he had to draw so much favourable attention to his work that it would never be forgotten. Hence more than half his verses are in this category. All of these are only about Europe; and most of them are about internal French politics. Some of these tell of incidents which, though doubtless of local interest at the time, did not even make the history books. So readers four hundred years later, who know little about French history anyway, can expect to find these verses the hardest to understand. It is, however, their very parochialism, which makes them easy to identify.

HIS SECOND HISTORICAL CATEGORY

The second category consists of the verses which deal with the period roughly between the years 1600 and 1900. The subject matter of verses in this category is better known. The reason why there are so few quatrains in this second category, in proportion to the long historical period which the category spans, cannot be more than conjecture. However, verse VI 2 contains a hint about the reason. For in it Nostradamus describes the 20th century as "strange", or "different". This implies that by comparison with the period preceding it, the 20th century will prove to have been more interesting or important. Which, if this proves to have been so, would account for his devoting more attention to it than to all the three preceding centuries put together. This in turn suggests that the sole purpose of his having written anything at all about the events between 1600 and 1900 may have been to keep interest in Les Prophéties alive. For if interest in his predictions were not somehow kept alive, those about this century would not have reached it.

HIS THIRD HISTORICAL CATEGORY

The third category, that with which this book is mainly concerned, consists of the verses about the period from 1900 onwards. Some of these bear dates. Others can be readily identified by words or phrases which only make sense in the context of this or some future century. These include references, some cryptic and others open, to air travel, space travel, submarines, and events we would have known about had they already happened. A further characteristic of verses in this third category is that though their subject matter is still confined to events of direct concern to Europe, the actual events described sometimes take place beyond its borders.

DOUBTS ABOUT CATEGORIES

When that first stage in the unscrambling procedure has been done, there may in practice still be doubt about the historical categories of some verses. No matter; they can be put aside for the moment and looked at again later. By then, when the reader has gained a little more experience, most of the doubts will have resolved themselves.

THE NEXT STAGE

The quantity of verses needing to be worked on together can now be further reduced. One starts with any verse in the chosen category, listing its significant words. This list will exclude conjunctions, prepositions, pronouns, verbs such as *être,* *mettre* and *venir* and all other words which have no self-contained meaning. Beside each word in the list can be briefly noted all its meanings, literal or idiomatic. Running through the resulting jumble of words there will be a theme. This will emerge as any word which is not connected with any of the possible meanings of the other words is deleted. The same treatment is now applied to another verse, and so on. This done, though few verses may yet make much sense, it will be possible to short-list their apparent subjects.

GROUPING VERSES

The verses can next be grouped according to their apparent subjects. Then be examined for more detailed connections between them. For example, any action will be set on one continent or another, or at sea or in the air. It will take place in peace or war. To begin with, that may be all that is clear. But as attention is now turned on each of these reduced groups separately, other things will be noticed. Among these will be that a story started in one verse is continued or added to in another.

All the words which were not self-contained can now be put back into their verses. And the links between verses having been found, the stories they tell will be complete. They will also be free of the ambiguities which deliberately misplaced punctuation marks had produced.

IMPOSING OUR OWN MEANINGS

This whole process does sound as if it risks the reader constructing his own predictions from Nostradamus' words, which is a subject to which we will return later. But in fact the danger of that resulting is very slight. A misunderstanding would not long stand up to scrutiny. The interwoven layers of meaning, which are Nostradamus' hallmark, are much too difficult to match, and were placed there by him partly to make sure that such mistakes should not be made.

Whether Nostradamus obtained his precognition from scrying or from dreams, it is known that he obtained it at night. Then he spent every daylight hour in working and reworking his grammar. So it would not be reasonable to expect that the unscrambling should prove a quick process, though it does become much faster with practice.

The 'conveyor-belt' procedure recommended above does indeed seem a boring method of analysis. But it would be pointless to work at unscrambling one verse at a time if part of its meaning lay in another verse. The process outlined, though perhaps slower than one would have liked, does prove to be the quickest in the long run.

Part Three

SAMPLE VERSES

"Some there are, though very few, to whom the divine grace has granted this, that they can clearly and mostly distinctly see, at one and the same moment, as though under one ray of the sun, even the entire circuit of the world, with its surroundings of ocean and sky, the inmost part of their mind being marvellously enlarged."

(The explanation given by Saint Columba when the monk Lubge asked how prophetic knowledge came to the saint.)

INTRODUCTION

Sample verses are arranged on the following pages in their historical sequence. It is an order which also illustrates Nostradamus' tightening techniques.

It will be noticed that nowhere does he appear to be puzzled by what he 'sees', despite the technological changes which have taken place since his lifetime. He takes all these in his stride, with none of the awe with which modern inventions have often been greeted when first seen by technologically backward peoples. It should nonetheless be borne in mind that Nostradamus is 16th not 20th century man. His blasé front should not lead to that being forgotten.

In preference to wielding always a broad brush, he usually paints the coming history in a series of cameos comprising its incidents. And his is everywhere a 16th century judgement of which incident, and which aspect of this, will communicate his meanings best. And these are not always the selections which a 20th century man would have made.

For the majority of readers, those whose interest in Les Prophéties is confined to learning about the future, there is though a compensation for this divergence in historical viewpoints. For we, when we read about the past, can see that our forebears often worried about things which did not in the long run matter, and that they tolerated or disregarded things which did. And conversely, without our short-term considerations to blinker him; but instead, with the hindsight of having seen our present and future, Nostradamus is able to hint at what we should not disregard. And, in what are headed 'The Lemming Verses' in Chapter Twenty-Seven, he does so.

CHAPTER EIGHTEEN

THE DEATH OF HENRY II

At one time it was not unusual for people to hint, darkly, that God had used Nostradamus as a channel through whom to speak to mankind. If this suggestion were true, then He may have taken the life of Nostradamus' patron, Henry II of France, to ensure He would be heard.

The date was 30 June, 1559. The place was Paris. The occasion was a royal double wedding. Princess Elizabeth, daughter of Henry II and Catherine de Medici, was to marry the most powerful man in the world, Philip II of Spain, who would be represented at the ceremony by the Duke of Alva. And Henry's sister, Marguerite, was to wed Emanuel Philibert the Duke of Savoy.

The attention of the whole of Europe was on Paris that day. Including those who had not been invited, and had come anyway, almost everyone who mattered in international affairs, or their representatives, were in town. These two marriages would influence the map of Europe for years to come, and there was no limit to what might be achieved by a lucky or contrived meeting here. So, although travelling 16th century roads was not something lightly undertaken, in this case very few ambitious men did not make the effort.

And that only covered statecraft. Daughters were taken down from the shelf, dusted, and packed off to Paris with their fathers. Those without single daughters to unload, or smart enough clothes to wear, or who were too sick or old to make the journey, had made arrangements to receive the latest news or gossip quickly, ...and ahead of their neighbours if possible. If anyone in Paris made the least social *faux pas,* all of Europe would hear about it in next to no time.

And poor Montgoméry's gaffe was a remarkably big one. He

killed the king.

It happened like this. The coming nuptials were celebrated by a jousting tourney. In this, King Henry's opponent was Gabriel, sieur de Lorges, Compte de Montgoméry, captain of his Scottish Guard. In their first course at each other, Henry was nearly unseated. His pride hurt, he announced that he would tilt once more with Montgoméry. Montgoméry protested, but the king insisted. This time when they clattered down the lists towards each other on their heavy chargers, for some reason the usual trumpets and drums accompanying a tourney were silent. Spectators, commenting on this silence afterwards, said it should have seemed ominous at the time. It certainly proved to be. In his first pass with the king, Montgoméry's lance had cracked, and while arguing against a further passage, he had forgotten to exchange his used lance for a fresh one. And this time, when it hit the king's shield its tip split and was deflected upwards to the king's helm.

Henry reeled in the saddle, and had to cling to his horse's neck until attendants lifted him off and laid him on the ground. By the time they had his helmet off, Henry was motionless, and they could see why. His helm seemed not to have been firmly secured, because a splinter from the shattered lance had passed under it and into his throat. And worse. Either Montgoméry's lance had then forced the king's visor upwards, or part of it had passed between the visor's bars, for another splinter had entered Henry's head, through his right eye.

When the king had been carried to a chamber in the Tournelles, still completely paralysed, only the dukes of Alva and Savoy, the Prince of Orange, the cardinal of Lorraine, the Constable of France, and doctors and apothecaries were allowed to enter. As result, if anything spread faster than the news, it was rumours. Within days the king's injuries became the talk of Europe, as did anyone who could be associated with them in any way. And, as we will see, Nostradamus fitted in this second category.

As soon as the steps necessary to secure the succession had

been taken, in case Henry died, censorship was relaxed and constant news updates followed. One newsflash concerned the progress being made in anatomy as result of the king's accident. 16th century knowledge about the inside of the human head was sketchy. That was admitted even by doctors. But now four criminals were collected from their cells in the Châtelet and Conciergerie, and decapitated; their heads then supplied to the half dozen doctors attending the stricken king, so that they might see which bits lay where. The next flash concerned the arrival at Henry's bedside of the famous Vesalius, personal physician to both Charles V and Philip II.

But in the early afternoon of 10 July, 1559, ten days after the joust, and through which his moments of consciousness had been agony, Henry died.

Now the gossip-mongers really let rip. Their original subject, the king's health, stolen from them by his demise, they concentrated on allegations about who had had a hand in his death. Henry, in one of his brief periods of consciousness, had absolved Montgoméry from blame, so they looked further afield. And because they could see from Les Prophéties that Nostradamus had known beforehand what would happen at the tournament, they turned their attentions on Salon, and him. The Paris mob burned him in effigy, and there was clamour for him to be brought to trial.

Though not in the way either would have chosen, Henry certainly achieved fame for Nostradamus. It was the latter's verse I 35 which had caused the commotion. Here it is.

"Le lion jeune le vieux surmontera,
En champ bellique par singulier duelle:
Dans caige d'or les jeux lui crevera,
Deux classes une, puis mourir, mort cruelle."

The literal translation of this is,

"The young lion the old will overcome,
In field of war by single duel:
In golden cage his eyes will tear,
Two wounds one, then to die, cruel death."

At first sight that verse appears harmless enough; indeed, so vague as to convey little if anything at all. But that is to a 20th century eye. In 16th century France its meaning had been suspected even before the fatal tournament took place. Suspected strongly enough for the queen, Catherine de Medici, to have sent for Nostradamus to ask him about it the year after it was published. So let us now look at it again, more carefully this time, and at the circumstances surrounding its first circulation.

Nostradamus does not write on zoology, so this is not about two lions fighting in a cage. But to describe a man who puts up a good fight the simile 'like a lion' is commonly used. So it is safe to assume that this is a fight between two men who are here compared with lions.

They are not, though, named; nor is the date or place of the fight given. However, the very absence of this information is itself the first clue. A fight between two men is not a rare occurrence, and is usually only of local interest. Which suggests that the incident described here took place in France, during or shortly after Nostradamus' lifetime. And it having been worthy of his attention, yet unnecessary for the participants to be named, - or even described beyond their relative ages, - one or both men would have been well known.

That is a start. More can quickly be deduced. Well known fighting-men of the 16th century were usually at least knights, and often noblemen or kings. And between such men, single combat was usually in a duel or a jousting tournament. Though neither of these would take place in a cage, many helmets of the period resembled cages in that the visors had bars. And though by Nostradamus' time full armour was obsolescent even on the battlefield, it was still worn in the lists. So this verse almost certainly predicts a famous jousting accident.

Proceeding from that deduction it is not now difficult to identify the accident concerned. Indeed, it had been predicted by someone else even before Nostradamus wrote this verse. The earlier prediction had been made by the Italian astrologer Luca Gaurico, under whom Nostradamus' one-time friend Scaligero had studied. Gaurico had personally warned Henry II of France not to engage in any sort of single combat, particularly in his forty-first year. Such combat, Gaurico had told the king, would be likely to result in the king's being blinded or killed.

It is thought to have been the queen's interest in this verse of his, which so clearly echoed Gaurico's warning, that caused her to summon Nostradamus to the court soon after Les Prophéties was first published.

Perhaps the king and queen had overlooked the fact that at forty the king was in his forty-first year. For despite both warnings, and as we have seen above, under the social pressure of a major state occasion, Henry did enter the lists, with fatal result.

Now let us look at the verse again. 'The young lion' can be recognised in the thirty-three year old Montgoméry, famed for his skill at arms. At forty, Henry was relatively 'old', and was 'overcome' by the younger man. It did happen in 'single' combat, in a stylised 'duel'. Henry's gilt helmet with its barred visor was a 'golden cage'. There were 'two wounds' from 'one' impact, one to Henry's 'eyes'. And the king was 'then to die', a 'cruel death' The apparent discrepancy between Nostradamus' mention of 'his eyes', and only one of Henry's being injured, can be seen to have been due to a printer's error. For an edition-variation of *les jeux* is *loeil*.

This may be as much as the casual reader wants to know. To a student of Nostradamian, however, there is more of interest. It concerns Nostradamus's use of the words *crevera* and *classes*.

Crevera is from *crever* = 'to burst open', and also 'to tear'. But coming too from O.F. *crever,* is *crevace* = 'narrow passage'. Put together, these words paint a graphic picture of Montgoméry's lance shattering against the king's helm, its splinters tearing between the narrow slits in the visor and into Henry's face And as in *cela lui a crevé un oeil,* 'it blinded him in one eye'.

In this verse *classes* comes from Gk. *klasis* = 'fracture' or 'break'. It therefore refers to the broken lance and also the king's injury. But not content with this, Nostradamus produces an edition-variation through which to extend it further. This is the English word 'plays'. 'Plays' can mean 'strokes', suggesting combat. It also confirms the 'play' nature of the 'duel'. And being plural it catches the fact that Montgoméry and the king had already passed down the lists at each other twice before the pass in which the accident happened.

Containing as it does, no literary references, verse I 35 is of only limited interest to the more serious reader. It has though been worth looking at. For it shows that such was Nostradamus' determination that his predictions should be recognised when they came true, he made those set in his own lifetime so simple that they could be understood before what they described happened. Hence, in general, the freer a verse from complex word-plays, the earlier its historical context usually proves to be.

And this simplicity, which led to Nostradamus establishing his reputation so quickly, also served another purpose. It allowed him to conserve most of his more involved ploys for verses about later generations. For those later generations would, inevitably have been accumulating knowledge of his techniques; and for them he would need a constant flow of unfamiliar tricks.

SUMMARY

For continuity in our unravelling of Les Prophéties, it must be mentioned that verse I 35 is of course an example of what we have in Chapter Seventeen labelled 'the first historical category', by which we mean the verses set in the 16th century or soon thereafter. And their effectiveness in ensuring that Nostradamus would make sufficient impact on his own times, to be remembered in ours, could scarcely be better illustrated.

CHAPTER NINETEEN

ENGLISH HISTORY

Both the following verses are about events in English history in which the political situation in the Netherlands was important and perhaps crucial. So although one of them is set in the 17th century and the other spans four centuries, they are linked by a common theme. And they also belong together as examples of the second historical category mentioned in Chapter Seventeen, which consists of events between the 16th and 20th centuries.

Verse X 100.

"Le[1] grand empire sera par Angleterre,
Le pempotam[2] des ans plus de trois cens[3];
[4]Grandes copies[5] passer par mer et terre,
Les Lusitains[6] n'en seront pas contens[7]."

"England will be the[1] great empire,
Glorious and all-powerful[2] for more than three hundred years[3];
Also[4] to move large forces[5] by sea and land,
The Portugese and Spanish[6] will not be pleased[7]."

1. Note 'the', not 'a'. England's empire is pointedly compared here with those of Portugal and Spain. The former's heyday was already over. The latter's would last only one hundred years.
2. This is a hybrid word, clearer in the edition-variation *pempotans*. 'Glorious' comes from the O.F. *pompe* = 'splendid display' together with the Latin *potens* = 'having power'. And 'all-powerful' from the Greek *pan* = 'all' together with *potens* as above.

3. In some editions the 't' has not been dropped from *cents* = 'hundreds'.

4. Nostradamus does not bother to employ the word 'also'. Instead, for brevity, he places the line where the described movement of forces applies equally to all three countries. In this line *par mer,* especially, strengthens the theme of competitive empire-building.

5. From L. *copia* = 'army' or 'force'.

6. In the Classical World the Lusitani were a people living in the western part of the Iberian peninsular, in what is now Portugal. But there had then been no division of the peninsular between Portugal and Spain.

7. The second 't' is dropped from *contents* in this edition to maintain its rhyme with cens.

When that verse was published, the last of England's old empire had just disappeared with the loss of Calais in 1558. And the first sign of its new empire would not appear until the settlement of Virginia in 1607. The first line was therefore a prediction for which there had been no apparent justification at the time. But to fully appreciate the verse as a whole, one should recall the wider European situation.

Spain already had settlements in North Africa, the Caribbean, Central and South America and the Pacific. She had dynastic commitments in the Netherlands, Germany, Austria and Italy. She was also the major partner in alliances stemming Turkish expansion in the Mediterranean. In short, she was a superpower.

This verse implied, however, that there would be a direct connection between the rise of an English empire and the curbing of the Spanish. There proved to be. Spain was over-extended. Her budget was so tight that four times in forty years her king had to declare her bankrupt. And it was in these circumstances that Hawkins and Drake were intercepting the gold and silver from the New World which comprised a fifth of the Spanish king's income. In 1588 Spain reacted with an

Armada, and within a decade with two more, each more ruinously expensive than the last. Drake responded with raids on Spain itself, the last of which cost Spain more than in a forty-year period her bullion revenue had totalled.

England's contribution to Spain's downfall was not only financial. With a usually-hostile France between her and her European possessions, Spain had only two lines of supply to her armies in the Netherlands which was in arms against her. One was via the Mediterranean and round half Europe. The other, which was through the Channel, England cut at will.

To illustrate the growth of the British Empire, its early contest with Spain is not the first choice a modern man would perhaps make. Nor does Nostradamus select it only for that purpose. He chose it partly because half the Netherlands, trying to hold which was to prove so ruinous for Spain, became independent in 1648. And that was the year in which the Netherlands, referred to in the first line of the next verse, briefly held the key to England's door.

Before looking at the next verse though, the reader might like to refresh his knowledge of the events which led up to and followed the English Civil War. Parliament was wanting more say in national affairs. King Charles believed in the divine right of kings to rule. They were on a collision course. Taxes became the instruments through which the struggle was conducted. Parliament was thwarting the king's foreign policy by denying him money to carry it out. Charles was responding with stratagems to raise money without parliamentary consent. The kingdom was dividing into two factions There were riots. By 1642 the tax issues were at an impasse which only a war could clear.

After the Civil War, not accepting defeat, Charles was continuing to plot, though with no troops to confront Parliament's Model Army. And then, in 1648, with the end of the Thirty Years War, mainland Europe was suddenly full of unemployed soldiers. These were Charles' last hope. His exiled supporters were in the Netherlands already, where many of the veterans were. Parliament saw the danger, and reacted quickly. It sent a mission to the Netherlands to work against foreign aid for the king. And on 30 January, 1649, it had his head cut off.

Now for the verse itself.

IX 49.

"Gand & Bruceles⁴ marcheront⁵ contra Envers⁶
Senat du Londres⁷ mettront à mort leur Roi¹⁰
Le sel & vin¹ lui seront à l'envers²,
Pour eux avoir le regne en dessarroi³."

"Taxes¹ will obstruct him²
And have the kingdom in disorder³.
Will Netherland⁴ armies march⁵ against⁶ the London Parliament⁷,⁸?
It⁹ will put to death its king¹⁰''.

1. Duties on salt and wine, such as the gabelle salt tax, are among the oldest sources of revenue.

2. Literally, 'will oppose him'.

3. Literally, 'For them to have the reign in disarray'.

4. a. *Gand* is the French name for Ghent;

   b. *Bruceles,* like the edition-variation *Bruxles*, is a homophonic cryptogram of *Brussel/Bruxelles;*

   c. in the 17th century, Ghent was a major port in the Netherlands which, here, like Brussels, it represents by synecdoche. The former already had particularly close links with England through the wool trade. Nostradamus' reference to Ghent in connection with the gathering of troops, with the potential consequences of this, may have been sparked by this line in Dant's Purgatory c.20, v. 16, "But if Doui and Lille and Ghent and Bruges were strong enough".

5. Cities or countries themselves do not march. 'Armies' from them do so.

6. After *contra* = 'against', *envers* = 'towards' is added to

rhyme and scan. An edition-variation is *Anvers* = 'Antwerp'. In 1648, with the silting up of Ghent's access to the sea, Antwerp was the principal port in the Netherlands, and was that from which the mercenary armies would have sailed.

7. *Senat du Londres* is placed where it will both end one line and begin the next.

8. Insertion of the question mark is for historical accuracy. Whether the Royalists could have assembled a foreign army must remain an open question.

9. An optional pronoun, avoiding repetition of 'the London Parliament'.

10. Charles was beheaded in 1649, which is the number that Nostradamus gives this verse.

The non-event of an invasion from the Continent to aid Charles is one of the less well known facts of English history. As too are some of the other connections between events in the Netherlands and the relative fortunes of the Spanish, Portugese and English empires. These verses illustrate the benefits to be had from checking its historical background once the broad subject of a verse has been identified, before proceeding.

CHAPTER TWENTY

LOUIS XVI

It is France in 1791. The revolution, which began in 1789, is gathering impetus. While a new constitution is being debated by revolutionary groups jockeying for power, Louis XVI is still on the throne. But his life, and that of Marie Antoinette his queen, are in danger. A plan is hatched for their escape across the border into the Austrian Netherlands.

On the night of 20 June the royal family creeps out of The Tuileries palace in small groups. They are soberly dressed, the Dauphin as a girl. They carry passports borrowed from a family due to go to Russia.

Meeting together at dawn, at a safe distance from the palace, they set off in two carriages which do not bear the royal coat-of-arms. As if there were no hurry, their route takes them through the Argonne forest, and they dawdle and picnic along the way.

But when they reach Varennes their plan miscarries. The queen's hairdresser, who has been sent ahead with the royal diamonds in another carriage, has taken all the available relay horses. While the fugitives are looking for other fresh horses, and also for an escort of loyal cavalry which is supposed to be waiting for them there, news reaches the village that the royal family is missing from the palace. That a warrant has been issued for the king's arrest.

Villagers surround the two carriages. The travellers try to bluff their way through, but the crowd grows and becomes suspicious. Louis eventually admits that he is the king.

The fugitives are detained overnight in Varennes. Louis and Marie Antoinette are lodged in a room over the shop of the village grocer who is named Saulce. And in due course the royal family is taken back to Paris.

Now let us read Nostradamus' account of this, contained in verse IX 20.

"De nuict[1] viendre[3] par[4] la forest[6,8] de Reines[5,7],
Deux[2] pars[10] vaultort[9] Herne[13] la pierre blanche[14],
Le main[17] noir[15,16] en gris[15] dedans[11] Varennes[12]
Esleu[19] cap.[18] cause[21] tempeste feu sang[21] tranche[20]."

"By night[1] a couple[2] will come[3] via[4] the queen's[5] doors[6] and[7] the forest[8], by a wrong[9] and roundabout[9] way[10], dawdling[9] into[11] Varennes[12]. The Queen[13] like a white stone[14] in grey and black[15], the king[16] looking like a monk[17]. The first[18] elected[19] king of France[18]; guillotined[20] in a violent[21] cause[22]".

1. Epenthesis of *nuit* = 'night'. Note that the journey ended as well as began at night.

2. Notice that *deux* is placed where it refers to the carriages as well as to the principal escapers. And the latter had been only 'two' when leaving the palace. The royal children with their governess, and those ladies and gentlemen-in-waiting who were to accompany the party, had already left separately.

3. *Viendra* in an edition-variation.

5. The king had donned his disguise in the queen's ante-room, and they left via her room and an empty one to which she had the key.

6. From L. *fores* = 'doors'. In Roman usage this word was frequently specifically used as in 'out of doors' and 'abroad'.

7. Commas are substitutes for 'and'.

8. *Forêt* in an edition-variation. And *forest* is an epenthesis of this.

9. An edition-variation of *voltorte*. From the latter comes *tort* = 'wrong', 'fault'. 'Roundabout' comes from *volte* = 'turn' as in *volte-face* = 'about turn'. 'Dawdling' is contained in *voltiger* 'to flutter', 'to hover while in flight'.

10. Epenthesis of *pas* = 'step'.

12. Also known as Varennes en Argonne.

13. A cryptogram of *reine* in which 'h', - usually silent anyway, - substitutes for 'i'.

14. A queen cannot literally be a 'white stone'. And in her memoirs Mme. Campan records that the thirty-six year old queen's hair had turned white during that night in Varennes. It is also recorded by others that during that night her body was as cold as stone from shock. But this phrase is as concisely complex as will be found anywhere in Les Prophéties. For in the sense of a diamond, 'white stone' also refers to the 'Scandal of the Diamond Necklace'. That had occurred in 1785-'86, when the queen was accused of having an immoral affair with a cardinal. It had so discredited the monarchy that the financial reforms which might have prevented the revolution were blocked. And it also refers to the smuggling of the queen's diamonds by her hairdresser, which in using the relay horses, led to the arrest of the king and queen and so eventually to their deaths.

15. The queen was wearing a black mantle and a grey dress.

16. *Noir* is a cryptogram of *roi*.

17. From the edition-variation *moine* = 'monk' or 'friar'. In the sombre brown clothes of his disguise the stout Louis resembled a friar rather than a king. And this is also a reference to Louis' earlier sexual immaturity, virginity and impotence.

18. An abbreviation of *'Capet'*. Since 897 AD every king of France traced his ancestry back to Hugh Capet, the 'first' king of their lineage. Nostradamus' use here of the king's name rather than title, reflects Dante's Purgatory c.20, v.17;

"On earth beyond I was called Hugh Capet;
from me have sprung the Louises and Philips,
rulers of France up to the present day".

In view of Louis' fate, it can be seen that by guillotining 'Capet' to *cap.*, Nostradamus fills the word with additional meanings. From O.F. *caper* = 'to seize', it refers to Louis' arrest. From L. *caput-* = 'of the head', - a word used by Livy in connection with danger to life, and by Cicero in connection with a chief or leader; from medieval L. *cappa* = 'a covering for the head'; and as in *de pied en cap* = 'from head to foot', it also refers to Louis' head which was to be cut off.

19. From *élire* = 'to elect'. Shorn of absolute power and therefore briefly a constitutional monarch, Louis was 'The first elected king of France'.

20. Literally, 'slice'. In modern idiom, 'the chop'.

21. Literally, 'tempest' - from *tempête* - of 'fire and blood'.

22. By moving the word *cause* to the end of the phrase, Louis is here made the victim rather than the 'cause' of the violence. That probably accords with the opinion of the royalist Nostradamus. This movement of the word is, however, optional.

The reader will have noticed that that last line of verse IX 20 jumps from the Varennes incident of June 1791 to Louis' execution in January 1793. The explanation for this is that Nostradamus scrambled that last line with the last line from verse IX 34. In doing so, duly adapting both lines to rhyme and scan in their respective new verses, he links the two quatrains.

Verse IX 34 continues Louis' story with an incident which happened at The Tuileries in 1792.

Fédérés, fanatical revolutionaries from the provinces, are in Paris for the Festival of the Federation. When it is over they refuse to go home. They demand a permanent camp near Paris. Louis refuses to authorise this. Now, on 10 August, they come to the palace to demand it. Louis is cut off in the mob.

"The nation has no better friend than me", he assures the crowd round him.

"Then prove it'', someone shouts. "Put this on". A stocking-cap, which is a revolutionary emblem, is thrust toward him on a pike.

Louis puts it on; and in doing so, for the moment probably saves his life.

> *"Le part[11] solus[10] mary[9] sera mitre[12],*
> *Retour[6] conflit[8] passera sur[5] la tuile[7]:*
> *Par cinq cents[13] un trahir[14] sera[17] titre*
> *Narbonne[16] et[15] Saulce[1] par couteaux[4] avons[2] d'huille[3]."*

"Saulce[1] stocks[2] oil[3] for knives[4]. On[5] returning[6] to The Tuileries palace[7], trouble[8]. The husband[9], cut-off[10], will play the role[11] of revolutionary[12] to five hundred traitors[13]. A traitor[14], too[15], the titled Narbonne[16] will be[17]."

1. Jean Baptiste Saulce, above whose grocery shop in Varennes Louis and Marie Antoinette passed the night of their arrest.

2. Literally, 'have'. But in a grocery shop 'stocks' is better.

3. An edition-variation of *huile* = 'oil'. And colloquially, *huile* = 'bigwig', which describes *Saulce,* the village procureur, in the role thrust on him by the times.

4. *Coutaux* in other editions. A two-syllable word was needed for the line to scan. *Coutaux* serves this purpose. The oil already mentioned is used to sharpen knives, and *Saulce,* who stocks it, being Louis' nominal gaoler, is seen by Nostradamus as a traitor, for whom the traditional symbol is the knife.

6. *Retour* = 'return'.

7. Literally, 'will cross the tile'. *Tuile* = 'tile'. The Tuileries palace was so-named because it was built on the site of an old tile-works. Its construction was ordered by Catherine de Medici in 1564, in Nostradamus' lifetime.

8. Literally, 'conflict'. 'Trouble' is more idiomatic.

9. An edition-variation of *mari* = 'husband'. This would be an irrelevance were this and verse IX 20 not read together. Here, with *solus,* it emphasises that the weak Louis is 'cut-off' specifically from his interfering wife. And the trouble which Louis is in, referred to in note 8 above, is emphasised here; for O.F. *marir* = 'to be afflicted', 'to be vexed'.

10. From O.F. *solu* = 'free', 'untied', 'single'; and L. *solus* = 'alone'. See note 9.

11. Abbreviation of *partie* = 'part', 'role'. And a 'role' is 'played'. As an abbreviation of *partenaire* = 'partner', this also relates to 'husband'.

12. The usually tall 'mitre' hat is a stiffened version of an

originally soft, sock-like headdress such as that adopted by French revolutionaries. It was one of these which Louis put on. And from Gk. *mitra* = 'girdle' also comes 'surrounded', adding to the reader's vivid mental picture of the incident.

13. The instigators of the mob's invasion of The Tuileries on 10 August 1792, and the largest contigent of Fédérés taking part, were the 'five hundred' odd from Marseilles. From the viewpoint of those who, like Louis and Nostradamus, identified the king with the state, those who marched against the king were 'traitors'. Hence *trahir* follows *cinq cents*.

15. Literally, 'and'.

16. *Narbon* in some editions. Compte Louis de *Narbonne* (1755 - 1813). Minister of War from December 1791 to March 1792. His dismissal by the king was condemned by the National Assembly and provoked threats of violent action against the court at The Tuileries. These were carried out in the mob's invasion a few months later. Although he was a moderate revolutionary who wanted no more than a constitutional monarchy, because he was an aristocrat who was also half-brother of the king most royalists considered Narbonne a traitor. And as a monarchist himself, Nostradamus shares this view.

Varennes' only claim to fame is that it was where Louis XVI and his family were caught. So there is no doubt about the subject of the first of these two verses. And as Louis' gaoler there, Saulce, is named in the second verse, nor is there doubt about the two quatrains belonging together. And as details of both incidents are well documented, a reader can unscramble and interpret them without fear of doing so incorrectly. They therefore comprise a Rosetta Stone against which beliefs about Nostradamus' writing techniques can be checked.

The two verses include abbreviations, cryptograms, edition-variations, epentheses, metaphor, misleading punctuation, a traditional symbol, and words which form parts of more than one phrase. That, though, does not make them particularly interesting by Nostradamus' standards. What should not perhaps be overlooked, however, is that the two words *Varennes* and *Saulce* ensured that these verses could not conceivably fail to be recognised after the events. The dates may therefore be significant. And, as several readers have commented, those dates being 1791 to 1793, they are just half-way between the date of publication of the verses and the time beyond which Nostradamus' predictions do not extend.

CHAPTER TWENTY-ONE

A RE-CAP

In Parts One and Two of this book we attempt to get inside Nostradamus, both as an individual human and as a man of his time. We cannot really enter another person's thoughts at will, even to know for certain what another person in our own century and culture means every time he speaks. But because we exist in a common environment we do usually interpret his words correctly. This almost automatic ability to understand each other though, extends far less often to words spoken or written in other languages and in a distant century. There, we have to exercise much more care. So in effect, in order to understand Nostradamus, we have to shift ourselves right out of our normal points of view, and temporarily adopt Nostradamus' 16th century perspective on the world.

Most of what understanding Les Prophéties entails has now been discussed. But before proceeding into verses about the 20th century it would be as well to recapitulate. Nostradamus employs several languages and dialects. These each involve their own grammar, so a comment here about syntax. The order in which words are placed in relation to each other varies with each language. It therefore alters in translation anyway, particularly when from verse to prose. Where two or more languages are mixed together, the syntax of one may not be more correct than that of the others. So though the vast majority of words in Les Prophéties are French, Nostradamus is theoretically free to mix his suffixes and syntax. And he does so. He even extends this liberty with words and their normal order into linked verses in which there may be no alien words.

To simultaneously convey and hide his meanings, Nostradamus also uses obsolete place-names, historical analogies, traditional symbolism, edition-variations, misplaced punctuation, more than a single system for dates, and verse which must be rendered into prose without losing information which is carried in the rhyme or scanning alone. And in addition, verses, lines and phrases are often displaced from where they would be more readily understood.

Aside from those reasons Les Prophéties does not lend itself to straight translation because it contains many figures of speech. The phrase, 'It's straight from the horse's mouth', meaning that something comes from an authoritative source, and which does not concern a horse at all, illustrates the difference between figurative and literal meanings. Even clearer illustrations of this difference can be seen in, for example, comparisons between any of Edward Fitzgerald's interpretations of Omar Kayyam's Rubaiyat and a literal translation of the original Persian text. But the main reason why it should be clear that straight translations will not suffice, is that Les Prophéties would not then puzzle Frenchmen.

So a line has to be drawn between what Nostradamus says and what he means. Any who do not draw this line are ignoring Nostradamus' warning, contained in the dedication to his son which prefaces the first edition. This bluntly describes Les Prophéties as "dark and abstruse sentences".

Straight translations of any texts unavoidably leave any riddles they contain unsolved. This always faces commentators with a dilemma. For if they report that a figurative passage means such and such, they can seldom prove it until, if it is a prediction, it is fulfilled. While if they say it does not mean that, this may be true only insofar as it is not expressed in the way in which they would express it. And how they themselves would express it is almost totally irrelevant; which is in itself a fact that all save a few commentators nowadays tend to overlook.

As with legal, medical, military or other professional jargons, an understanding of the writings of Nostradamus has to be picked up as one goes along. His readers are fortunate that his style is so 'way-out' that it can seldom be mistaken for conventional communication. It would certainly be pointless to try to impose on it any rules of grammar which it does not itself employ.

Although their jargons are already familiar to those among whom they circulate, even legal documents and political communiques are carefully studied by their recipients for what may be written between the lines. That is, for what the words do not say, yet do imply. But that done, the conclusions reached are usually no better than strong probabilities. For it is almost impossible to say anything which is not open to more than one interpretation.

Nostradamus' verses are more difficult, yet, at the same time, easier to interpret correctly than are other writings. They are more difficult because he has found a variety of ways in which to withhold his meanings from superficial examination. But they are also easier in that, by corroborating each other, his multiple layers of detail put most of his meanings beyond all reasonable doubt. They are easier too in that we have learned to distinguish whose writings influenced his. And by checking in them we can sort out which, in a range of otherwise equally likely meanings, he has intended each of his words to convey.

Nostradamus' literary and astrological references are further hurdles. But with a very modest amount of research, these too can be cleared. There still remains, however, a potential obstacle which it is much more difficult to deal with. This last obstacle is our own, often unconscious, interference. For whether they be gloomy or optimistic, we have preconceptions about the future, and expect or hope to find these supported by Les Prophéties. In this connection it may be worth pointing out that even the newspapers we each buy are those which will present the news to us in the way that will confirm our opinions. So when a particular interpretation of Les Prophéties achieves this, we tend to dig no further. Thus, without consciously intending to do so, we fail to find out what Nostradamus really says, and have only ourselves to blame for this.

OUR OWN REJECTIONS

This interference, arising within ourselves, is in part a natural reaction to our fears about whether mankind can survive its own Achilles heels. The result is that interpretations of Les Prophéties are not always judged to be correct or wrong according to a real balance of probabilities, the criterion we have learned to apply to almost all other subjects.

Instead, the greater the probability that an unwelcome interpretation is correct, the more stubbornly it is sometimes rejected. The reader will then have wrapped himself in a self-image of sophistication and scepticism, oblivious to the trick his mind is playing on him. The 18th century explorer Captain James Cook encountered a comparable trick among islanders who were unable to see his ship riding at anchor in plain view a few hundred yards away. There was nothing wrong with their eyes. Their blindness extended no further than an inability to see his ship. They did not wish to see it because its presence upset their chosen preconceptions about the world. So they reacted to its arrival by dropping a curtain of psychologically induced blindness between themselves and it.

We can only too easily do what those islanders did. Or err in the other direction, by manufacturing from Nostradamus' words, meanings which are our own not his. For readers of Les Prophéties it is these risks which are the real Scylla and Charybdis, and which must be at least acknowledged to exist if they are to be avoided.

HIS CHANGING METHODS

In the remaining chapters it will be seen that Nostradamus realised that by the twentieth century many of his literary stratagems would have become familiar to his readers and so have lost their power to puzzle. To off-set this he begins to increase the frequency of his references to mythology, the flow of symbolism, and the need for reading between the lines. This does not bring with it though any less certainty as to whether or not an interpretation is correct. The multiple layers of meaning remain as a very effective guide to this. But, as always, no interpretation should be accepted while any part of the verse concerned remains unexplained.

Chapter Twenty-Two

ENTER THE TWENTIETH CENTURY

In verse VI 2 Nostradamus introduces the 20th century. As has been seen in Chapter Nineteen, when dealing with any lengthy period it is his practice to portray it through some of its main events. To fulfil this purpose, those events required to be carefully chosen. They had to at least reflect their times. Preferably, once complete, they would have a major effect on European history. And to suit his overall purpose and style, they or their effects should have been unexpected. The invention of the aeroplane and the collapse of Communism both satisfy these criteria.

"En l'an cinq cent octante[3] plus et moins[2],
On attendra[5] le siècle bien étrange[4]:
En[6] l'an sept cent et trois[7] cieux en témoins[1],
Que plusiers[8] regnes[10] un à cinq[8,9] feront change[11]".

"Judged by the skies[1] around[2] 1905[3], a strange century[4] will be in store[5]. And from[6] 1985[7], one after another[8] five[9] states[10] will change[11] their political systems[12]."

1. Literally, 'skies as witness'.
2. Literally, 'more or less'.
3. Literally, 'In the year five hundred', to which 'eighty', from Gk. *octa* - is added. To this 580, 325 is added as the key-date of the Council of Nicaea. (See Chapter Sixteen). This totals 905. This could not be complete because 905 AD was already in the past, and this is a prediction. So the prefix '1' is added, giving '1905'. Note: the first powered flight took place in 1903, and by 1909, when Bleriot flew the Channel, aircraft had arrived to the extent that there had already been international air races.

But which year between these dates marked the start of the 'air travel' to which Nostradamus later refers must remain indefinite. Hence the 'around 1905'.

5. Literally, 'one will wait for'.

6. Literally, 'in'. But 'from' better conveys an unfolding of events which began 'in' the year given.

7. Literally, 'the year seven hundred and three'. To which is added the keydate '327', - that of the reconvened Council of Nicaea because this is the second date in this verse, - giving 985 AD. And, as usual, with the prefix '1', '1985'. Note. This was the year in which Michail Gorbachev came to power in the Soviet Union, and therefore from which the changes referred to came about.

8. Literally, 'several ....one to five'. The 'one to five' conveys that the changes would take place successively. Had they been simultaneous, the 'five' would have sufficed.

9. Nostradamus gives the exact number of states which would make the change within the span of time justified by the doubt about the year in which Christ was born. (See Chapter Sixteen again). And by inserting *plusiers* = 'several', he even deliberately makes the 'five' less certain, suggesting by so doing that beyond the legitimate range of time from the date given, other states too would begin that change.

10. Literally, 'kingdoms'. In Nostradamus' time, 'kingdoms' were almost universally synonymous with 'states'. With hindsight, these can now be seen to have been Czechoslovakia, East Germany, Hungary, Poland and Rumania.

12. This is not stated. But it is implied because 'kingdoms' are states which are governed in a particular way. And any lesser change would neither balance the importance of the aeroplane nor satisfy the criteria for the nature of the verse.

Both the subjects of verse VI 2 were successions of events, and not incidents which happened at a single moment. Nostradamus' making full use here of a dating system based on the Council of Nicaea which, having failed to solve its problems at the first attempt, was obliged to reconvene, is very appropriate.

Verse 1 63 also deals with this century in broad terms, and foresees the importance of the aeroplane. It does not directly follow verse VI 2 in the sequence in which all Nostradamus' verses eventually fit together. But because, here in this book, the selection given from his quatrains is intended only to illustrate his techniques, it can suitably be looked at next.

"Les fléux[11] passés[12] diminue[4,5,12] le monde[3],
Longtemps[1] la paix[2] terres inhabitées[14];
Sûr[9] marchera[7] par ciel[8], terre, mer[10] et onde[6],
Puis[15] de nouveau[17] les guerres[16] suscitées[18]."

"During a long period[1] of peace[2] the world[3] will in effect[4] have been shrunk[5] by radio[6] and by safe[9] travel[7] by air[8] over[9] land and sea[10]. And diseases and wars[11] will be over[12] or fewer[13] in developed lands[14]. Then[15] wars[16] of a new sort[17] will start[18]."

1. Literally, 'long time'.

4. The world does not of course actually get smaller.

6. *Onde* = 'waves', as in water or radio waves. The former do not fit the context.

7. Literally, 'will go'.

9. a. i. *Sur* = 'reliable', 'secure';

　　ii. and the edition-variation *Seur* is an anagram of the feminine form of *Sûr*;

　　b. *Sur* = 'above', 'over'.

11. Literally, 'the scourges'. A scourge is a whip only in its most literal sense. The word has long and far more widely been applied to a person or thing which causes widespread suffering. For example, to Genghis Khan, 'The Scourge of Asia'. Traditionally, the twin scourges of mankind have been wars and epidemic diseases. The application here of this more customary meaning is confirmed by the edition-variation *fleurs* = 'flowers'. This is a reference to the rashes which are symptoms of many epidemic diseases such as smallpox, and particularly of plague from which comes the nursery rhyme,

"Ring a ring o' roses,
Pocket full of posies,
Atishoo, atishoo,
We all fall down."

And as red marks upon the body are also produced by a 'scourge' in the literal sense of that word, *fleurs* is a doubly apt edition-variation.

14. 'Diseases and wars' could scarcely occur in lands which were literally 'uninhabited'. 'Developed' is more sensible in the context.

18. Verbs such as *recommencer* = 'to resume', and others which also mean 'to restart' or 'to start again' were available to Nostradamus had they conveyed his meaning. But he selects none of these. Instead, he uses *susciter* = 'to create', and draws attention to this with *nouveau* = 'new'. Other verses make all too clear what these new forms of warfare are to be. But the first hint of that does in fact appear here, in *onde,* which is so similar to *ondée* = 'shower' - which happens, also, to be the link showing where in the final order this verse is properly placed.

Nostradamus' economy with words is well illustrated above by his placing *diminue* where it will apply to *Les fléaux* and also to *le monde.* And his supporting 'travel by air' with *sur* = 'over', while unnecessary, is an example of his reinforcing actual meanings. Note that 'will be' is added to the text in the interpretation, because this is a prediction. Its addition to the text is everywhere optional.

Verse VIII 96 traces the origins of Arab-Israeli discord. Before reading it, it is best to recall these.

In 1900, Palestine was in the Turkish Empire. Arabs, then a poor and subject people, accepted the homeless and equally poor Zionists who, from 1882, had begun to settle among them. But from 1905, pogroms in Russia increased the flow of Jewish immigrants to Palestine, and the Balfour Declaration of 1917 indicated that this would continue. Meanwhile, during the First World War, T. E. Lawrence encouraged an awareness of an

Arab identity which was not satisfied at the Peace Conference afterwards. From then on, Zionist and nationalist Arab aspirations had to collide. And since Israel became a state in 1948, it and its Arab neighbours have distracted each other from progress in other fields.

Now here is the verse which predicted that that would happen.

"La synagogue[1] stérile sans nul fruit[2]
Sera reçue entre[3] les infidèles[5]
De Babylon la fille[7] du poursuit[8],
Misère[4] et triste[6] lui tranchera les aisles[9]".

"Jews[1], with nothing and no future[2], will be accepted[3] by poverty-stricken[4] Arabs[5]. And rueful[6], the children of the Arabs[7] will harry them[8]. They will hold each other back[9]."

1. A synagogue is a specifically Jewish building. And it is also a place where Jewish people come together.

2. Its fruit contains the seed of a plant; in other words, its future. That which should, but does not have fruit, has no future.

5. In Nostradamus' day this term was specifically applied to Moslems and identified with Arabs in general.

7. A carefully constructed phrase. Literally, 'The daughter of Babylon'. Usually, by metonymy, *Babylon* =. 'Iraq' specifically. But Nostradamus continually harps on the theme of the Arab desire for unity, represented by the ancient empires of Assyria, Babylonia and Persia, of which *Babylon* was both in sequence and geographically the centre. So here, as in *les infidèles, BABYLON* represents Arabs in general. The descendants of the Arabs who had earlier accepted the Jews are represented here by *la fille* = 'the daughter', in contrast to the 'fruit' of the Jews. This is because *Babylon* is pictured as a woman, from 'The Whore of Babylon' in Revelation XVII and XVIII. Though Nostradamus was of Jewish origin himself, this does not automatically carry a

disparaging connotation. It is merely a literary reference. But as he uses the same reference in several verses, it is evident that this is the reason for *la fille* rather than *le fils* = 'the son'.

8. Literally, 'of the chase', from *poursuite* = 'the chase', 'the harrying'.

9. More literally, 'will clip the wings'; a figure of speech which is common in England too. From epenthesis of *ailes* = 'wings', with *tranchera* = 'will cut'. Note, a bird's wings are cut so that it cannot fly. And Nostradamus says nothing to connect this action with only one of the sides involved, or with either in particular.

CHAPTER TWENTY-THREE

THE ABDICATION

In January 1936 King George V died. He was succeeded
on the throne by the Prince of Wales as King Edward VIII.
Among the prince's friends had been a Mrs. Wallis Simpson.
Shortly after Edward became king, Mrs. Simpson began divorce
proceedings from her second husband. This divorce would have
freed her to marry Edward. But as a divorcee she would have
been unsuitable as a royal Consort. Earlier, her friendshlp with
Edward had not been widely known about in Britain; but as
gossip about the royal liaison now spread, so did controversy.
Edward was advised that, as king, he could not marry Mrs.
Simpson. He did not agree. But he was eventually forced to
accept that if he did so he would have to vacate the throne.

On 10 December, 1936 Edward announced his abdication.
And two days later his brother the Duke of York, who had not
expected to become the king, took his place, as King George VI.
Had Mrs. Simpson remained married to her American husband,
her friendship with the king might have been tolerated. It was
the pending divorce which made this impossible. And this, as can
be seen in the following verses, Nostradamus clearly understands.

X 40.

"Le jeune[3] né au regne Britannique[4],
Qu'aura[5] le père mourant[1] recommandé[2]:
Icelui mort[7] LONOLE[9] donnera[8] topique[10],
Et à son fils[11] le regne[12] demandé[13]."

"The dying father[1] will entrust[2] Britain to the young man[3]
born to rule it[4]. Who[5], the former[6] dead[7], will give[8] London[9] a
topic of gossip and controversy[10]. And from his son[11] the throne[12]
will be demanded[13]."

2. The future tense because this is a prediction.

3. *Le* shows that this is not a young woman.

4. *Britannique* is placed at the end of the line to show that it is what is entrusted, as well as what is to be ruled.

6. A cryptogram of *celui-ci*.

9. *Londres* in an edition-variation.

10. A hybrid word from Gk. *topos* = 'commonplace', L. *topica* = 'topic', and O.F. *topiquer* = 'to quarrel', 'to dispute'.

12. Literally 'reign' or 'kingdom'. A metonymy.

13. Again, the future tense for a prediction

X22

"Pour[8] ne vouloir consentir[4] au divorce[5],
Qui[5] puis[10] après[1] serra[6] connu[2] indigne[7]:
Le Roi des Isles[3] sera chassé par force[9],
Mis à son lieu[11] qui[12] de roi[14] n'aura signe[13]."

"After[1] it is known[2] that the King of the Isles[3] does not want to agree[4] that a divorce[5] will be[6] unsuitable[7] for[8] him[3], he[3] will be forced out[9]. Then[10], in his place[11], one who[12] had no expectation[13] of kingship[14]."

2. From *connaître* = 'to know'. And from L. *cognoscent* = 'knowing' in the edition variation *cogneu*.

3. *Roi des Isles* is positioned in the verse where it is 'The King of the Isles' who will not agree, where it is for him that a divorce is not suitable, and where it is he who will be forced out.

4. Literally, 'not want to agree'.

5. Literally, 'that to a divorce'. The text does not say *divorcée*. But as that would translate into better English, it would be a permissible alternative because Nostradamus habitually dispenses with accents and full word-endings.

7. Literally, 'unworthy'. Note that through *indigner* = 'to make indignant', this is connected with the 'controversy' alluded

to in verse X 40.

9. Literally, 'chased out by force'.

12. Literally, 'who'. The 'one', which clarifies without changing the meaning, is added for correct grammar in translation.

13. Literally, 'no sign'.

14. Literally, 'of king'. A synecdoche.

The abdication of King Edward VIII had little effect on history. That Nostradamus devotes two verses to the subject confirms his special interest in royalty. And also that this interest is well-meant. For by naming *Britannique, Londres* and *Roi des Isles* he was drawing the attention of the British people, including Edward himself, to both verses before the events took place. In this way he appears to have sought to warn the latter in time for him to avoid the consequences of failing to understand his position.

But this sympathetic approach to mistakes where royalty is involved, is noticeably absent where Nostradamus deals with errors of judgement by people who are not royal. To the latter, he owed no favours.

CHAPTER TWENTY-FOUR

THE AYATOLLAH

Until he reaches the 20th century in Les Prophéties, Nostradamus husbands and even keeps back some of his literary tricks. But from now on he no longer does so. He moves into a higher gear. Allegories and extended metaphors begin in some places only to hint at meanings. There are more references to mythology. And, more often now, there are incomplete phrases to which more than one word in that verse can be added; by which means several phrases are supplied where only one is immediately apparent.

It should be borne in mind that all the interpretations supplied in this book, except in Chapter Twenty-Eight, are simplified, intended for the casual reader. But the more serious student will find that if he subjects them to further analysis, some of the verses will prove to be like onions; in that as he probes beyond each layer of meaning, another, confirming it will be revealed.

Becoming aware of every layer of meaning in what Nostradamus predicts in these verses is a cryptic-crossworder's delight. And this is a stage at which the would-be Nostradamian might profitably try out his own interpretations before looking at those given or at the dictionary in Part Four. For everyone who is an adult now in the 1990s has lived through the events described below by Nostradamus. So there is no need to turn first to history books.

However, a few reminders about the events of 1979 and 1980, and what led up to them, may be useful.

In dragging Iran towards Western standards for the 20th century, the Shah of Iran had made enemies within his country. The most stubborn of these was the Ayatollah Ruholla Khomeini, who wanted Iranians to live by the Koran. He was arrested in

1963 and expelled to Turkey. He later moved his base for subversion to Iraq; from where, in 1978, to curry favour with the Shah, Saddam Hussein in turn expelled him.

For the Iranian government and those wishing to overthrow it, assassinations and threats to families were methods of political persuasion which spread to Iranians in Europe. And world opinion could be far more easily influenced from Europe than from the Middle East. So on 6 October 1978 Ayatollah Khomeini flew to France. There he waited until, back in Iran, the time was ripe for revolution.

As is his custom with subjects to which he devotes several verses, here Nostradamus scrambles his predictions among them, rather than dealing with each event in a separate quatrain. But those who wish to do so can readily extract the relevant parts of each and reassemble them into a single, ordered narrative.

V 84.

"Naître du gouffre et cite[3] immesurée[2],
Né de[4] parents obscurs et ténébreux[5]
Qui[1] la puissance du grand Roi révérée[11],
Voudre[6] détruire[10] par[7] Rouan[8] et Eureux[9]."

"One[1] to be born at an unknown[2] place[3] in the Gulf, of[4] obscure parents[5], will want[6], via[7] France[8] and Europe[9], to destroy[10] the power of a great and respected king[11].''

1. Literally, 'Who'.
2. Literally, 'unmeasured'. To take the measure of something is to know it.
3. Literally, 'city'. But this cannot be accepted literally, for it could not then also be 'unknown'. And the Ayatollah's exact birthplace is not known. The name Khomeini is that of a then small town in West Central Iran, probably in or near which he was born or spent his infancy.
4. Literally, 'born of'.

5. Literally, 'obscure and mysterious parents'. It is interesting that The Penguin Dictionary of Twentieth Century History actually describes Ayatollah Khomeini's early life with this same word, 'obscure'.

6. *Voudra* = 'will want' in an edition-variation.

8. A metonymy. But more than that; as the sea-port of Paris, *Rouan* is a synecdoche for what is to be exported from France. In this case, and for which France produced the prototype, revolution.

9. The word-ending is adjusted in order to rhyme.

11. The Shah's armed forces were the most powerful in the Gulf area, in which he was the regional 'policeman'. But in his choice of word to express this, Nostradamus does once more display some bias where a monarch is involved.

II 29.

"L'Oriental[4] sortira de son siège[5],
Passer[8] les monts Apennins[9] voir la Gaule[6]:
Transpercera[1,8] le ciel[2] les eaux[3] et[7] neige[9],
Et un chacun frappera de sa gaule[10]."

"He will go through[1] the sky[2], overseas[3] from his eastern[4] base[5], to see support in France[6]. Then[7] he will pass over[8] Italy[9], and will goad everyone[10]."

3. Literally, 'the waters'. To 'go through the sky' in connection with these is to go over the waters, and hence 'overseas'.

5. Or 'seat' or 'headquarters'.

6. A pun. *Gaul* is an ancient name for France. *Gaule is* 'a stick'.

7. Literally, 'and'. But 'then' is preferable for clarity.

8. *Passer* = 'to pass'. But here it is with *transpassera* = 'will pass over' in an edition-variation of *transpercera*.

9. Literally, 'the Apennine mountains snow'. A metaphor.

Nostradamus is correct about the routes. On his outward journey to France Ayatollah Khomeini flew along the Mediterranean. On his return journey to Iran he flew over northern Italy.

10. A figure of speech. Again, Nostradamus puns with *gaule*. Here, as a 'stick', it suggests an old man as a user. And with *frappera* = 'will hit', the stick becomes a synonym for a goad.

III 59.

"Barbare empire³ par le tiers² usurpé⁴,
La plupart⁵ de son sang mettre à mort⁶.
Par mort sénile⁸ par lui⁷ le quart frappé¹,
Pour peur que⁹ sang par¹¹ le sang ne¹⁰ soit mort¹¹."

"The time ripe¹, a third² of the barbarian empire³ will be usurped⁴ and most of its leaders⁵ put to death⁶. For him⁷, his own hour come¹, death of old age⁸ in fear that⁹ more of his kin¹⁰ would die violently¹¹."

1. Literally, 'the quarter struck'.

3. That of classical times. This was successively Assyrian, Babylonian and Persian; and later that of Tamerlane. The 'third' is therefore Syria, Iraq or Iran. Note that in the completed sequence of Les Prophéties, this is the first reference to the rivalry between these three states for hegemony over the modern Middle East.

4. The future tense because this is a prediction.

5. From *plupart* = 'the majority'; with the edition-variation *La plus grand* = literally, 'the more great'.

8. Ayatollah Khomeini was born between 1900 and 1902. He died on 3 June 1989, of old age.

10. *Par lui ....le sang ne* = 'born of his blood'. Nostradamus omits the accent from *né*, as he does from many words. Here though he does so to directly link this verse with verse V 84 above, in which he otherwise uneconomically

accompanies naître = 'to be born', with *né* its past participle. 'More' is not in the text; it is inserted here with hindsight, because many of Ayatollah Khomeini's family, including his eldest son, had at this stage in the story already been killed by Savak, the Shah's internal security organization.

11. Literally, 'will be dead by blood'.

II 62.

"*Mabus[2,4] puis tôt alors mourra viendra[5]*
De gens et bêtes[9] une horrible défaite[10]:
Puis[6] tout a coup[3] la vengeance on verra,
Cent, main[7], soif, faim[11] quand[1] courra la comète[8]."

"When[1] an Ayatollah[2] will suddenly[3] seize power from a Shah[4], he will then soon die[5]. Afterwards[6] will come the vengeance of the poor[7]. This will be a herald[8] of all living creatures[9] ravaged horribly[10] by thirst and hunger[11]."

2. A cryptogram of *Magus* = 'a Persian priest'.

4. A cryptogram of MegAByzUS who was a leading figure in the coup which removed the magus Smerdis from the Persian throne and replaced him with another usurper. This is an extended analogy. (See Chapter Fifteen.)

5. Shah Muhammed Reza Pahlevi left Iran on 16 January 1979, was deposed in that March, and died on 27 July the following year.

6. 'Then', in this sense.

7. 'Will come' is not in the text. But to be grammatical the sentence requires a verb, and this one does not affect the meaning. *Cent main* = 'a hundred hand' - or 'hands'. Figuratively, this is 'a mob'. And here the words which follow these suggest a more specific connotation.

8. A comet traditionally foretells great events. Nostradamus introduces one here in order to stress that the consequences of the Shah's overthrow will prove to be very

serious. He is not associating these events with any actual comet. (See Chapter Fourteen).

9. From L. *gens* = 'a group of families having a common origin'. Hence, more literally, 'mankind and beasts'.

Having established his reputation for accuracy in his many verses about his own times, Nostradamus scoots through the following three hundred years. To major events in European history he pays little more attention than he gives to its minor incidents such as those concerning royalty.

Then, suddenly, when he reaches 1979, this changes. To the fall of the Shah of Iran he devotes more verses than he has done to any earlier subject. It is as though he sees all else as merely leading up to and from this. In itself and its immediate effects, the Ayatollah's coup does not seem to rate this much attention. In the last line of verse II 62, however, Nostradamus alludes to the reason why he thinks it does so.

CHAPTER TWENTY-FIVE

THE SHAH, HOSTAGES AND WAR

Extra-sensory perception is not unusual. Animals too seem to experience it. But what sets Nostradamus' precognition aside from that of most other people is that he understands so clearly the symbolism in which it is often conveyed to the conscious mind, and that his is about subjects so far removed from his own lifetime. And more than this, that he evidently understands not only what he 'sees', but also the connections between these things. In the three verses below, which cover events in Iran in the decade between 1978 and 1988, this awareness is well illustrated.

The background to the first of these, quatrain I 70, is that Shah Muhammed Reza Pahlevi had ruled Iran since 1941, but the Iranian mullahs were opposing his westernisation of their country. Shortly before he was overthrown, the Shah spoke on British television of his confidence in the stability of his regime. He had, though, overestimated the ability of his internal security forces to control the opposition. And when, in 1978, religious incitement by the mullahs, orchestrated by the Ayatollah Khomeini from his retreat in France, produced ever-larger demonstrations against the Shah's rule, it suddenly collapsed.

Once in power, Ayatollah Khomeini alienated the West. The West responded with a trade embargo which affected living standards in Iran. And he purged the Iranian armed forces, possession of which had in 1975 allowed Iran to get the better of Iraq in their border dispute. This unilateral disarmament in Iran encouraged Saddam Hussein to attack his neighbour. And in September 1980 Iraqi forces invaded Iran in a war which lasted until August 1988.

"Pluie[11], faim[12], guerre[13] en Perse[10] non cessée[13],
La foi trop[1] grande[3] trahira[2] le monarque[3],
Par la finie[9] en Gaule[7] commencée[5].
Secret[6] augure[4] pour à un être parque[8]."

"Religious fanaticism and over-confidence[1] will betray[2] the great Shah[3]. And when he judges that the time is ripe[4], an ayatollah[4] will start out[5] from a retreat[6] in France[7] to stop him[8]. The result[9] in Iran[10]:- widespread need[11,12] and a long war[13]."

1. Literally, 'too much faith'. This applies to the fundamentalist belief in Islam with which the ayatollah motivated his followers. It equally represents that of the Shah in the state apparatus which failed him *par la finie.*

3. Persia, now Iran, is the stated setting. There, *le monarque* is styled 'the Shah'.

4. From L. *augor* = 'a priest in ancient Rome who, by testing the auguries, decided when the time was ripe for a venture to start'. In the stated location, Iran, an ayatollah is a priest.

5. The future tense for continuity and because this is a prediction.

6. From L. *secretus* = 'set apart', and L. *secretum* = 'retired place', 'retreat'.

8. Literally, 'for one to be stopped'. From *parquer* = 'to stop'.

9. Literally, 'the end'.

10. Persia is the obsolescent name for Iran.

11. Here *Pluie* = 'rain' is used figuratively, as in 'a rain of blows'. Through its association with a rainbow, which is a traditional symbol of war, the proximity within the line of *Pluie* to *guerre* speaks for itself.

12. Literally, 'hunger'.

13. Literally, 'unceasing' or 'without end'. This cannot have been meant literally, because all wars eventually end. The Iran - Iraq War lasted for eight years. Figuratively, however, the

on-going struggle between Iran, Iraq and Syria for supremacy in the Middle East, now in its third millennium, fully justifies Nostradamus' phrase.

The following two verses are linked by a common date. The events they describe interlock with each other and expand on those met in verse I 70 above. The following is what else happened in the period they deal with.

In January 1979 the Shah left Iran and went to Egypt. From there he moved round the world seeking political asylum. After sanctuary had been denied to him elsewhere, in March 1980 he was again taken in by Egypt. There, three months later, he died.

Meanwhile, the Ayatollah cancelled trade contracts with the West. And urged his supporters to deal "without pity" with the Left-wing fedayeen. This they did, with religious fervour.

By now, over a hundred thousand skilled workers had fled Iran, many with visas from the U.S. embassy. This left two and a half million bread-winners unemployed and caused widespread shortages. One escape route from Iran could be closed, however. And on 4 November 1979 the Ayatollah's supporters seized the American embassy. Fifty-three Americans and some European nationals were then held hostage, partly to back a demand for the Shah to be handed over to "Islamic justice".

The West responded with sanctions. These did not work. An attempt by American Special Forces to rescue the hostages ended in fiasco. The West was impotent; unable to enforce international law, even to protect its own citizens. Its humiliation was protracted and complete. When, at last, on 20 January 1981, the hostages were released, it was because the Iran - Iraq War had first call on the Ayatollah's attention. And even then, he made the West purchase their release.

III 77.

"Le tiers climat sous⁶ Aries⁹ compris⁴
L'an mil sept cent¹ vingt et sept en Octobre⁶,
Le Roi² de Perse³ par ceux d'Egypte⁵ pris⁴:
Conflit, mort, perte¹⁰: à la croix⁸ grand opprobre⁷."

"In 1980¹ the Shah² of Iran³ will be taken⁴ by the Egyptians⁵. The autumn⁶ will comprise⁴ great humiliation⁷ to the West⁸, and the start of⁹ conflict, death and loss¹⁰."

1. To the given year '1700', 325 is added because that is the base-number of Nostradamus' dating system. (See Chapter Sixteen). From the resulting 2025 AD forty-five years are subtracted because the Julian calendar was introduced in 46 BC.

2. 'The King of Persia' is termed 'The Shah'.

3. The modern name for Persia.

4. The future tense because this is a prediction.

5. Literally, 'by those of Egypt'.

6. Literally, 'Under the third climate'. Climatic divisions are seasons. 'The third' of these is 'autumn', which spans 23 September to 21 December. These were the relevant events of the autumn of 1980. The Shah was moving from country to country seeking sanctuary. The hostage crisis was at its height. And the Iran - Iraq War had begun on 22 September. Hence in this way Nostradamus connects the hostage crisis with the Iran - Iraq War which led to its solution. '27 October' can be seen from the text to have been the particular date that was the subject of Nostradamus' 'vision'.

8. In this context, in which it is opposed to Islam, 'the cross' is particularly clearly a symbol of Christendom, and by metonymy, of 'the West'. Equally, in this context, 'the cross' symbolizes the money with which the West purchased the hostages' release. For as an emblem widely minted on Western coinage, the cross has long been used in literature in puns about coins. In Act 1, scene 2 of Love's Labour's Lost, Shakespeare, for example, uses it in this way.

9. In this instance *Aries* cannot mean the zodiacal Ram, because Nostradamus makes it clear that it relates here to a season, not to a month. But that is not its only meaning. In astrology, Aries also represents the original impulse through which a potential becomes actual; that is, to the dawn or start of something. Note, *Aries* is also a pun on Ares the Greek god of war who, in contrast to his Roman equivalent Mars, is bloody and merciless, yet cowardly.

10. In the Iran - Iraq War, Iranian casualties were note-worthily high. Iran also lost industrial facilities, territory and the war.

I 49.

"Beaucoup, beaucoup avant telles menées[1]
Ceux d'Orient[3] par la vertu[6] lunaire[5]:
L'an mil sept cent[2] feront grands emmenées[4],
Subjugant presque[7] le coin[9] Aquilonaire[8]."

"Well before such moves[1] in 1980[2], those of the East[3] will take important captives[4]. With Islamic[5] fervour[6] they will almost get rid of[7] the Northern[8] presence[9]."

1. Literally, 'Much, much before such manoeuvres'.

2. To the '1700', 325 is added because this is the start-year of Nostradamus' dating-system. From the resulting 2025 AD forty-five years are subtracted because the Julian calendar began in 46 BC. (See Chapter Sixteen).

4. More literally, 'will make greats taken'. From *emmener* = 'to take', 'to take away', 'to capture'.

5. The crescent moon is the universal symbol of Islam.

6. Literally, 'by the virtue'.

7. Literally, 'almost vanquish'. Here with Aquilo who was the Roman god of the North East wind, in an abbreviation of *Aquilonaire*.

8. A cryptogram of L. *aquilonaris* = 'northern'. Note, the

Ayatollah's regime was as opposed to Communism as it was to the West, as was seen in its treatment of the fedayeen.

    9. Literally, 'the wedge', 'the corner'.

CHAPTER TWENTY-SIX

SADDAM HUSSEIN AND THE GULF WAR

Saddam Hussein Takriti acquired absolute power by murdering his political opponents and then his rivals within the Iraqi Ba'ath Party. The legal penalty for joking about him became death. Those who laughed at the jokes, or failed to inform on those who did, also died. Iraq became a nation of terrified informers.

During the 1980 to 1988 Iran - Iraq War, Iraq received tens of billions of dollars in aid from her Arab neighbours. And the United States helped finance grain sales to feed Iraq, while American warships prevented the Iranians from closing the Gulf to Iraqi shipping. But in February 1990 Saddam responded to this assistance with threats that if Saudi Arabia and the other Gulf States did not pay Iraq thirty billion dollars more he would take it. And in that December he threatened worldwide action against U.S. interests. These things are the subjects of verse VIII 70.

"*Il[4] entrera[8] vilain, méchant, infame[3],*
Tyrannisant[1] la Mesopotamie[2]:
Tous amis[10] fait[5] d'adulterine dame[6],
Terre horrible[7] nois de physionomie[9]."

"Tyrannizing[1] Iraq[2], an evil[3] man[4] will make[5] of it[6] a horrible land[7], and will come[8] to threaten[9] all its friends[10]."

2. From Gk. *Mesopotamus* = 'Between rivers'. Since it was so-named in Classical Greece, 'Mesopotamia' has been the area between the rivers Tigris and Euphrates; now Iraq.

3. Literally, 'nasty, malicious, vile.'

4. Literally, 'He'.

6. *Adulterine* from L. *adultrinus* = 'unlicensed', and from L.

adulter = 'adulterer' or 'adulteress'. With *dame* from L. *domina* = 'mistress', this is 'a whore'. In association with Mesopotamia in which Babylon is situated, this is a reference to the Whore of Babylon in Revelation XVII and XVIII.

9. *Noir* in an edition-variation. Hence literally, 'black of face'; or, figuratively, as in The Concise Oxford Dictionary, 'threatening'.

10. Whose 'friends' is not stated, but is implied by the context.

On 1 August 1990, Saddam Hussein's Iraqi forces invaded Kuwait. Reacting, on 8 August American forces began landing in Saudi Arabia. While other European nations dithered, Britain supported America's lead and an Allied expeditionary force was eventually assembled there. This was of mixed racial colours. There were black men from Niger and Senegal; brown men from Bangladesh, Egypt, Morocco, Pakistan, Syria and the Gulf States; and white men from more than a dozen countries. The assembling of this force to oppose Iraq is the subject of verse X 86.

> "Comme un griffon[3] viendra[2] le Roi d'Europe[1],
> Accompagné[4] de ceux d'Aquilon[1]:
> De rouges et blancs[7] conduira[5] grande troupe[6],
> Et iront contre[8] le Roi[9] du Babylon[10]."

"The Europeans[1] will come[2]: Americans[3] accompanied by[4] the British, and then others[3]. They will lead[5] a great military group[6], coloured and white[7], and go against[8] the leader[9] of Iraq[10]."

1. Literally, 'the King of Europe'. In Nostradamus' time 'a king' was synonymous with 'government'. And here, with *blancs* = 'whites', it also has a racial connotation. Appearing too with *ceux d'Aquilon* = literally, 'those of the North' from L. *Aquilo* = 'North', there is considerable detail concentrated here. First; *Aquila,* a cryptogram of *Aquilon,* is a constellation of the Northern

Hemisphere in autumn, so that its appearance in the sky coincided with the despatch of European forces to the Gulf. Secondly; the constellation *Aquila* lies in that part of the Milky Way known as The Rift, between its eastern and western branches. Thirdly; for over five thousand years this constellation was known as 'the eagle', which is the emblem of the United States. Fourthly; the brightest star in *Aquila* is *Altair* = 'the flying vulture', from the Arabic. Lastly; this carries a suggestion that the United States is here 'the king', or 'leader' of Europe.

3. *Gryphon* in an edition-variation. The text reads, 'Like a griffon', but *griffon* could not in any case have been meant literally because a *griffon/gryphon/griffin* is a fabulous beast. As such, it was invented to express symbolically and in a single word what each of the real animals which make up its parts are associated with. It has the head and wings of an eagle, which is the animal emblem of the United States. It has the body of a lion, the animal emblem of Britain. It also has a serpentine tail, and serpents are of many colours. The mythology of the griffin is appropriate too. Its ethics are dubious, and it is associated with the protection of treasure drawn from underground. (See under *GRIFFON* in Part Four for further information).

7. Here, with *blancs, rouges* = 'red' represents colours as different from 'white'.

9. Literally, 'the King'; historically the holder of absolute power. And in that the Allies stressed that their quarrel was with the Iraqi leader rather than with the Iraqi people, this is another carefully chosen word.

10. The capital city of the ancient empire of Babylonia. Its ruins lie sixty miles from Baghdad in modern Iraq.

Iraqi forces invaded Kuwait at 11 pm GMT on 1 August 1990. As the Allies assembled in the Gulf to oppose them, Saddam Hussein boasted that he would unleash "a holocaust", and threatened that he would send the Allies home in bodybags. Hostilities were suspended at 5 am GMT on 28 February 1991. The Iraqi invasion had lasted exactly seven months. The Allied land offensive began at 1 am GMT on 24 February 1991, seven full days before the formal ceasefire on 3 March 1991. Nostradamus gives this precise timetable, and other details, in verse V 81.

"L'oiseau royal[11] sur la cité solaire[12],
Sept mois devant[1] fera nocturne augure[3]:
Mur[6] d'Orient[2] cherra[4] tonnerre éclair[5],
Sept jours[8] aux portes[10] les ennemis[9] à l'heure[7]."

"For seven months[1] the East[2] will make nightly threats[3], and boast[4] a thunder and lightning[5] defence[6]. In exactly[7] seven days[8] the enemies[9] could have crossed the border[10], and the United States Air Force[11] will fly over the city in the sun[12]."

1. Literally, 'Seven months ahead', or 'Seven months in advance'.

3. Nostradamus uses *nocturne* = 'nightly' because 'daily' would unintentionally connect this phrase with *Sept jours* which appears later in the verse. *Augure* = 'omen', which is a warning traditionally more often of harm than good. It is in the singular in order to rhyme.

4. From *cherrer* = 'to talk big', 'to boast'.

5. In this phrase Nostradamus catches Saddam's threat of 'a holocaust'; and also the 'Storm' in 'Desert Storm' which was the code-name of the Allied offensive.

6. Literally, 'wall'. Both literally and figuratively, a wall has always been the primary means of defence.

7. Literally, 'to the hour'.

10. Literally, 'at the gates'. These gates are of course in the 'wall'. In the Classical Age a wall and a border were often effectively synonymous. 'At the gates', rather than 'At the wall', implies that entry could have followed. Note: it will be recalled that Allied forces were authorised by the United Nations only to evict Iraqi forces from Kuwait. They had not been authorised to invade Iraq, which they could in fact have done without

SADDAM HUSSEIN AND THE GULF WAR

significant opposition.

11. Literally, 'The royal bird'. Traditionally this is the eagle, which is the animal emblem of the United States where it had also been an emblem in pre-Columbian times. But as a symbol of authority, power, war and victory throughout Europe since the Ancient World, here the word does not exclude the other Allied air forces which took part. Nostradamus could simply have said 'eagle'. Instead, he uses this phrase in order to emphasise its general 'bird' characteristic, its capacity to fly.

12. Literally, 'over the solar city'. For a 'bird', this implies flight. And in a prediction the future tense is required.

Allied air supremacy was the outstanding feature of this campaign. The Allied ground attack did not begin until Iraqi positions had been pounded from the air, mainly by the United States Air Force. This air assault continued when the Allied land forces advanced. The Iraqi army's withdrawal became a rout. And when its retreat over the border into Iraq was cut off, it surrendered. These stages in the fighting are predicted by Nostradamus in verse III 7.

> "Les fugitifs[8], feu du ciel[7] sus les piques[6]:
> Conflit[2] prochain[1] des corbeaux[4] s'ébattants[5],
> De terre[3] on[12] crie aide, secours[14] celiques[13],
> Quand[9] près de murs seront[11] les combattants[10]."

"Leading up to[1] conflict[2] on the ground[3], American aircraft[4] will hop[5] over the land forces[6] and attack from the sky[7] those running away[8]. When[9] the combatants[10] are near the border[11], it[12] will be to quickly swelling[13] cries of 'Help, help![14]'"

1. Literally, 'impending'.
3. Literally, 'of the ground'.
4. Literally, 'crows'. Here, as in *corbeaux blancs* = 'vultures'. This is a reference back to *Aquilon* in the linked verse X 86 above; for the brightest star in the constellation *Aquila* is

Altair from the Arabic word for 'flying vulture'. And for five thousand years *Aquila* was known as 'the eagle', which is the animal emblem of the United States. Note; 'vultures', as carnivorous birds, are a particularly effective parallel to aircraft attacking or preying on land targets.

5. From *ébattre,* as in *les oiseaux s'ébattent* = 'the birds are hopping'.

6. Pikes, when in use, were infantry weapons.

7. Literally, 'fire of the sky'. A metaphor.

8. Literally, 'The fugitives'.

11. Literally, 'near the walls'. In the Classical Age walls were often effectively and sometimes literally synonymous with borders.

13. A hybrid word from L. *celer* = 'swift'; Gk. *kele* = 'swelling'; and *céliaque* = 'artery' which is an important route, and also from where blood runs rapidly.

CHAPTER TWENTY-SEVEN

THE LEMMING VERSES

Nostradamus' verses about what still remains in the future are dominated by pollution of the environment, terrorism and counter-measures. But his quatrains on those subjects are so numerous, so detailed and so closely linked to each other that they should be read together.

For that reason the six verses in this chapter, which are about other subjects, do not reflect in accurate proportion what most of the as-yet unfulfilled verses say. They are included here because in five instances they deal with the corruption which Nostradamus sees as among the causes of the pollution and terrorism.

This is not to suggest that Nostradamus was particularly moralistic, nor that he is preaching to us here; for little else would support that view. On the contrary, he lived in an age when, for example, authority to gather taxes was widely farmed out to men who intended to profit personally from handling the revenue. And who were actually expected to do so.

Rather than react with impatience to Nostradamus' implied criticisms of corruption and permissiveness in the modern world, therefore, the reader might reflect on this. That being widely read in the classics, Nostradamus would have very closely connected corruption with the fall of Rome and the end of the Classical World. Indeed, he effectively draws this parallel. For in Les Prophéties he often refers to Europe by allusions to Rome, through the Roman Empire, the Holy Roman Empire and the Church based at Rome. He did this although there were other ways in which he could, more often, had he wished, have identified Europe. His choice of Rome with which to convey the connection between behaviour and the future is traceable especially clearly to The Early History of Ancient Rome, which

Nostradamus would have read, and in which Livy had written this.

"Of late years wealth has made us greedy, and self-indulgence has brought us, through every sort of sensual excess, to be, if I may so put it, in love with death both individual and collective."

Greeks had already foreseen that corruption would always weaken and might ultimately destroy civilization. Plato's precaution, suggested in his Republic, never got off the ground. But that of Lycurgus did. And by naming the latter in his Epistle to Henry II, Nostradamus has already drawn attention to this. It is the only instance in Les Prophéties in which he actually indicates a remedy. This implies that he attaches a special significance to corruption, and that he is aware of no other measures which will work, other than those instituted by Lycurgus.

Preceding the verses as it does, the name of Lycurgus sets the stage for verses which climax in the otherwise difficult to explain use of the word *MARBRE*.

Lycurgus was the legendary founder or re-organiser of the Spartan state. His reception by the oracle at Delphi ensured the attention of Nostradamus. This is how Herodotus speaks of it in Book One of The Histories.

"The circumstances which led to their being well-governed were the following:

Lycurgus, a man of distinction among the Spartans, had gone to Delphi, to visit the oracle. Scarcely had he entered into the inner fane, when the Pythoness exclaimed aloud,

'Oh! thou great Lycurgus, that com'st to my beautiful dwelling,

Dear to Jove, and to all who sit in the halls of Olympus,

Whether to hail thee a god I know not, or only a mortal,

But my hope is strong that a god thou wilt prove, Lycurgus.'

Some report besides, that the Pythoness delivered to him the entire system of laws ....which he took care should be observed by all."

Lycurgus instituted military national service. But more to the point, he ensured that mobs would no longer be tools for ambitious politicians. He replaced a self-seeking establishment with leaders raised from childhood to put duty before self-interest. And for centuries thereafter, Sparta thrived in safety. Nostradamus uses only a name with which to point this out. But in no way could he have expressed his meaning more clearly; nor more emphatically.

We too, of course, have read history. The difference between Nostradamus and ourselves is that he also seems to have seen our future. The purpose of the verses below will become clear when Les Prophéties' quatrains have been arranged in date order. These will then be seen as an introduction to the stripping of banks - and, by implication, of building societies, insurance companies, pension funds and state benefits - by embezzlers, and to the inevitable social and other consequences of this. In verse IX 62 Nostradamus speaks of drug-running by Common Market officials.

"Aux grand de[7] Cheramon agora[8],
Seront croisés[9] par rang tous[10] attachés[11],
Le pertinax[2,6] Oppi, et Mandragora[3],
Raugon[5] d'Octobre le tiers[1] seront l'âchés[4]."

"On the third of October[1] habit-forming[2] narcotic drugs[3] will be released[4] from Turkey[5] to the greedy and internally-destructive[6] leaders of[7] the Common Market[8], and will be passed[9] by all ranks[10] involved[11]."

1. It is possible that this refers to an isolated incident. However, with drug-trafficking already widespread, one incident would be unlikely to warrant a verse. It is more likely to refer to a general practice involving Common Market officials; the

date being merely that seen by Nostradamus in his vision.

2. From L. *pertinax* = 'tenacious'.

3. *Oppie* in an edition-variation. From Gk. *oppie* = 'opium'. And *Mandragora* officinarum/Mandrake, from Gk. *Mandragoras* and L. *Mandragora* is another narcotic plant. Nostradamus' citing of *Mandragora* in fact suggests more than simply a narcotic drug. It implies the breakdown of the personality which follows its use. For in primitive magic mandrake represents the negative and minimal aspects of the soul.

4. From *lâcher* = 'to release'.

5. A cryptogram of Agron. Agron, a king of Lydia which is now in Turkey, appears in Herodotus' The Histories. The latter are among Nostradamus' chief sources of historical references.

6. An extended analogy. With a capital letter in an edition-variation. Having killed him, the palace guards of the emperor Pertinax auctioned the Roman Empire to the highest bidder.

7. Literally, 'to the great of'.

8. *Cheramonagora* in an edition-variation. A composite word constructed from *chercher* = 'to look for'; *chère* as in *la bonne chère* = 'good living'; *chèrement* = 'dearly', 'at a high price'; and *commun* = 'common'. With Gk. *agora* = 'market'.

9. From *croiser* = 'to pass'.

10. Or 'grades'.

11. Literally, 'attached', 'tied up'.

Verse VIII 28 concerns fraud involving 'wine lakes', and perhaps - by extension through this imagery, - also 'food mountains'.

> "*Les simulacres[5] d'or & d'argent enflez[9],*
> *Qu'apres[1] le rapt[10] au lac[6] furent[4] gettez[6]*
> *Au desouvert[11] estaincts tous[4] & troublez[3].*
> *Au marbre[7] script prescript[8] intergetez[2].*"

"After[1] questioning[2] a disturbing[3] theft[4] from what is called[5] a 'lake'[6], false[7] documents[8], a swollen account[9] and theft[10] will be uncovered[11]."

2. From *interroger* = 'to question'.

3. From *troubler* = 'to disturb'.

4. *Éteints tous* in an edition-variation. Literally, 'extinct', 'all gone'. With *furent* from L. *fur* = 'thief'.

5. From L. *simulacrum* = 'an image', 'a pretence'.

6. Literally, 'thrown into the ....lake'. From *jeter* = 'to throw', in the edition-variation *jetés*. But though that is good imagery, the context clearly demands 'from what was carelessly put in the 'lake'.

7. Literally, 'in marble'. A metaphor. In architecture marble is used to convey an impression of stability and wealth, and conceal cheaper materials; to inspire confidence. And stuffs such as cake and the edges of books are 'marbled' to look like that which they are not. Marble is also the traditional material on which inscriptions are written over graves. But Nostradamus does not use the word here only for that range of meanings. With it he connects this verse to IX 62, at which we have just previously looked. That quatrain contains the word *rang* of which the edition-variation is *ranc*. And in the 16th century, and more commonly used then than it is now, 'rance' was the name of a blue and white veined marble. It predicts more than this, however. It also warns about the disappearance of national borders, the planet plundered, official corruption and moral collapse. These things are described here in one of Nostradamus' favourite sources, Pliny's Natural History, where in Book XXXVI the latter comments on the effects of using marble. "Nature is levelled. We carry off materials which were meant as barriers between nations ....The authorities said nothing. Indeed, they made concessions in the interests of pleasing the populace! But why this excuse? How do vices infiltrate other than through official channels? How else have ivory, gold and precious stones come to be used by private persons? ....The moral considerations

were naturally disregarded because standards had already collapsed."

9. Literally, 'gold and silver swollen', from *enfler* = 'to swell'. Because these substances do not literally swell, this is a metaphor. Placed with *simulacres* and with *enflez,* this relates to the false accounting which conceals the theft, and also to the bank accounts of the thieves. Note that *simulacres* is plural.

10. Literally, 'abduction'.

11. *Découvert* in an edition-variation. From *découvrir* = 'to discover'. The future tense in a prediction.

POSTSCRIPT

By 1992 the known frauds involving the Common Market's agricultural policy alone amounted to £6 billion.

Verse VIII 62 predicts that, involved in them themselves, governments will fail to punish for these crimes.

"Lorsqu'on verra[1] expiler[3] le saint temple[2],
Plus grand du Rhosne leurs[4] sacrés[6] profaner[5]:
Par eux[8] naître[10] pestilence si ample[9],
Roi[7] fait injuste[11] ne fera condamner[12]."

"When one will see[1] Europe[2] robbed[3], its leaders[4] to abuse[5] good[6], Government[7], by whom[8] so much moral destruction[9] was cultivated[10], will unjustly stand[11] back and not punish[12]."

2. Literally, 'the holy church'. A metonymy. 'The Church' for Christendom based on Rome. A connection made throughout Les Prophéties.

3. From L. *expilare* = 'to pillage', 'to plunder'.

4. *Rhosne* is a cryptogram of 'Rhone', the European river which rises at Geneva. Note, Nostradamus' references to this always concern the doings of European governments.

6. Literally, 'sacred'. As in the idiom 'sacred cow', which is an institution which does not justify the faith put in it. Note;

it sustains the imagery in *le saint temple*.

7. Literally, 'King'. A metonymy. Kings are the oldest form of central government; and in Nostradamus' time they were still its most usual form.

8. Literally, 'by them'.

9. By definition. What is 'pestilent' is morally destructive.

10. Literally, 'to be born'.

11. Literally, 'will flee', 'will shun'. From *fuir* in the edition-variation *fuit*.

12. Literally, 'will not make to sentence'.

In verse I 53 Nostradamus foresees that with the discovery of oil, power would pass to non-Western states. And this verse includes his first allusion to terrorism.

> *"Las!¹² qu'on verra grand peuple tourmenté⁹*
> *Et⁸ la loi⁶ sainte⁵ en totale ruine⁷,*
> *Par autres lois¹¹ toute Chrétienté¹⁰,*
> *Quand¹ d'or, d'argent³ trouve⁴ nouvelle mine².*"

"When¹ a new source² of wealth³ is found⁴, Western⁵ hegemony⁶ will be gone⁷. And⁸ how a great people will be tormented⁹ throughout the world¹⁰ by other powers¹¹, alas!¹²"

2. Literally, 'new mine'. 'Mine' was required to construct an imagery of gold and silver being mined. But here these metals are used in metaphor, and 'source', with its broader meaning, fits both this and the original imagery.

3. Literally, 'gold and silver'. A metaphor. But the 'gold' is more specific than merely a metaphor for 'wealth'. It is the colour of refined oil. Oil is called variously 'black gold' and 'liquid gold'. It is also obtained, like the metals in the imagery, from underground. And it is the 'new' form of wealth.

5. Literally, 'holy'. In Nostradamus' circumstances, what was 'holy' was definitely Christian. And Christianity is named in the next line. Still generally synonymous with the Church of

Rome in Nostradamus's time, this is a synecdoche for Christendom, Europe or 'European'. The context extends this meaning to 'Western'.

6. Literally, 'law'. A metonymy.

7. Literally, 'in total ruin'.

10. Literally, 'all Christendom'. By definition, 'Christians everywhere'.

11. Literally, 'by other laws'.

Verse I 51 predicts that from 1996 fear will produce major changes in European attitudes.

"Chef⁵ d'Aries, Jupiter et Saturne⁶,
Dieu éternal quelles mutations¹⁰!
Puis⁴ par long siècle⁷ son malin temps⁸ retourne⁹,
Gaul¹ et Itale² quelles émotions³."

"France¹ and all Europe² will be frightened³. Then⁴, chiefly⁵ from 1995⁶, after a long period⁷, common sense⁸ will return⁹. And God eternal, what changes¹⁰!"

2. Literally, 'Italy'. A syncope of *Italie*. *A* synecdoche of 'Rome', the centre of Christendom. The naming of two European states suggests that here 'Christendom' does not extend beyond Europe.

3. Literally, 'what frights'.

5. Literally, 'chief'.

6. The next conjunction of these planets is due in December 1995.

8. Literally, 'one's shrewd time'.

9. The future tense in a prediction.

In verse VII 38 Nostradamus the monarchist uses an accident involving royalty as a vehicle with which to express regret at his impotence to alter history through his warnings.

"*L'aîné Royal[3] sur coursier[2] voltigeant[1],*
Piquer[4] viendra si rudement[5] courir[4,6]:
Gueule, lippée[7], pied dans l'etreinte[9] plaignant[5,8],
Traîne, tiré[10], horriblement mourir[11]."

"Playing[1] on a fast horse[2], the eldest Prince[3] will spur[4] too hard[5]. It will bolt[6], with the bit between its teeth[7]. And alas[8], foot stuck in the stirrup[9], he will be dragged, and pulled[10] to a horrible death[11]."

1. From *voltige* = 'trick-riding', and from *voltigeur* = 'acrobat'.

2. O.F. *coursier* = 'swift horse'.

4. Literally, 'To prick to go'.

5. Literally, 'so hard'. Note that the horse's reaction to this is conveyed in *plaignant* = 'complaining', and the O.F. *plainte* which is the past participle of *plaindre* = 'to protest'.

6. Literally, 'face to run'. Note that *courir* is placed where it forms part of two phrases.

7. Literally, 'thick-lipped'. This because a horse's jaws are necessarily apart when it has the bit between its teeth.

8. From O.F. *plainte*. An expression of sorrow.

9. Literally, 'clutch', 'grip' or 'hold'. *Étrier* = 'stirrup' is a cryptogram of *étreinte*. The edition-variation *estrein,* which is a cryptogram of O.F. *resne* = 'rein', is also relevant to the context.

10. *Traîne,* as in *être à la traîne* = 'to be in tow', and *tiré* = 'pulled'.

11. Literally, 'to die horribly'.

The lamentation in *plaignant,* though sincere, is more than a royalist's regret at a fatal accident to a prince. Following as it does in Les Prophéties the equestrian accident of Henry II, which also resulted from a warning not being heeded, here Nostradamus ruefully shows he is aware that his prophecies may always be ignored. This was something with which, in common with all prophets, he would have had to come to terms. In his case it may also have contributed to his impatience with people he regarded as foolish, and to the style in which he couched his predictions. It was not a lesson he had had to learn from experience. In his youth he had certainly read about that prototype of unheeded prophets, Cassandra. She had claimed that Apollo, the god of prophecy, gave her the ability to see into the future as a free gift, with no strings attached. But he insisted that she had known the score full well; that the gift had been pre-payment for 'personal services' to be rendered, ...which she now refused to render. The upshot of this disagreement was that, unable to take back a gift once given, Apollo made it a burden for her, by ensuring that no one believed her predictions until too late.

CHAPTER TWENTY-EIGHT

THE FINAL STAGE:
FULL UNDERSTANDING

There can be a great deal of difference between any straight translation and its full interpretation. And in the case of Nostradamus, as will by now be apparent, beyond even his sometimes complex figures of speech much also needs to be 'read between the lines'.

Hence at one extreme there is a literal translation which may not make much sense but will be what Nostradamus actually wrote. At the other extreme there can be a full interpretation which may be either more than, or even, in a literal sense, nothing to do with what he actually says; and worse than that, which cannot for certain be known to be what he means until after the event.

Most of the interpretations in Chapter Twenty-Seven are compromises between those extremes. But such compromises can result in clumsy mixtures in which all that it is likely Nostradamus means is not revealed. Attempts to render complete interpretations, however, do involve some degree of conjecture, and are therefore unsafe.

There is only one way in which to escape from this dilemma. It is to avoid mixing a version which shows what Nostradamus actually says with a version which tells what the interpreter thinks that Nostradamus means. This calls for three versions instead of one. First, a literal translation. Secondly, an interpretation in which every phrase and word is directly reflected from the original text, - allowing only adjustments of pronouns, conjunctions and so on, and these only as may be grammatically necessary. Thirdly, a version constructed from meanings contained in the second version, but in which none of the actual words used need be those in the literal translation.

Three such versions of verse X 70 are given below. Before we examine these though, there is another matter for which that treatment of the verse will serve as an example.

This concerns verses for which the usual method of analysis is not adequate. These can be subjected to a method different from that previously recommended. It is one which might seem to be a short-cut and suitable for use anywhere in Les Prophéties. But it is not. It would be completely unsuitable for application to verses which are linked to other verses. And it should never be used by recent initiates to Nostradamian, because the risk of inadvertently imposing one's own presuppositions is too real.

The technique is best explained by comparing it with a practice in arithmetic. Suppose there are decimal fractions to be multiplied. All too often the answer is wrong in that the decimal point has ended up in the wrong place. This error can be avoided simply by recognising that, for example; 7.539 is approximately 8, and 3.498 is approximately 3; and 8 times 3 is 24. So if the exact answer is not also roughly 24, something is wrong.

Applied to analysis in Les Prophéties, the equivalent to that process also involves getting an approximate answer to begin with, and then working towards it with the details. First, the significant words, usually nouns, have to be identified. Then, round each of these are gathered the words which might directly relate to them. Some of these, which are usually adjectives and pronouns, may be equally applicable to more than one of the nouns. That does not matter at this stage because Nostradamus habitually makes more than one use of a single word.

It is rarely that Nostradamus deals with unrelated subjects within a single verse. So when the reader reviews the words he has grouped together he will begin to see connections between the groups. This part of the process employs lateral thinking, but the connections will be there. The broad subject of the verse will usually now be evident. And from here on the reader has the literary parallel of the mathematician's approximate answer to guide him. The value of having this can be seen when we take verse X 70 as an example. Here is the original text and its literal translation.

> "*L'oeil par objet fera telle excroissance,*
> *Tant et ardente que tombera la neige:*
> *Champ arrosé viendra en décroissance,*
> *Que la primat succombera à Rege.*"

> "The eye by object will make such lump,
> So much and blazing that will fall the snow:
> Field watered will in decrease,
> That the primate will succumb to King."

That fourth line appears to be a cause or a result of something, and more or less self-contained. So it can be examined later. That leaves the following nouns: eye, object, lump, snow and field. Of these, 'object' is different from the others in that its nature is not stated. So, for the moment, it too can be put aside. As too can 'lump', because although this could be a lump of snow, *excroissance* properly refers to a lump on an animal or plant.

The only descriptive word, 'blazing', could apply to most of the nouns. To the eye in the sense, for example, of its 'blazing with anger'. To the field in the sense of a blazing crop. To the lump in the sense of a painful swelling. And it might also apply to the as yet unidentified 'object'. As there is therefore only a one-in-four chance of putting it with the right noun, pending more information as a guide it too is best left out at this stage.

This process of elimination has left only 'eye', 'snow' and 'field'. But between these, obvious connections can be made. One is 'snow' with 'field', in the sense of an expanse of snow, or snowfield. The other is 'field' with 'eye', in the sense of a field of vision.

And now, immediately, a third connection becomes

apparent. For a snowfield can affect the eyesight, and therefore the field of vision. The glare of daylight reflected from an expanse of snow causes what is called 'snowblindness'. The symptoms of this are that the eyes become sore, and water, and sight is reduced.

But that these connections do hold Nostradamus' meaning in this verse is as yet only conjecture. This must now be tested against the text. It is with this result.

> *"L'oeil[1] par objet[9] fera telle excroissance[10],*
> *Tant[6] et ardente[3] que tombera[7] la neige:*
> *Champ[4,8] arrosé[2] viendra en décroissance[5],*
> *Que la primat[11,12] succombera[13] à Rege[12]."*

"The eye[1] will water[2] and burn[3], its vision[4] reduced[5] so much[6] that one will fall[7] in the snowfield[8]. And it[9] will make such mole[10] that mankind[11] to the highest[12] will succumb[13]."

2. The future tense in a prediction.

3. Literally, 'blazing'.

4. 'The eye' itself cannot be reduced. Only its 'field' of vision can.

5. From *décroître* = 'to diminish', 'to decrease'.

7. The gender is not stated.

8. Though it is on another line, *Champ* is placed next to *la neige*. This indicates that in one sense of 'field' they are connected, and that in another sense of this same word they are not.

9. The nature of the 'object' which causes the symptoms then described is still not specified. Perhaps, although he clearly knew that an expanse of snow causes these symptoms, Nostradamus lacked the necessary knowledge of physics to account for its doing so. Or he may have understood but preferred to be brief.

10. An 'excrescence' is an abnormal growth on the body.

11. Literally, 'primate', the animal order to which

mankind belongs. Because, unlike 'beast' for example, 'primate' embraces only man-related species, it stresses the inclusion of 'mankind'.

12. Literally, 'to the King', from L. *rex regis* = 'king'. Figuratively, this is applicable to any person pre-eminent in his own field, which is not necessarily associated with government. And placed here in the same line as L. *primate* = 'of the first rank', this figurative meaning is confirmed.

13. From *succomber* = 'to die', 'to succumb'.

All that now remains to be done is to identify what it is that Nostradamus alludes to as an 'object'. According to the text, it will be the cause of what happens to the eye; and perhaps, directly or not, of deaths.

This is not likely to be a long-lying universal snowfield, because that would be accompanied by intense cold, of which there is no mention in the text. However, for protection from the medical condition known as 'snowblindness', polar explorers wear goggles. They do so because the eyesight is harmed by exposure to excessive ultra-violet light, ...which also causes skin cancer. And from its effects neither man nor beast would indeed be immune.

Here, therefore, is the full interpretation of verse X 70; the wood as different from the trees.

"Ultra-violet light will cause skin-cancer and blindness. All men and animals, even the most powerful, will succumb."

It is a prediction about the consequences of the current destruction of the ozone layer, which was sounded three centuries before the warnings of scientists today.

"What can be avoided
Whose end is purposed by the mighty Gods?"
(SHAKESPEARE. JULIUS CAESAR II, 2.)

THE TIME-MACHINE

Les Prophéties can be like a time-machine. Though we can only land it where Nostradamus did so, in it we can travel backwards and forwards at will across four centuries. The pleasure this can lead to is limited only by our imaginations. There is no need to be interested in past events only for the purpose of assessing Nostradamus' accuracy.

Let us try, for example, pretending that all the people involved in them had already recognised themselves in the prophecies, as Henry II had done, and then attempt to understand their reactions.

Why did Henry tempt Fate by entering the lists in his forty-first year? O.K., the royal double-wedding was a big event. Yet had he been a few years older he would not have done so anyway. At any age he could have avoided doing so. No one had challenged him. He was himself the challenger. So why did he? Now that we have looked at his life, it is not impossible to come up with a reason. For perhaps that use of witchcraft in order to beget an heir had afterwards worried him? If this were so, then his appearance in the lists was an invitation to God to punish him directly, rather than through his family.

We will never know what actually motivated Henry. But the process of wondering about this, of facing ourselves in our imaginations with the choices which confronted him, will be found to lend an extra something to one's interest in history.

Similarly, what would it have felt like to be Charles I, squabbling with Parliament over taxes for money for one's foreign policy, having already read the outcome? Remember, one is a man of narrow principles, whose kingship along with its responsibilities is God-bestowed; here faced with a prophecy which is already unfolding, yet may have been written by a servant of Satan. And a few years later, in those last moments on the scaffold. What would your thoughts have been then? Had God deserted you? Or had He inspired the prophecy to guide you, ...and you had misunderstood that?

And in recent years what would have been your thoughts had you been the Shah of Iran? You could not show the verses to your allies, to dissuade them from deserting you, even had you also shown them the verses detailing the consequences for them. To do so would in their eyes cast doubt on you sanity, and hasten your downfall. And later, abandoned and dying, do you console yourself with your knowledge of what will be the cost to them?

Questions; all without sure answers. Yet if they go unasked, if we do not wonder about such things, are we perhaps missing out on more than just an interesting pastime? Are we also missing out on a chance to rehearse what to think if Nostradamus' predictions continue to prove right?

THE PRICE TAG

As you are finding, understanding Les Prophéties adds a new enjoyment and dimension to life. But there is a small price tag attached to this.

After a while you will alter, beyond the ordinary changes that come with the years. You will start to see many things differently from the ways your neighbours do. Increasingly you will tend to avoid other people, in case the conversation turns to subjects on which there will and can be no meetings of your minds. You will feel a sort of loneliness and frustration you have never encountered before. This will happen. Have no doubts about that. So before you learn what you will not be able to unlearn, think about the warning on Imperial Roman passports. These read; "Before interfering with the bearer, consider whether you be able to wage war with Caesar."

That is not a much exaggerated warning; because if life can be viewed as a journey through unknown terrain, you will have fragments of a map. And that difference between you and your friends will prove to be a real one.

You will sit with others in front of your tv set as bankers, churchmen, industrialists, politicians and assorted experts pontificate about what is wrong and what to do about it. You will still be able to admire the sheer professionalism with which their furrowed brows, thoughtful eyes and measured tones convey that they know what they are talking about. You will, though, envy in those sitting beside you the reassurance which they are obtaining from the experience. But, depending on the subject, you yourself will often need a keen sense of humour, or considerable self-control, if you are not to say what you will be thinking, which will be, "What a prat!"

Always remember, though, that speaking out like that would be unfair. That the poor dear on the box is doing his best. And that had you not read Les Prophéties you would probably be agreeing with him.

RE-WRITING LES PROPHÉTIES

Having spent so many years immersed in such things as Nostradamus' writing style, it is not perhaps surprising that I eventually wondered how other writers named in this book would have presented his predictions. In my mind's eye I invited two of them to do so. But, neither of them wishing to bother, with twinkles in their eyes they outwitted me. This they did by giving away, in their new titles for the work, too much about the text.

Dante came up with, "The Divine Comedy II". And the bluff Rabelais, in his forthright style, with a phrase which translates into English best as, "One Almighty Pratsville!"

Since then, and as it is an old tale which Nostradamus could have heard, I tried to approach the author of The Emperor's New Clothes. But not knowing when it originated, I was not able. So instead, although he would probably have been illiterate, I asked the child it features to have a stab at it. He is, after all, remembered for having told the truth. But I fared no better with him. Laughing, he moved further back into the crowd. As he did so, what he called back to me was,

"*Che sara sara!*"

PART FOUR

THE DICTIONARY

*"There is only one good, knowledge,
and one evil, ignorance."*
(SOCRATES)

PREFACE

Nearly all words in most languages have more than one meaning. Where several languages are in use together, the range of their meanings is even wider. Where definitions cater for more esoteric subjects such as are encountered in Les Prophéties, they are further stretched. And changes in usage, to keep pace with social change and technological progress, adds yet another tier to definitions and translations.

The meanings of many words in Les Prophéties differ between one verse and another, so that a definition or translation applicable in one instance might be misleading if applied elsewhere. A result of this is that the more comprehensive the scope of a dictionary of Nostradamian usage, the less precise the guidance it would afford.

For this reason, although in most cases the definitions and translations contained below are applicable to all of Nostradamus' verses, they are specifically intended for use with the quatrains dealt with in this book, or which are about future events. These are the relevant verses.

I. 1, 2, 9, 13, 16, 18, 26, 35, 41, 49, 51, 53, 55, 56, 62, 63, 64, 70, 73, 87, 91, 94.

II. 1, 2, 5, 18, 22, 28, 29, 30, 34, 35, 41, 43, 46, 47, 48, 62, 89, 91, 95, 96, 97, 98, 99, 100.

III. 4, 5, 7, 11, 13, 27, 31, 34, 59, 61, 64, 77, 79, 81, 90, 92, 93, 94, 95, 97, 99.

IV. 20, 23, 39, 43, 46, 50, 67, 82, 84, 94, 95, 96.

V. 8, 11, 14, 23, 25, 27, 34, 35, 47, 48, 50, 59, 62, 63, 65, 80, 81, 84, 86, 90.

VI. 2, 5, 7, 21, 33, 44, 58, 80, 81, 90, 98, 100, 100.

VII. 18, 21, 22, 38.

VIII. 2, 14, 15, 17, 21, 28, 46, 49, 55, 59, 62, 70, 77, 91, 96, 97.

IX. 20, 34, 42, 43, 44, 49, 55, 60, 62, 73, 83, 97, 99, 100.

X. 1, 2, 10, 21, 22, 31, 40, 49, 53, 66, 70, 72, 74, 86, 100.

Several of Nostradamus' quatrains do not appear in some editions of Les Prophéties, or are differently numbered in different editions. Verses III 79 and VI 100 are examples of this. Fortunately there are few of these, and though they may cause a little initial confusion, they do not significantly affect use of the dictionary because entries in it are alphabetical.

ENTRIES IN THE DICTIONARY

These include some five hundred and fifty definitions, with linguistic bases where required. Also brief relevant notes on alchemy, astrology, astronomy, geography, history, literary references, mythology and symbolism.

USING THE DICTIONARY

Cross-references permit the meanings of words where they appear in one context to be weighed against their meanings in other contexts, and also against their edition-variations.

As in Parts One to Three, words in italic capitals and perpendicular brackets refer to headings in the dictionary, - except where they were already in capitals in Nostradamus' text.

The numbers immediately following each heading are those of the verses in which that word or its edition-variations appear. And under each heading, those edition-variations are given.

REMINDER

In everyday speech and writing, the meaning accorded to a word in any particular instance usually turns on a balance of probabilities. If it is the word's usual meaning, and it also fits its context, that is assumed to be what it means. And as we are living in the same century, and are all exposed to the same ideas, we do understand each other without much difficulty. This remains true even when that meaning is figurative rather than literal. But when we are dealing with Les Prophéties, the facts, on which the probabilities to be balanced are based, are different. For this reason, before any meaning is accepted, we should have asked ourselves the following questions.

1. Do all the literary tricks involved in this use of the word conform to Nostradamus' usual practices?

2. Is the word being given a meaning which it had in classical literature and mythology, or even in the 16th century ....and not just in the 20th?

3. What, if any, is its astrological meaning?
4. Does it have multiple meanings which support each other?
5. Does it follow traditional symbolism?
6. Does it suggest an analogy? And if so, would the story which it suggests be too lengthy for telling in some other way?
7. Might its use have been triggered by Nostradamus' own travels or personal experiences?
8. Have all its figurative meanings been examined?
9. Does its use come naturally from such a man as we now know Nostradamus to have been?
10. Is this meaning free from the influence of one's own hopes or opinions about the future?

Acquitaine. II 1.
(Aquitaine.)
See *AQUITAINE*.

Adrie. V 27.
Ancient Hadrie, Hatria and Atria.
l. Town in northern Italy. Once
a flourishing Adriatic port, now
silted up in the river Po delta.
2. Adriatic Sea, named after the
town.
(See *HADRIE*).

Adultère. VIII 14, X 10.
(Adultres.)
1. Forger, cause of monetary
inflation. From L. *adulterare* =
'to adulterate'.
2. A reference to the Whore of
BABYLON in Revelation XVII and
XVIII. From L. *adulter* =
'adulterer', 'adulteress'.
(See *ADULTERINE* and *DAME*).

Adulterine. VIII 70.
1. Adulterous.
2. Born of adultery.
3. False, illegal.
All from L. *adultrinus* =
'unlicensed'.
4. *BABYLON*. From the Epistle to
Henry II in which Nostradamus
writes of "….the procreation of
the New Babylon, a miserable
prostitute large with the
abomination of the first
holocaust".
(See *ADULTÈRE* and *DAME*).

Adust. IV 67.

1. Ashes, dust. From L. *adustus* =
'burned', 'charred'.
2. Droplets. From L.G. *dunst* =
'vapour'.

Aenobarbe. V 59.
1. Redbeard. From L. *Aeneus* =
'copper-coloured'; and *barba* =
'beard'. Traditional nickname for
a comet/*COMÈTE*.
2. Roman. From Aeneas, hero of
Virgil's Aeneid, who was
legendary founder of Rome.
Aenobarbus, also spelt
Ahenobarbus, was the name of
many notable Romans including
the consul L. Domitius
Ahenobarbus and his son Gnaeus
Domitius Ahenobarbus who
became Emperor Nero.

Affrique. V 11, V 23, V 48.
1. African. Afri,
Berber/*BARBARE*,
Mauri/Moorish, Numidian,
Tripolitan.
2. Africa. In the Classical World,
though occasionally embracing
Egypt/*EGYPTE* and Ethiopia,
usually only applied to the
Mediterranean coastal territories
which became Roman provinces
after the 3rd Punic War ended in
146 BC. These included
Mauretania, now western Algeria
and Morocco, and Numidia, now
Morocco, after the original
Roman conquest of Afri, modern
Tunisia, was extended.
3. Relating to 'Africus' the

South-West wind blowing from Africa to *ROME*. (See *VENT*).

Agath. IV 94.
Agde. From apocope of Agatha. (See *AGDE*).

Agde. VIII 21.
1. Site of ancient Agatha/*AGATH*. Now a fishing port on Canal du Midi near mouth of river Hérault. Industries include fertilizers, ship-building and wine. Thirteen miles from Béziers/*BLYTERRE*.
2. Saint Agatha was martyred in Sicily in 251 AD. But legends about her were not recorded until the 16th century, during Nostradamus' lifetime. Her name is invoked against fire and lightning.

Agora. IX 62.
Market. In Greek.

Ailes. VIII 96.
(Aisles.)
Wings.

Alegro. V 27.
With high expectations, optimistically. From It. *allegro* = 'briskly', 'lively'; and O.F. *alegre* = 'joyful'.

Alein. III 99.
(Alleins.)
1. A village near Salon in S. E. France.

2. Aleiyan or Kedemoth, twenty miles East of the Dead Sea.

Alemagne. IV 94.
(Alemaigne.)
1. German.
2. Germany.

Almatie. IX 60.
1. Dalmatia. That part of modern Yugoslavia along the Adriatic coast between the Gulf of Kotor and Fiume. Incorporated by the Romans into Illyrium in 33 BC, it was made a separate province from Pannonia (see *PANNONS*) in 9 AD after an Illyrian revolt. Among its tribes was the Parthini (see *PARTHE*). It was overrun by Goths in the 5th century, and became part of the Byzantine empire (see *BISANCE*) in the 6th. All but its coastal towns was settled by Slavs (see *ESCLAVONIE*), mainly Croats, in the 7th century. And by the 10th century it had separated into Croatia in the North and Serbia in the South. The region's North and South became known as White and Red Croatia. From c.1100, though administered by a Croatian *BAN,* it passed under the Hungarian throne. In the 14th century it fell to the Ottoman Turks.
2. The people of Dalmatia.

Alus. VI 33.
1. Iran. By apheraesis of Halus,

near modern Qasr-i-Shirin in Kermanshah in western Iran. Ancient trade centre serving the purposes of both Persia and Mesopotamia.
(See *MESOPOTAMIE, PERS* and *PERSIENS*).
2. Saul. Anagram. An 11th century BC king of Israel. Chosen by the prophet Samuel as a war-leader to unite the twelve tribes against the Philistines. Not being a murderous religious fanatic, Saul later lost Samuel's political support. But out of jealousy Saul did try to kill the young military hero David, and latterly became deranged.
3. The ruler of wind/*VENT*. By syncope of Aeolus in whose cave, according to Ovid in Metamorphoses Book I, *BOREAS* had been confined by *JUPITER/IOUË*. In Virgil's Aeneid, Aeolus scatters a Western fleet, blowing it onto the coast of North Africa. In Homer's Odyssey, while grubbing for gold and silver the crew open the bag containing the winds, given to them by Aeolus, and are blown back whence they came.
4. Secret contact between Syria and Europe. By syncope of Alpheus the underground river between Syria and Sicily along which Arethusa/*ARETHUSE* was conducted by Artemis/*DIANE*.
5. Hippalus is a wind peculiar to the Persian Gulf.

Americh. X 66.
American, America, the United States.

Amphitheatre. VI 100.
Arena. (See *THÉÂTRE*),

Angleterre. X 100.
1. England.
2. Britain.

Angloise. V 34, V 35, V 59.
(*Anglois.*)
English, England.

Angolmois. X 72.
Mongol. Apocope and cryptogram of Mongolois. The Mongol Moslem Timur i Leng/Timur the Lame/Tamerlane made a reality in the 14th century of the Mohammedan dream of Iraq, Iran, Syria and Turkey united within an Islamic empire.

Annibal. II 30.
1. Hannibal - The letter 'H' is frequently silent. According to Livy, at an early age Hannibal swore eternal enmity towards Rome. He became the outstanding Carthaginian commander in the 2nd Punic war between Carthage and Rome. He invaded Europe through Spain and France. According to Livy, Hannibal tried to put the blame for his own destruction of Italian property onto Fabius the Roman leader, by the simple expedient

of leaving only the latter's home unpillaged. After his defeat in battle Hannibal was pursued from one neutral state to another by Roman diplomats until he committed suicide.

2. Carthage. By association with Hannibal. Founded in the 9th century BC by Phoenicians from Tyre (see *TYRREN),* and named Cartago or New City, it was razed by the Romans in 146 BC. From 439 to 533 AD it was the Vandal's capital. Destroyed by Arabs in 698 AD, it became an image of a fallen materialistic existence. Though now the site of a suburb of modern Tunis, its Phoenician origins connect it with Libya. (See *LIBYQUE).*

Anibalique. III 93.
North African. (See *ANNIBAL, BARBARE* and *PHOCEAN).*

Antechrist. VIII 77, X 66.
Antichrist. From L. *Antechristus* and O.F. *Antecrist.*
1. From biblical references in I John 2, 18, and 22, and II John 7, combined with Persian dualism, medieval Christians produced a mythology about an opponent of Christ and Christians, the Antichrist, who was expected to appear shortly before the end of the world. In this mythology he is;-
a. a pseudo-saviour;
b. a tyrant;

c. a flying beast with a huge head, flaming eyes, iron teeth, and the ears of an ass. In mid-16th century France the Antechrist was the bogey-man with whose title parents struck fear into their children, ...and into themselves in the process.

2. Iran. In the theology of the early and medieval Church, the original Antichrist was Simon Magus. This arose from Acts VIII 18-24 in which Simon the Magus (see *MAGUES)* tries to bribe the Apostles to share with him their power.

Antenne. II 2.
(Anthene,
Anthenne.)
1. Aerial.
2. Feeler, spy.
3. Outpost, sub-branch.
4. Sail-yard.
5. Outcome, progeny. As that part of a tree/*ARBRE* which bears the blooms and fruit, the branch symbolically represents what it bears.

Anvers. IX 49.
(Envers.)
1. Antwerp. Province and city in modern Belgium. Unofficial capital of Flanders. Once part of the Netherlands. A major port since 2nd century AD on estuary of rivers Meuse, Rhine and Scheldt. (See Chapter Nineteen).
2. a. To, towards;

b. other side, wrong side.

Apennins. II 29.
(Appenins.)
1. Apennines.
2. Italy.

Aquilon. II 91, VIII 15, IX 99,
X 86.
1. Northern land. From L. *Aquilo*
= 'North'. Aquilo was also the
Roman god of the North and
North East winds, equivalent to
the Greek *BOREAS*.
2. Aquila is an autumn
constellation of the Northern
Hemisphere, in that part of the
Milky Way known as The Rift,
between its eastern and western
branches. Known to ancient
civilisations for over five thousand
years as 'the eagle', of which the
brightest star is Altair from the
Arabic word for 'the flying
vulture'.
3. L'Aquila is a city in central
Italy.
4. Italy. As in Caesar's The Gallic
Wars, Aquila was the Roman
eagle standard; of which
Renaissance readers were
reminded by Dante's The Divine
Comedy in which "Under the
eagle triumphed in their youth
Scipio and Pompey".
(See *AQUILONAIRE*).

Aquilonaire. I 49.
Northern. From cryptogram of L.
aquilonaris = 'northern'.

(See *AQUILON*).

Aquitaine. II 1.
(Acquitaine.)
Aquitania. In Caesar's The Civil
Wars, the area between the river
Garonne and the Pyrenees.
Region of S.W. France inhabited
by Iberians in Gallic times,
conquered by Rome in 56 BC
and belonging to England from
1154 to 1453.

Arabe. III 27, III 31, IV 39,
V 25, V 27, V 47.
Arab. From L. *Arabis*.
(See *ARABIQUE*).

Arabique. I 49.
(Arabiq.)
1. Arabian.
2. Arabic.
Both from Gk. *Arabikos*. (See
ARABE).

Araon. II 22.
(Arton.)
1. Iran. By cryptogram of Aryan,
the ancient race of Iran.
2. NATO. An acronym of North
Atlantic Treaty Organisation.
From cryptogram of *Arton*.

Araxes. III 31.
Ancient name of the river Aras
which rises in Turkish
Armenia/*ARMENIE* and flows six
hundred and sixty miles between
Iran, Russia and Turkey.

Arbre. III 11.

Tree. Traditionally representing survival and regeneration, its roots reach the centre of the world - which, on early Christian maps, was always Palestine. From the Trees of Knowledge and of Life in Genesis, and also from the concept of the sacred tree which came to Western thought mainly from Iran, the tree represents that which needs to be respected. As a symbol it usually takes its meaning from the context in which it is used. Standing as it does for life, in the context of a city it represents the government which sustains social life. It is sometimes associated with the *GRIFFON*.

Arche. III 13

1. a. Survival;
   b. defence.

Both, from the ancient Greek belief that the arch of the sky might fall down at any time and therefore needs support. The former also from Noah's ark, a craft built for survival, from L. *arca* = 'ark'.
2. The Church. Of which the ark was an emblem used by early Christians.
3. Triumph. From O.F. *arche* the architectural arch through which victorious armies parade.
4. That which is sacred. The Ark of the Covenant, holding the Torah scrolls, is kept in the central sanctuary of the synagogue and represents the presence of God.
5. Danger of disease. From L. *arx* = 'a box'. When the Ark of the Covenant was captured by the Philistines, they returned it because plagues broke out in every city into which they took it.

Ardente. II 96, X 70.
*(Ardent,
Ardant.)*
1. Blazing, burning, raging, hot. From L. *ardere* = 'to burn'.
2. Ardent, eager, fanatical, fervent, passionate, zealous. From O.F. *ardant*.

Arethusa. I 87.
(Arethuse.)
1. A town with Roman ruins in W. Syria.
2. In Greek myth, a wood nymph attendant of Artemis/*DIANE*. To assist Arethusa escape the attentions of a river god, Artemis changed her into a spring of water, westward in Sicily. But the river god flowed under the sea, found and merged with her.

Argent. I 53, III 13, VIII 14.
1. Silver.
2. With *or* = 'gold', wealth from any source.
3. In alchemy, the colour of the moon/*LUNE*.
4. Banking. From L. *argentaria* =

'a banker's office' in Cicero and Livy.

Argiels. I 73.
(Argal,
Argils,
Argel.)
Algiers. An anagram.

Aries. I 51, III 77.
1. The zodiacal Ram, 21 March to 20 April.
2. In Greek mythology, associated with the Golden Fleece.
3. In astrology;
a. Dawn;
b. Spring;
c. the *CYCLE/SIÈCLE* of existence;
d. the original impulse through which a potential becomes actual;
e. control over the head or brain;
f. ruled by the planet *MARS,*
Aries is the sign of the primal fire which both creates and destroys.
4. In Caesar, a battering-ram.

Armenie. III 31, V 50.
1. Armenia. Now includes E. Turkey and the Soviet Republic of Armenia.
The source of the rivers Aras/*ARAXES,* Tigris and Euphrates. The oldest Christian state, in it is Ararat where Noah's Ark landed. (See *ARCHE* and *ARQ).*
2. Turkey. (See *ARMENIQUE).*
3. Location of a decisive defeat of a Romany army by the Parthians (see *PARTHE)* in 36 BC.

Armenique. IV 95.
(Armonique,
Armorique.)
1. Armenian.
2. Turkish.
(See *ARMENIE).*

Arq. II 35, II 48.
(Arc.)
1. See *ARCHE.*
2. Aquarius. An abbreviation.
a. The zodiacal sign governing 21 January to 18 February;
b. as the 'Water Carrier', originally god of the Nile and later a Babylonian water god, Aquarius is depicted as a man pouring water over the earth. All eastern and western traditions connect this, through Noah's, Deucalion's and other floods, with the end of an age/*CYCLE/SIÈCLE.* The Flood also corresponds in mythology with the three days of the death of the moon. Water symbolises birth, regeneration and purification. In Exodus VII 19 and 20, and Revelation VIII 8, water is changed into blood.
(See *DELUGE, EAU, LUNE* and *SANG)*

Artois. V 59.
Region in northern France. Between Flanders and Picardy, for centuries a battleground.

Arton. II 22.
(Araon.)

1. NATO. Acronym of North Atlantic Treaty Organisation.
2. Iran. By cryptogram of Aryan, an ancient race of Iran.

Ascop. II 22.
(Asop.)
Rash. From Gk. *askopos* = 'imprudent', 'unseeing'.

Asiatique. V 11.
Asiatic. From L. *Asiaticus*. (See *ASIE*).

Asie. IV 50, VI 80 .
1. Asia. From Gk. *Asianos*. (See *ASIATIQUE*). Named after the wife of Prometheus, according to the Greeks.
2. In Tacitus' Agricola and Germania, and also in Caesar, this refers only to the Roman senatorial province of Asiana in western Anatolia.

Auge. I 16.
(AUGE.)
1. Grow. From L. *augere* and O.F. *augmenter* = 'to increase'. Also from the Arabic *awj* = 'height'.
2. Trough.
3. Gloss. From Gk. *auge* = 'lustre'.
4. Filthy. From the Augean stables through which Hercules/*HERCLE* diverted a stream to clean them.
5. Auge was a priestess of Athena and, in Ovid's Heroides, was one of the many women seduced by Hercules/*HERCLE*.

Augure. I 70, II 98, II 99, V 81.
1. Oracle, prophet, seer, soothsayer. Particularly a priest in ancient Rome who divined when an enterprise should start. From L. *augur* = 'interpreter of auguries'.
2. Portent, prophecy, sign, threat, warning. From L. *augurium* and O.F. *augurie* = 'omen'.

Aure. VI 100.
1. Breath, breeze. From L. *aura*.
2. Death, after a warning has not been understood. In Ovid, Procris misunderstands the nature of Aura the breeze, and, while following her husband Cephalus, she is killed.
(See *VENT*).

Ausone. VII 22.
(Ausonne.)
1. Italy. Ausonia was a name used by Latin and later Greek poets including Virgil and Apollonius to denote Italy. In Nostradamus' time Ausone or Ausonia was more specifically in the kingdom of Naples.
2. Bordeaux. The modern name of Burdigala from where the Roman writer and herald of French literature, the 4th century Ausonius came.

Autour. III 92.
1. Around, about.
2. Goshawk.

Aux. VIII 2.
Auch. Town in Gascony, S.W.
France. (See *AUXERRE).*

Auxerre. IV 84.
Town in North Central France.
Ancient Autessiodurum, city in
Roman Gaul mentioned by
Ammianus. (See *AUX).*

Avignon. III 93.
City in S.E. France. Industries
include wine trade and transport.

Babel. II 30.
Confusion, disorder, disunity. In
Genesis XI God confused,
scattered and disunited men by
giving them many languages when
they had joined together to build
the Tower of Babel at the site,
later, of *BABYLON.*

Babylon. VIII 96, X 86.
(Babilon.)
1. Iraq. Babylon was an ancient
city sixty miles South of modern
Baghdad. It was site of the
Hebrews' Captivity. Capital of
the early civilization, city-state
then empire of Babylonia which
for centuries vied with Assyria
and Persia for hegemony over the
Middle East and Egypt. And it
was the breaking away of
southern Babylonia from the

Parthian empire/*PARTHE* which
decisively delayed Parthian
expansion westward.
2. In literature, a symbol of a
corrupt and fallen existence,
where matter is perverted by
spirit. An example is in
Revelation XVII 5, in which,
"This title was written on her
forehead: 'Mystery, Babylon the
Great, the Mother of Prostitutes
and of the Abomination of the
Earth'." In another example,
Petrarch refers to the often
dissolute papal court at *AVIGNON*
as 'an earthly Babylon'.
(See *BABYLONIQUE).*

Babylonique. I 55.
Babylonian. (See *BABYLON)*

Bagues. X 21.
1. Rings, jewels, treasure.
2. Methods, tools, ways,
weapons.

Balance. IV 96.
1. Balance.
2. Scales. (See *LIBRA).*

Ban. IX 73.
1. Ban, exile, prohibition. From
O.F. *ban.*
2. Persian 'lord'. And since the
12th century, 'lord' in what is
now Yugoslavia, as in the c.1300
AD Paul Subic who was 'Ban of
Croatia and Dalmatia and Lord of
Bosnia'. In the 1920s, Yugoslavia
comprised nine 'banats'.

Barbare. III 59, III 97, V 80,
VI 21, VI 100, IX 42, IX 60.
(Barbari,
Barbar.)
Barbary. From L. *Barbaria,* O.F.
Barbarie, and also Arabic *Barbar* =
Berber. The coastal region of
North Africa now forming
Algeria, Libya, Morocco and
Tunisia. The Berbers were its
early inhabitants. Now, the only
true Berbers live in remote parts
of Algeria and Morocco; but, for
example, 97% of Libyans are
Arab-Berbers. From Barbary,
Europe was invaded by
Carthaginians in 218 BC, and by
Moslems in 711 AD. Barbary
pirates, mainly from Tripoli,
raided across the Mediterranean
from 1551 until 1911.

Barbarin. VIII 49.
1. Berber. (See *BARBARE).*
2. Barbarian, uncivilized,
primitive, foreign, heathen. From
Gk. *barbarismos, Barbaroi* and L.
Barbari. Originally, anyone who
could not speak Greek. Later
applied more specifically to
German, Turkish and Slav
peoples of eastern and central
Europe including Serbs and
Croats.
(See *BARBARIQUE).*

Barbarique. V 80.
Cruel, uncivilised. From L.
barbaricus = 'barbaric'.
(See *BARBARIN* and *BARBARE).*

Barcelone. I 73, IX 42.
(Barcelonne.)
Barcelona. City on North East
coast of Spain.

Barriques. V 34.
Barrels, casks.

Bellique. I 35, II 100.
Disposed to fight, warlike. From
L. *bellicosus* = 'bellicose'. Bellona
was the Roman goddess of war.

Bestes. II 62.
1. Animals. From *bête* and O.F.
beste = 'beast'.
2. Supplies. Cattle, goats and
sheep comprised an army's
mobile rations.

Bisance. V 25, V 80, V 86,
VI 21, IX 73.
(Bizance.)
Byzantium. A city on the
European shore of the Bosporus,
founded by Greeks in 658 BC. It
fell to Rome in 196 AD. Named
Constantinople in 330 AD.
Became capital of the Eastern
Roman or Byzantine empire in
395 AD. By 569 AD the latter
included Turkey, Palestine,
Lebanon, Jordan, Syria, western
Saudi Arabia, Malta and other
Mediterranean Islands, Egypt,
Libya, Tunisia and Algeria. After
the fall of Rome it remained a
Christian bulwark against heathen
and then Islamic expansion for a
thousand years. In 626 AD, four

years after it had attacked Persia, the city was itself besieged by an alliance of Slavs and Persians. It fell to Turks in 1453 AD and is now Istanbul, Turkey. Its emblem was a crescent.

Bisantinois. V 47.
1. Turks.
2. Byzantines. (See *BISANCE*).

Blanc. IX 73, X 86.
(Blancs,
Blancz.)
White.
1. a. The racial colour;
   b. the White Horde of western Siberia warred against the Moslem empire of Tamerlane, which included Iraq, Iran, Syria and Turkey. In the late Middle Ages northern Croatia was known as White Croatia.
2. Syrian. A white banner was the emblem of the Umayyad Moslem dynasty which ruled Islam from Damascus. The Assyria of Apollonius' The Voyage of the Argo was in northern Asia Minor, where the Leucosyri inhabitants were 'White Syrians'.
3. The Moors of N. Africa were also Umayyad.
4. Cowardice, surrender.
5 Good. As in Western mythology and symbolism.
6. In Homer's Odyssey the White Rock is a landmark on the way to the underworld.

(See *BLANCHE*).

Blanche. II 2, IX 20, X 53.
1. Whiten.
2. Pale, from fear or shock. Both from O.F. *blanchir* = 'to whiten'.
(See *BLANC*).

Blennis. VI 100.
(Blenni.)
Fool. From Gk. *blennos* = 'blockhead, 'idiot', 'simpleton'. Also from L. *blennus* = 'a stupid fellow'.

Bleu. II 2, VI 80.
(Bleue,
Bleux.)
Blue. Sometimes a symbol of monarchy. In Amores II, Ovid refers to 'woad-blue Britain'. (See *PERS* and *CEIULEE*).

Blois. V 34.
Ancient town in North Central France. Industries include wine trade.

Blyterre. IV 94.
Béziers. Founded in 6th century BC and called Baeterre Septimanorum by the Romans, whose arena still stands there. Site of 12th century massacre of Catharists, an heretical sect distinguishing good from evil. A town on river Orb and Canal du Midi in southern France. Industries include fertilizers,

shipbuilding and wine trade. Thirteen miles West of AGDE/AGATH.

Boeuf. VIII 49.
(Beuf.)
1. Beef, meat.
2. The zodiacal *TAURUS* 'The Bull', 21 April to 20 May.
3. Europe. From the bull symbol of Europa. The connection between the Cretan bull of mythology and the zodiacal *TAURUS* originates in the spots appearing on the bull's hide in ancient vase paintings; these spots sometimes being thought to depict stars.
4. *DELUGE.* The Cretan bull of Europa was also the symbol of the Minoan civilisation which was destroyed by flood.
5. a. Fertility;
   b. the Underworld. From Osiris represented by Apis the holy bull of Egypt. (See also under *GRIFFON).* In astrology, the Bull is a feminine sign and ruled by the planet *VENUS.*

Boreas. II 99.
1. Greek name for the North and North East wind, equivalent to the Roman Aquilo, renowned by the Greeks for its importance at the naval battle of Artemisium in 480 BC, where it favoured them against the Persians. (See *AURE* and *VENT).*
2. Northerners. From a Greek

myth in which a people called Hyperboreans live in a land of perpetual sunshine - midnight sun - beyond the North Wind. Their "land comes down to the sea", says Herodotus; they are continually encroaching on others' lands, and are associated with the *GRIFFON.*
3. Violence. Boreas has a wider mythology than other winds, so more is known about him. The son of Astraeus the stars and Eos the dawn, he kidnaps back to his native Thrace an Athenian princess by whom he has three children, Zetes, Cleopatra and Calais. And *JUPITER/IOUË* punishes him with confinement in the cave of Aeolus (see *ALUS)* the ruler of the winds. His violence is contrasted with the gentleness of Zephyrus the West wind; and this persists into Renaissance literature. By then, however, unpredictability is appearing among his attributes. In Samuel Rowlands' poem 'Boreas', Boreas is equated with a drunken knight who has to be restrained from spitting peasants on his sword for fun. And in Dante's Paradise c.28, v.27, "Boreas blows from his milder cheek". But back in the 8th century BC, Hesiod's Boreas, a "terrible lawless brute", is a carrier of moisture, dust and refuse. And here in Ovid's Amores I, Boreas is asked to, "Strike these deaf portals with

your whirlwind's roar,
The whole town's silent now,
and damp and dewy
The night is slipping by; unbolt
the door.....
Or I'm all set to raid your
haughty mansion
Myself with my strong sword and
torch's flame."
(See *ADUST* and *POUDRE*).

Boristhenes. III 95.
(Boristhynes.)
1. The river Dnieper. A literary
reference from The Histories by
Herodotus, according to whom
its banks produce abundant food,
but also salt/*SEL*. The people of
the region are forbidden to
associate with foreigners, upon
whom they spy. Their leader at
last succumbs to the dissolute
ways of the Greeks.
2. Russia.

Braise. V 65.
(Brasse.)
1. Hot coals, charcoal.
2. Brewery. From O.F. *brasse* =
'beer'.

BRANCHES. I 2, II 2.
(Branche.)
1. Tree branch.
2 Olive branch.
3. Side-piece; legs, as of a tripod.
4. Prophecy. From Branchus, son
of Apollo. And also from his
legendary descendants the
Branchidae, the hereditary priests

of the oracle at the temple to
Apollo at Didyma near Miletus in
Asia Minor.

Brassières. VIII 91.
1. Vests.
2. Teams, sides.

Briges. VIII 49.
See *BRUGE*.

Britannique. II 1, IV 96, V 34,
VI 7, X 40.
(Britanniques.)
British, Britain.

Brodde. III 92.
1. Brown, black, dusky, feeble.
From O.F. *brode*.
2. Goad, prick, spike. From Old
Norman *broddr*.

Bruceles. IX 49.
(Bruxles.)
Brussels. Homophonic
cryptograms of Dutch and French
versions, Brussel and Bruxelles.

Bruge. VIII 49.
(Briges.)
1. Bruges. City in N.W.
Belgium. Once major port in
Netherlands, with close trade
links to England from 13th
century. Silted up in 16th century
and superseded by
Antwerp/*ANVERS* and Ghent/
GAND. In Canto 20, verse 16 of
Purgatory, Dante says, "But if
Doui and Lille and Ghent and

Bruges were strong enough".
(See Chapter Nineteen).
2. La Brigue. Region in S.E.
France.
3. Corruption. From *briguer* = 'to
canvas for', and *brige* = 'corrupt
practices'.
4. Disunity. From medieval L.
brigue = 'contention', 'strife'.

Bruine. IV 46, V 35, IX 100.
(Bruyne.)
1. Drizzle, fog, mist.
2. Confusion.
3. Substance suspended in air;
droplets.

Caché. I 41, II 47, II 48, V 8,
V 34, V 65.
(Cachez.)
1. Hide, smuggle.
2. Concealed, hidden, secret,
smuggled.
(See *CACHERA).*

Cachera. X 2.
See *CACHÉ* and *COUVERT.*

Calcine. IV 23.
1. Viscous substance.
2. A chemical.
3. A substance which is burned.
All from O.F. *calcina* = 'lime'.
4. Ashes. From L. *calcinare* = 'to
burn to ashes'; 'to reduce to
powder by heat', an instruction
much used by medieval
alchemists.

Cap. IX 20.
1. An abbreviation of Capet.
Since 897 AD every king of
France had traced his ancestry
back to Hugh Capet, the first
king of their lineage. A fact
emphasised by Dante in Purgatory
c.20, v.17, in which;-
"On earth beyond I was called
Hugh Capet;
from me have sprung the Louises
and Philips,
rulers of France up to the present
day".
2. Caught. From O.F. *caper* = 'to
seize'.
3. Head. From L. *caput-* = 'of
the head', and as in *de pied en cap*
= 'from head to foot'.
4. A hat. From medieval L. *cappa*
= 'a covering for the head'.

Caper. II 35.
Capricorn.
1. The zodiacal Ram, 23
December to 20 January.
2. As the Greek form *aigokeros*
shows, this zodiacal sign was
originally a goat with a fishlike
tail, a prototype originating in
BABYLON. Its goat shape also
identifies it with the god Pan.
3. Astrologically, Capricorn is
ruled by Saturn/*SATURNE,* and
marks the exultation of *MARS.*
4. The Southern Hemisphere.

Captive. III 13, V 14, VI 100,
VII 18, VIII 77, X 1.
(Captifue,

Captifve,
Captif.)
In Romans VII 23 Saint Paul equates captivity with sin, and in II Corinthians with disobedience. In the Old Testament, captivity is mainly associated with that imposed by *BABYLON*. (Also see *RAYPOZ*).

Caques. VIII 55.
Casks.
(See *BARRIQUES.*)

Car. VIII 46.
1. For, because.
2. Abbreviation of *CARMANIE*.

Carmanie. III 90, X 31.
In Tacitus' Annals Carmania was the Roman named for Kerman, a province in S.E. Iran at the mouth of the Persian Gulf.

Cavées. X 49.
1. Caves. From L. *cava*.
2. Warnings. From L. *cave* = 'beware'.

Ceiulee. IX 73.
(Cerule.)
Blue. From L. *caeruleus* = 'sky blue'. See *BLEU* and *PERS*.

Celiques. III 7.
1. God. From L. *caelum* = 'heaven'.
2. Airborne, air force. From O.F. *celestial* = 'of the heavens or sky'.

3. Swiftly swelling. A composite of L. *celer* = 'swift'; Gk. *kele* = 'swelling'; and, used figuratively, *céliaque* = 'artery'.

Cerule. IX 73.
(Ceiulee.)
1. Blue.
2. 'Of the sky', in Ennius' Annals.
Both from L. *caeruleus* = 'sky blue'.
See *BLEU* and *CEIULEE*.

Chaîne. III 79, IV 84.
(Chaisne,
Chaines.)
1. Chain, line, range.
2. Channel.
3. Sequence of events.

Cheramon. IX 62.
Common, as in 'The Common Market'. A hybrid word constructed from *chercher* = 'to look for'; chère as in *la bonne chère* = 'good living'; *chèrement* = 'dearly', 'at a high price'; and *commun* = 'common'.

Cicle. I 62.
(Cycle.)
See *CYCLE*.

Cite. I 41, I 87, II 97, III 11, III 13, III 79, III 81, IV 82, V 8, V 35, V 81, V 84, V 86, VI 80, VI 98, VII *22,* VIII 17, X 49.
City.

Classe. I 9, I 35, I 73, II 5, II 22, II 99, III 13, IV 23, V 8, V 23, V 34, V 48, VI 44, IX 42, X 2.
(Plays.)
1. From L. *classis* = 'army' or 'fleet'. In Caesar, Cicero and Virgil it is applied specifically to a fleet.
2. Break. From Gk. *klasis* = 'fracture'.
3. For *plays* see Chapter Eighteen.

Climat. I 55, III 77.
1. Climate.
2. Season.

Combust. IV 67.
1. Bright, fiery.
2. Burned, consumed, destroyed.
All from L. *combustus* = 'combustible'.

Comète. II 62.
1. Comet, meteor.
2. Warning.
Seneca suggested that a comet preceded Noah's flood. (See *DELUGE*).
The Magi were warned of Jesus' birth by the Star of Bethlehem which may have been a meteor or comet. A comet in 66 AD preceded the fall of Jerusalem in 70 AD, as did another the death of Attila in 451 AD. Halley's comet in April 1066 preceded the Norman Conquest. The list of connections men have made between comets and important events which coincided with or followed them is very long. Since the times of the Chaldeans and ancient Egypt, comets have traditionally warned of the births and deaths of leaders, and of famines, plagues and wars. Comets appearing in the East may foretell pleasant events. But seldom those appearing in Aquarius or in the West. Hence, in The Sibylline Oracles, "In the West a star shall shine, which they call a comet, a messenger to men of the sword, famine and death". While, in Historia Naturalis, Pliny summed up the belief in the classical world that "A comet ....is usually a very fearful star and announces no small effusion of blood". It is to Book II, where Pliny deals with comets, that some of Nostradamus' word-plays can most easily be traced. Here we find that, "The Greeks call them comets; we call them long-haired stars.... The Greeks call those that have a mane spreading out from their lower part like a long beard 'bearded stars'. The Ethiopians and Egyptians saw a terrifying comet to which Typhon, the king at that time, gave his name" (See *TISON*.) "In the head of the Northern or Southern Serpent it brings poisonings." (See *SERPENT*.) Pliny also tells of a comet which marked a public games/*JEUX*.

Like many myths, those concerning comets are almost universal. And the time elapsing between their appearance and the events to which they relate is everywhere as elastic. Comets of 1490 and 1499 had thus predisposed the Aztecs in 1519 to accept Cortes as the returning god Quetzalcoatl. (Also see Chapter Fourteen).

Condon. VIII 2.
1. Condom. Town in S.W. France, twenty-one miles from Agen.
2. Sacrificed. From L. *condono* - = 'give up', 'sacrifice'.

Conflit. I 26, I 41, I 91, III 7, III 99, V 14, IX 34, IX 60.
(*Conflict.*)
Battle, conflict, fighting, war.

Connisse. V 90.
Harmful dust. From Gk. *konnisse* = 'dust'; and L. *connissus* = 'used', 'striven against'. In Acts XXII 23 the crowd throws dust into the air to show their anger towards Paul. And in Deuteronomy XXVIII 24 God shows his anger by raining dust. In Leviticus XVII 13 dust is used to cover blood.
(See *ADUST, POUDRE, POUSSIÈRE* and *SANG).*

Contentieux. III 81.
1. Argument, contention,

controversy, disagreement, opinion, quarrel. From O.F. *contention* = 'dispute'.
2. Ambition, case, intention. From L. *contentio* = 'I rival'.

Convert. I 18, V 27, X 31.
(*Couvert.*)
See *COUVERT.*

Copie. II 48, III 31, VI 7, IX 97, X 100.
(*Copis.*)
Troops. From L. *copia* = 'army', 'force'.

Coq. V 14, VIII 46.
Cock.
1. France. From the *Coq gauloise,* an emblem of France since the Revolution.
2. Repentence. As in Matthew XXVI 75.
3. Associated with ;-
a. bragging, crowing;
b. supremacy;
c. vigilance.

Corbeaux. III 7.
1. Black birds.
2. Crows, jackdaws, ravens, rooks.
3. Pillagers from the air. From *corbeaux blancs* = 'vultures'.
(See *AQUILON.*)

Corinthe. V 90.
(*Perinthe, Perinthus.*)
See *PERINTHE.*

Cornette. IX 60.
(Cornere.)
1. Pennant or cavalry standard. Introduced to Europe from the Middle East.
2. A junior cavalry officer who carried the regiment's Colour or battle-standard.
3. A nun's winged headdress.

Corruer. III 97.
Crumble. From L. *corruere* = 'to collapse', 'to fall to the ground', 'to be overthrown'; and C. *corroer* = 'to decay'.

Coultre. VIII 55.
Knife. From O.F. *coultre* and L. *culter*.

Coup. II 62, III 94.
1. Blow, chime, knock, shot, stroke.
2. Illegal seizure of power, as in *coup d'état*.
3. Suddenly. As in *coup de main* = 'sudden vigorous attack', and in *tout à coup*.

Coursier. VII 38.
Fast horse. From O.F. *coursier* = 'courser'.

Couvert. I 18, V 27, X 31.
(Convert.)
Covert, disguised, secret, undercover. From O.F. *covert* = 'covered'. (See *CACHÉ* and *CACHERA*).

Croisés. III 77, VI 80, VIII 91, IX 62.
(Croisez,
Croix.)
1. Crusaders.
2. Crosses.
3. Christian Church, Christendom.
4. Europe, Europeans.
5. Western, the West.
6. Money. For many centuries a cross was minted on coinage of Christian countries including Byzantium/*BISANCE*. As result, 'crosses' became a common slang term for coins. This punning use of the word even crossed the Channel to England, as can be seen in Act I, scene 2 of Shakespeare's Love's Labour's Lost.
(See *CRUCIGÈRE*).

Croistre. VIII 97.
(Croître.)
To grow, to wax.

Crucigère. III 61, IX 43.
1. Crusade, crusader, crusading.
2. Christian, Christendom.
3. European, Europe.
4. Western, the West.
5. Suffering.
All from L. *crux-gerens* = 'cross-bearing'.
(See *CROISÉS*).

Cuve. X 49.
Tank.

Cyclades. III 64, V 90.
A group of Greek islands in the
Aegean and Sea of Crete.

Cycle. I 62.
(Cicle.)
1. A planetary orbit.
2. Set of seasons or years.
Both from L. *cyclus* and Gk.
kuklos.
(See *SIÈCLE*).

Dace. VI 7.
Dacia. Southern East Central
Europe. The tribal lands of the
Daci or Dacians lay along the
Danube, mostly North of the
river in what is now Rumania.
As the Dacians were pushed
westward by tribes migrating
from the Steppes they met the
eastward push of Roman armies.
In 107 AD, after five years of
warring, Trajan annexed Dacia to
the Roman Empire as an Imperial
province. Pressure from the East
shifted the province southward
and it eventually consisted of part
of what is now Hungary,
southern central Yugoslavia,
North West Bulgaria and the
northern tip of Albania. Its
western neighbour was then the
Roman province of Illyricum (see
PANNNONS). In the mid-3rd
century the original Dacia North
of the Danube was lost by the
Romans to Germanic tribes. At
the division of the Roman Empire
the remainder of Dacia was
alloted to Byzantium/*BISANCE*,
and later invaded by Mongols and
Slavs. In the 11th century it
passed to the Hungarian crown,
and though invaded by Mongols
and Turks in the 13th century
was still part of Hungary in
Nostradamus' time. In the 17th
century its possession passed to
the Austrian Hapsburgs. But the
name 'Rumania' and of its
'Romance' language originates
with its Roman colonists.

Dame. I 94, V 65, VII 18,
VIII 70.
1. Lady.
2. Mature woman.
3. Mistress. All above from L.
domina.
4. The Whore of *BABYLON* in
Revelation XVII and XVIII. (See
ADULTÈRE and *ADULTERINE*).

Dechassera. VI 80.
Expel. From O.F. *dechasser* = 'to
drive out'.

Deffraieur. I 94, II 30, V 23,
V 65, VI 21, VI 81, X 72.
(Effrayeur,
Frayeur.)
See *EFFRAYEUR*.

Deluge. I 62, VIII 91.
Flood myths exist throughout the
world. And they have strong
similarities to each other. For
example, the Guianan version has
the waters flood from the stump

when a man cuts down the Tree of Knowledge. Their meanings too are similar.

1. A flood.

2. A new start. Associated with the zodiacal Aquarius, and then, through *PISCES,* with the final stage of a *CYCLE.* In mythology the deluge is never presented as final. There are survivors, as in Noah and his family in Genesis, Deucalion and Pyrrha in the Greek equivalent, Bergalmer and his wife in the Prose Edda, Utnaphishtim and his family in the Sumerian myth, and Yima and a thousand couples in the Persian tradition.

3. a. Violence;
   b. corruption;
   c. overpopulation. As in Genesis VI and VII, floods are widely associated in scriptures with human violence and corruption, and are sent to punish or reduce the human population for these faults. *"Par déluge punis"* leaves no doubt about this being the meaning in verse VIII 91.

4. War. In the Celtic creation myth the heroes who escape the flood in a ship to Innisfail are killed when a large red moon appears. (See *LUNE*). And in traditional symbolism the flood corresponds to 'the death of the moon', which turns red. (See *ROUGIR).* In the Norse Ragnarök a flood accompanies war, as it

does in the Anglo-Saxon story of Beowulf. In the Persian flood myth the means of survival is an underground shelter which would be useless in a flood, but handy in a war. And the dove and olive branch, the signs that Noah's flood is over, are the symbols also of peace from war. Note, the original connection between flood and war was the water with which, in primitive societies, returning warriors washed away guilt about those whom they had slain.

Desouvert. VIII 28.
(Découvert,
Descouvert.)
Discovery, uncovering. From *découvrir* and O.F. *descourir* = 'to discover'.

Destrois. VIII 46.
1. Oppressed. From O.F. *destrois.*
2. A pass or sound. From *détroit* = 'a narrow place' on land or sea.
3. A charger From *destrier* = 'war-horse'.
4. Defeat. From O.F. *destruire.*

Determine. III 97.
Ended, over. From O.F. *determiner* = 'to finish'.

Diane. II 28.
Diana, the Roman form of Artemis, Greek goddess of nature, fertility and the

moon/*LUNE*. Her characteristics vary with phases of the moon, so that she sometimes has three heads, Diana, Jana and Janus. Bearing arrows and other weapons for the hunt, as the night huntress she is accompanied by dogs. And linked with the Greek Hecate, she is 'She who succeeds from afar', whose attributes are key, dagger and torch. She is also associated, through Hecate, with Lilith who was Adam's first wife and is the dark aspect of the great Mother Goddess. In this latter identity she is the personification of the moon, responsible for obsessions and madnesses, and whose particular time is the three days before a new moon, during which it is dangerous to try to work magic. As a night phantom, Lilith is the enemy of childbirth. As a despised mistress, (see *DAME)* she is associated with the Whore of *BABYLON* of Revelation XVII and XVIII. As daughter of *JUPITER/IOUË* and *LATONA,* she is also Phoebe/*PHEBÉS* the twin sister of Phoebus Apollo. And as Seline/*SELENE* she was originally a titaness.

Dix. IX 43, X 2.
Ten.

Durance. III 99.
1. The river Durance in S. E. France, which turns West at the Lubéron mountains.
(See *LEBRON).*
2. Captivity, durance, imprisonment. From L. *durare.*

DUUMVIRAT. V 23.
(Duumvirat.)
An alliance of two. From L. *duum virum* = 'of two men'; and *duumvir* = 'one of two co-equal officials'. According to Livy's The History of Rome From It's Foundation, duumvirs were special officials appointed to enquire into cases of high treason.

Eau. II 29, IV 20, V 86, VIII 49, VIII 77, X 10, X 49.
1. Water.
a. The astrological symbol of purification and regeneration;
b. to Arabs and Egyptians a symbol of birth and life;
c. rain (see *PLUIE);*
d. *DELUGE;*
e. in Exodus VII 19, 20, water is turned into blood (see *SANG);*
f. in Revelation VIII 8 - 11 water when turned into blood becomes a poison.
2. Aquarius.
a. The zodiacal 'Water Bearer', 21 January to 19 February;
b. an autumnal constellation of the Northern Hemisphere.

Eclipses. VIII 15.
1. Passing of the moon/*LUNE* between the sun and earth.

Note: the next eclipse of the sun which will be visible in England is not due until 1999.
2. The cutting out of light; figuratively, of learning, and hence of civilisation. Both the above from Gk. *ekleipsis* = 'to fail to appear'.
3. Decline, loss of importance.
4. To surpass.

Effrayeur. I 94, II 30, V 23, V 65, VI 21, VI 81, X 72.
(Frayeur,
Deffraieur.)
From O.F. *effrayeur* = 'terror'.

Egypte. III 77, V 25.
Egypt.

Elisees. IX 97.
(Helisees.)
See *HELISEES*.

Embleront. VIII 21.
1. Capture.
2. Kill.
Both from O.F. *embler* = 'to carry off'.

Empiera. X 66.
(Tempiera.)
See *TEMPIERA*.

Emprinse. V 63.
(Emprise.)
1. Project. From O.F. *emprinse* = 'enterprise'.
2. Initiative, control, hold, ascendancy.

Ennosigée. I 87.
1. NEPTUNE/Poseidon 'the earth-shaker'.
2. Volcanic.
Both the above from Gk. *ennosigaeus* = 'earth-shaking'.
3. NOCG. The syllables of *ennosigée* phonetically resemble this acronym.
i. 'N' as in *naturel* = 'natural', as in 'natural gas'; also as in *national* = 'national'. And, with 'O', as in *Nord* = 'North'.
ii. 'O' with 'N' as in *Nord* = 'North'. And also phonetically as in *EAU* = 'water'.
iii. 'C' as in *compagnie* = 'company, 'corporation'. And phonetically, as in 'sea' and northern European versions of this.
iv. 'G' as in *gaz,* as in *gaz naturel* = 'natural gas'.
4. The letters involved are themselves traditional symbols:-
'N', for the waves of the sea;
'O', for a solar disc; 'C', for the crescent moon; 'G', for the creator.

Envers. IX 49.
(Anvers.)
See *ANVERS*.

Esclavonie. IV 82.
1. Slavs.
2. Russia.
3. Yugoslavia.
4. Croatia. Slavonia is now that part of northern Yugoslavia lying

between the Danube, Drava and Sava rivers. (See *PANNONS*).

Escosse. X 66.
Scotland. From *Écosse*.

Espagne. IV 94, V 14, V 59.
(Espaigne.)
Spain.

Estenique. V 80.
(Unique.)
1. Heathen. From L. *ethnicus* and Gk. *ethnikos* = 'pagan'.
2. Culture, race. From Gk. *ethnos* = 'nation'.
3. A usually non-European minority national or cultural group.
4. Unique.

Étang. I 16.
(Estang.)
1. Pond.
2. Water/*EAU*.
3. Aquarius, the zodiacal 'Water Bearer'.
4. Point. From N. *tang* = 'tip', as of a sharp object.

Éteints. IV 82, VIII 28.
(Estaincts,
Estaindre.)
1. Metal. From *étein* = 'tin'.
2. Exhausted, extinguished. From *éteint* = 'extinct', 'gone', 'lacklustre'; and *éteindre* = 'to quench'.

Étincelle. II 46.
(Estincelle.)
Spark. In metaphor, as in the tail of a meteor or comet/*COMÈTE*. Also metaphorically, as in a shooting star. (See *ÉTOILE*).

Étoile. II 41, II 43, V 59.
(Estoille,
Estoile.)
1. A star.
2. When 'bearded', a meteor or comet/*COMÈTE*.
3. When "burning for seven days", a comet.

Etreinte. VII 38.
(Estrein,
Estrain.)
1. Clutch, grip, hold, rein. From L. *retinere,* and *rêne* and O.F. *resne* = 'rein'.
2. Stirrup. From *étrier*.

Etrusque. 1 26.
1. Tuscany.
2. Italy.
3. Europe.
By the 8th century BC there was a prehistoric tribe, the Rasna/Rasena in central Italy. The Greeks named them the Tyrsenoi/Tyrrhenoi (see *TYRREN*) and the Romans the Etrusci/Tusci. In the area later known as Etruria/Tuscany, with other tribes including the Volci (see *VOLSQUES*) they created the Etruscan League of city states. In the 3rd century BC the League

was destroyed by its southern neighbours the Romans. In the Middle Ages Tuscany became part of the Duchy of Lombardy. Florence, its capital, was one of the leading powers of Europe during the 14th and 15th centuries, and was still so during the 16th in which Islamic expansion westward was halted. And Florence, birthplace of Dante, was the centre of arts, learning and literature throughout the Renaissance.

Eureux. V 84.
(Evereux.)
EUROPE.

Europe. II 22, VI 80, VIII 15, X 86.
(Eurotte.)
1. Europe.
2. a. Europa was a Phoenician princess, daughter of the king of Tyr. (See *TYRREN*). She was kidnapped by Greeks and carried away to Crete on the white bull *TAURUS:* - in Ovid's version, in his Metamorphoses, Europa is taken not from Tyr but from Sidon, and the bull is *JUPITER* in disguise, who, with Europa, sires Minos the legendary founder of the first great European civilisation;
   b. the zodiacal *TAURUS,* from the bull symbol of Europa in Minoan mythology.
   c. One of Europa's relevant

characteristics is described here by Rufinus, c.550 AD, in The Kiss.
"When Europa kisses me
She takes no gentle honey-sips,
But sucks my soul insatiably
Out of my very finger-tips."
(See *EUREUX*).

Evereux. V 84.
(Eureux.)
1. *EUROPE.*
2. Évreux. Town in N. W. France, destroyed by fire in 1119 and again in 1365. Le Vieil-Evreux, the Roman Mediolanum, is four miles from the present town.

Excroissance. X 70.
1. Abnormal or morbid growth on outside of the body.
2. Mole.
3. Skin cancer. (See Chapter Twenty-Eight).

Exercites. II 18.
(Excercites,
Exertites.)
Military formations. From L. *exercitus* = 'army'.

Expiler. VIII 62.
1. Forced out. From L. *expellere* = 'to expel'.
2. Plundered, robbed. From L. *expilare* = 'to pillage'.

Faim. I 55, I 70, II 62, II 91, V 63, VIII 17.

Famine, hunger, need, shortage. (See *FAMINE*).

Faincte. I 53, IV 43, VIII 62, IX 83, X 31.
(Sainte,
Sainct.)
See *SAINTE*.

Famine. I 16, II 46, II 96, V 90, VI 5.
Famine, hunger, want. (See *FAIM)*.

Faux. I 16, V 90, X 66.
(Faulx.)
1. Fake, false. From L. *fraus fraudis* = 'deception'.
2. Mistake.
3. Wrong.

Faypoz. IX 44.
(RAYPOZ)
See *RAYPOZ*.

Femme. I 41.
1. Woman.
2. As in *femme de joie,* = 'prostitute', in reference to the Whore of *BABYLON* in Revelation XVII and XVIII.

Fer. II 5, II 34, II 46, IX 44, X 10.
1. Iron, steel.
2. Weaponry.
3. War.

Fez. VI 80.
1. Cap worn in some Moslem countries.
2. A city in Morocco. This is a major religious centre where, in 788 AD, a North African Shiite dynasty was founded.

Fille. VI 100, VIII 96.
1. Daughter.
2. Descendant.
3. Girl.

Fils. I 41, X 21, X 40.
1. Son.
2. Descendant.
3. Someone associated with a particular attribute, as in 'son of the soil'.

Fléaux. I 63.
(Fleurs.)
1. Scourges, whips.
2. Droughts, epidemic diseases, famines, wars. 'Scourge' is a metaphor for a person or thing which causes widespread suffering; e.g. Genghis Khan the 'Scourge of Asia'. *Fleurs* = 'flowers' is a reference to the rashes which are symptoms of many epidemic diseases such as smallpox, and particularly of plague from which originates the nursery rhyme,
"Ring a ring o' roses,
Pocket full of posies,
Atishoo, atishoo,
We all fall down."
And as red marks upon the body are also produced by a scourge, in the literal sense, *fléaux* and

fleurs are well-chosen as edition-variations of each other.

Flèche. VIII 49.
(Fleiche.)
1. Arrow.
2. The zodiacal Sagittarius 'The Archer', 23 November to 22 December.
3. Dart. From *fléchette*.
4. Missile.
5. Disease. In Homer's Iliad the arrows shot by Apollo deliver *PESTILENCE*.
6. Poison. The arrow with which Hercules/*HERCLE* accidentally wounds Chiron the friendly and constructive centaur is poisoned, and the pain so great that Chiron forfeits eternal life and goes to Hades in preference to enduring it.

Fleuve. I 87, II 35, II 97, III 61, VI 33, VI 98, VIII 55.
River.

Fois. IX 73.
(Foix.)
Town in S. W. France.

Forêt. VI 7, IX 20.
(Forest, Forestz.)
1. Forest.
2. Doors. From L. *fores*. From Roman usage, particularly as in 'out of doors', 'abroad'.

Franche. V 80.
(France.)
1. A Frenchman.
2. French or German.
3. A free man.
All from L. *Francus* = 'Frank'. The Franks or Francs were a German tribal coalition which conquered what is now France in the 6th century AD. And only Franks had full freedoms in Frankish Gaul.
4. A European. In the Middle East and North Africa a Frank can be anyone of a Western nationality.

Frayeur. I 94.
See *EFFRAYEUR*.

Frères. II 34, II 95, IV 94, IV 96, V 50, VI 7, VIII 17.
Brothers. (But see Chapter Thirteen.)

Frofaim. VI 81.
(Fromfaim, Tochsain.)
Hunger, for both animal and vegetable foods. A composite word from *faim* = 'hunger'; *from*, an abbreviation of *froment* = 'wheat'; and *fromage* = 'cheese'.

Fouldre. I 26, III 13, IV 43, VIII 2.
(Fondre, Foudre.)
1. To strike;
a. down or severely;

b. suddenly, stunningly;
c. with a loud noise and a dazzlingly bright light.
All from *foudroyer* = 'to strike as lightning', and O.F. *fouldrer* = 'to flash and thunder'.
2. a. Anger, hostility;
b. a thunderbolt, a bolt from the blue, a disaster.
All from *foudre* = 'wrath' and 'unexpected event'.

Galère. IX 43, X 2.
(Gallere.)
Ship. From Gk. *galaia* = 'galley'.

Galiotes. V 63.
(Galiotz,
Gallots.)
Launches, frigates, small ships. From L. *galea* and O.F. *galie* = 'boat', and O.F. *galiot* = 'galley'.

Gand. IX 49.
Ghent. In Flemish, Gent; in French, Gand. In the 16th century Ghent led the opposition to Spanish rule in the Netherlands. It declined in importance when it lost access to the sea in 1648, the year in which, with the end of the Thirty Years War, part of the Netherlands achieved independence. Thirty-seven miles from Brussels/*BRUCELES* and thirty from Bruges/*BRUGE.* Canto 20, verse 16 of Dante's Purgatory ponders, 'but if Doui and Lille and Ghent and Bruges were

strong enough". (See Chapter Nineteen.)

Garonne. VIII 2.
1. River Garonne, which rises in Spain and flows past Toulouse, Agen, *MARMANDE* and Bordeaux (see *AUSONE)* into the Gironde/*GYRONDE* estuary. It drains the *AQUITAINE* basin.
2. S. W. France.

Gaul. I 51, I 70, II 29.
(Gaule.)
1. France. In his The Gallic Wars, Caesar seems to exclude what is now the North West and the South of France, the areas he was not then invading. In the later Roman empire, however, 'Gaul' extended up to the Rhine and so included what is now Belgium.
2. Italy. Distinguished from Transalpine Gaul in France, was Cisalpine Gaul in northern Italy.
3. Stick, as in 'a goad'.
4. Stick, as in 'walking-stick' or 'crutch'.

Gelée. II 1, X 66.
(Gellee.)
1. Frost. From L. *gelare* = 'to freeze'.
2. Jellified, viscous. From O.F. *gelee* = 'jelly'.

Geneve. IX 44.
(Genesvue.)
1. Geneva. From O.F. *Genevre* =

'Geneva', and also from O.F.
Genevese = 'from or connected
with Geneva'.
2. Disarmament. Geneva is the
venue of international discussion
about disarmament and reducing
the harshness of wars.

Gens. II 62, II 99, III 64, VI 81,
VII 22, IX 42.
(Gent,
Gennes.)
1. Clan, nation. From L. *gens* =
'people'.
2. Genoese, people of Genoa.
Italians.
3. People of Ghent. Belgians.
4. People of Geneva. Swiss.
5. Disarmers (See *GENEVE*).

Germanie. X 31.
(Germaine.)
1. German, Germany. From L.
Germanus. In his Agricola and
Germania Tacitus sites Germany
as East of the Rhine and North of
the Danube. He does not indicate
where its eastern borders then
were: but so far as these would
have existed, they are likely to
have included parts of modern
Czechoslovakia, of Hungary, of
Poland and of the Ukraine.
2. European, *EUROPE.* The Holy
Roman Empire, latterly German,
was an early attempt to unify
Europe.
3. Related. From L. *germanus* and
O.F. *germain* = 'closely
connected'.

Gettez. VIII 28.
(Jettez,
Jetés.)
Placed carelessly. From *jeter* =
'to throw'.

Glaive. II 91, II 96, III 11.
1. Blade, sword.
2. Weaponry, military hardware.
From O.F. *gleive* = 'spear',
'lance'.
3. Force, violence.

Globes. V 8.
1. Spherical containers. From L.
globus.
2. As in globe-lightning.
3. Having neither corners nor
edges, a globe denotes freedom
from difficulty.
4. Bombs, explosions. As in *globe*
de compression = 'an overcharged
mine, which produces a crater
which is wider than it is deep'.
(See *ROND*).

Gouffre. V 84, VI 44.
(Gouphre,
Goulfre.)
1. Gulf. A deep sea inlet with a
narrow mouth. From O.F. *golfe.*
Note that Herodotus called the
Persian Gulf 'the Arabian Gulf'.
2. An abyss.
3. Difference, division.
4. Greed. Figuratively, as in
Spenser's Faerie Queene in
which:-
"That is the Gulfe of Greediness,
they say,

That deepe engorgeth all this worldes pray....
For whiles they fly that Gulfes deuouring iawes,
They on this rock are rent, and sunk in helplesse wawes."

Grêle. VIII 2, VIII 77.
(Grêler,
Gresle,
Gresler,
Guerre.)
1. Hail.
2. Ravaged by disease. From *grêlé* = 'pock-marked'.
3. Airborne pollution, contamination.
4. War-associated. From *guerre*.
5. A chemical-biological warfare agent.

Griffon. X 86.
(Griphen,
Gryphon.)
Force in protection of financial interests. The griffon/griffin/gryphon is a fabulous beast, a composite of several real creatures. Like other fabulous beasts it was invented in order to express in a single word or picture the several characteristics with which each of the real animals which made up its parts are associated. It was a sort of shorthand. A griffon appeared in Egyptian art before 3300 BC, from where it spread to the Cretan and Greek cultures. It may have originated independently in Babylonia/ *BABYLON;* and Aristeas' poem Arimaspeia suggests it may have done so in Russia too, where there were already legends about monsters guarding treasure. The griffon has several forms, in the most common of which it has the head and wings of an eagle, the body of a lion, and a serpentine tail. Those early forms of griffon in Ezekiel I and Revelation IV originated with the sculptured human-headed, winged lions outside the palaces of Assyria. In Book 7, chapter 2 of Pliny's Natural History, the griffons fight to protect the treasures which were theirs to mine. And in wider mythology, griffons not only stand beside the Tree of Life, guarding the roots of salvation, but are, too, particularly associated with the protection of wealth, for which their claws are well suited. In Book Four of his Histories, Herodotus actually describes them as "the gold-guarding Griffins". The griffon's ethics are vague. While it is of generally good character, in medieval Christian art it was variously used to represent both Saviour and Antichrist. Perhaps, good for the wrong reasons. And it was consecrated by the Greeks to both Nemesis and Apollo. Nemesis is the goddess of retribution. Apollo, or Phoebus

Apollo (see *PHEBÉS),* has several
roles. As the Greek god of crops
and herds he protects from
disease and wild animals. As god
of prophecy he communicates the
future to men. He also tells them
their guilt and purifies them of
this. As the god of divine distance
his bow, with which he threatens
from afar, is associated with awe,
terror and death. In his Egyptian
form he is Horus/Orus, a falcon
god of the sky. The son of Osiris,
god of fertility and the
Underworld whose representative
is Apis the bull (see *BOEUF,
EUROPE* and *TAURUS),* Horus'
eyes are the sun/*SOL* and
moon/*LUNE.* His left eye, the
moon, is injured in a fight with
the murderer of his father.
Herodotus says that, "It was Orus
who vanquished Typhon". (See
TISON.)

Guele. VII 38.
(Guelle.)
Mouth. From *gueule* = 'face',
'mouth'.

Gyronde. V 34.
(Garonne.)
l. Gironde.
a. Region in S.W. France;
b. estuary of river *GARONNE.*
2. French xenophobia. During the
French Revolution the Girondin
group which took its name and
was drawn from the Gironde
region, pursued an aggressive

foreign policy. Almost all its
members were eventually
imprisoned or executed.

Hadrie. I 9, III 11.
Neglect. From Aidrie, a North
Italian city once a flourishing
coastal port but now silted up.

Hécatombe. X 74.
1. Blood-spilling, carnage,
slaughter.
2. Atrocity, massacre.
3. Public sacrifice.
All from Gk. *ekato* or *hekaton* =
'a hundred'; and Gk. *bous* = 'ox';
and L. *hecatombe* = 'the sacrifice
of a hundred oxen' in Juvenal.
Figuratively, a sacrifice of many
victims.

Helisees. IX 97.
(Elisees.)
1. Elysium, paradise.
2. Death.
In Greek mythology the Elysian
Fields were the abode of the
blessed after death. In Hesiod's
Works and Days the Isles of the
Blessed Ones are a home for
heroes, with three harvests a
year. The location of the 'Isles' is
vague. Referred to in Homer's
Odyssey, Book IV, the Isles of
the Blest lie at the western
extremity of the world and
contain the garden of the
Hesperides (see *HESPERIES).* In
Plutarch's Sertorius, they are sited
in Madeira and Porto Santo in the

Canary Islands.

Hercle. IV 23.
(Chercher.)
1. Hercules/Heracles. An
abbreviation. A hero of Greek
mythology. The trial in which he
triumphs over the Amazons
represents his overcoming the
threats posed by Lilith (see
DIANE). As a composite figure he
is the personification of several
things;-
a. he is the Roman god of
physical strength, illustrated as a
very muscular figure armed with
a club and wearing the skin of
the nemean lion - symbolizing the
sun/*SOL,* but which began its life
in the moon/*LUNE,* - as which he
is the wielder of overwhelming
force, able to annihilate rather
than just to win;
b. although shown in art as a
large man with a small head,
suggesting a lack of intelligence,
it is he who mediates with Zeus
on behalf of the condemned titan
Prometheus, and his cunning
described in the myths suggests
that his use of physical force is
carefully timed;
c. in alchemy he is associated
with the spiritual trouble which
ends in his taking the golden
apples representing immortality;
d. as their traditional founder he
represents the Olympic Games;
e. it is he who captures the
Cretan bull;

f. Apollonius describes Hercules
as cruel, evil and savage in
pursuit of wealth, and, by
implication, a humbug. For when
Hercules enters the garden of the
Hesperides he carries a club of
olive-wood, a token of peace, and
appears to want only a drink of
water like other travellers. But he
is really after the golden apples,
and, with poisoned arrows, kills a
snake with a 'dark spine', 'a son
of the Libyan soil' (see *LIBYQUE)*
to get them. (See *BOEUF,
EUROPE* and *TAURUS).*
2. Monaco. From the Roman
Herculeis Monacei/Portus
Herculis Monoeci. In the 6th
century BC Phoenicians erected
on the site a temple to Herakles-
Monoicos in memory of the
demi-god said to have passed that
way with the three golden apples
from the garden of the
Hesperides. (See *HESPERIES).*
3. *Chercher* = 'to look for'.

Herne. IX 20.
1. Queen. *Herne* is a cryptogram
of Reine.
2. Abbreviation of *Héroine* =
'heroine'.

Herodde. V 14.
(Heredde.)
1. Hereditary. From *héréditaire.*
2. Rhodes. A cryptogram.
3. Herod I 'The Great', (73 to 4
BC.) Roman-appointed king of
Judea from 37 to 4 BC. Ally of

Rome. Made a citizen of Rome, and president of the Olympic Games. Though a practising Jew, both his parents were Arabs. He murdered many of his own family and ordered the slaughter of the infants of Bethlehem. On his deathbed he ordered that his death should be a signal for the murder of the leaders of the Jewish nation, in a hippodrome. (See *AMPHITHEATRE*).

Hesperies. IV 39, IV 50.
l. Hesperus/Hesperos, the Evening Star.
2. The West. From L. *Hesperia* = 'the lands in the West'; and from L. *Hesperius* = 'western'. Greek poets gave the name 'Hesperia' to Italy, and Roman poets sometimes gave it to Spain. In mythology, the Hesperides were the daughters of Atlas and Hesperus/Hesperis, and they lived in the extreme West, 'at the world's edge hard by Night', according to Hesiod; and, according to Apollonius, 'near the Tritonian lagoon', - to Herodotus, 'Lake Tritonis', - which was a salt lake on the coast of Libya/*LIBYQUE*. There they resided in a garden with trees bearing golden apples watched over by a dragon or snake (see *SERPENT*) with a 'dark spine', 'a son of the Libyan soil'. The day after Hercules/*HERCLE* kills the garden's guardian with

poisoned arrows, "the Hesperides turned to dust and earth on the place where they had stood." (See *HELISEES* and *HERCLE*).

Hiérarchie. IV 50.
Priestly government. From Gk. *hierarkhia,* in which *hieros* = 'sacred', and *arkho* = 'rule'.

Hircania. III 90.
(Hyrcanie.)
See *HYRCANIE*.

Hoires. I 9, IV 39.
(Hoirs.)
Descendants, heirs.

Hommasse. VIII 15.
1. A mannish woman.
2. A woman who is less than a woman. (See *ADULTÈRE*).

Honnissement. VI 90.
1. Disgrace, humiliation, shame.
2. Appeasement.

Huille. IX 34.
(Huile.)
1. Literally 'oil'.
2. Idiomatically, 'a bigwig', 'a big shot', 'high and mighty'.

Hurne. IX 73.
(Urne.)
1. Urn.
a. A container for ashes of the cremated dead;
b. ballot box.
2. Vase. A container for

water/*EAU*.
3. Aquarius the zodiacal 'Water Carrier'.

Hyrcanie. III 90.
(Hircania,
Hyrcania.)
Iran. In Tacitus and Xenophon, Hyrcania was a province of ancient Persia, on the South East shore of the Caspian Sea.

Icelue. X 40.
(Iceluy.)
The former. A cryptogram of *celui-ci*.

Ieux. VII 22, X 74.
(Jeux.)
See *JEUX*.

Ile. I 9, II 22, II 100, IV 96, V 34, VI 7, VI 58, VI 81, X 22, X 66.
(Isles,
îles.)
1. Isle, island.
2. The British Isles.

Immesurée. V 84.
(Emmesuree.)
Immeasurable, obscure, uncertain. From O.F. *immesuree* = 'unmeasured'.

Impos. II 28.
(Imposts.)
1. Impossible. From L. *impossibilis*.
2. Powerless, subject, subjection.

From L. *impotens* = 'impotent', 'feeble'; and from L. *impos* = 'having no power over'.
3. Deceive, exploit, inflict. From L. *imponere imposit* = 'to put upon'.
4. Duty, tax. From L. *imponere* = 'to lay upon', 'to impose'; and *impôt* from O.F. *impost* = 'taxation'.

Infidèles. VIII 96, IX 83.
(Infidelle.)
1. Unfaithful.
2. Infidels.
3. Atheists.
4. Historically, people who do not belong to a particular religion. Within Christendom, especially applied to Moslems.

Iniustement. IV 43.
(Injustement.)
1. Unjustly. From L. *iniustus* = 'unfair', and *iniustitia* = 'injustice'.
2. Effectively.

Inscium. VI 100.
Uneducated. From L. *inscius* = 'ignorant', 'inexperienced', 'untaught'.

Insuls. II 1.
(Insultes.)
1. Isles. From L. *insula* = 'island'.
2. To cross over or jump. From L. *insultare* = 'to leap'.
(See *INSULTE*).

Insulte. II 1.
(Insuls.)
Abuse, insult, provocation. From
L. *insultare* = figuratively, 'to
insult'.
(See *INSULS).*

Ionique. III 64.
Ionian. Ionia included the
PHOCEAN towns of Chios,
Clazomenae, Colophon, Ephesus,
Erythrae, Miletus, Myus, Priene,
Samos, Sebedus and Teos along
the Aegean coast of what is now
Turkey and adjacent islands.

Iouë. VIII 48.
(Jove.)
See *JUPITER.*

Ireux. VI 33.
See *IREZ.*

Irez. VII 22.
(Yrés.)
Angry, irate. From L. *iratus* =
'anger'. (See *IREUX).*

Iris. VI 44.
1. Rainbow. Iris was the Greek
goddess of rainbows.
a. In Genesis IX 11 - 17 the
rainbow is the sign of God's
promise that further floods would
never kill everyone;
b. in classical Greece the rainbow
was an omen of war;
c. in the Norse Ragnarök the
invasion from the East comes
across a 'rainbow bridge';

d. in mythology the rainbow
drinks in the sea;
e. in astrology the rainbow
represents the *CYCLE/SIÈCLE* of
world ages;
f. a rainbow is produced by
refraction of light in airborne
moisture, from the sun usually,
but occasionally from the
moon/*LUNE.*
2. The river Iris, now Yeshil
Irmak. Once in the Assyria of the
White Syrians (see *BLANC),* now
in Turkey, it flows into the Black
Sea.
(See SERPENT).

Isles. I 9, II 22, II 100, IV 96,
V 34, VI 7, VI 58, VI 81, X 22,
X 66.
See *ILE.*

Ismael. IX 60.
See *ISMAELITES.*

Ismaelites. IX 43, X 31.
Arabs, particularly northern
Arabs. The Arab peoples claim
descent from Ishmael the son of
Abraham and Hagar.

Itale. I 51.
(Italie,
Italy.)
1. Italy.
2. Christendom.
3. Europe.

Iters. III 59.
(Tiers.)

1. A third. As in:-
a. a fraction;
b. a sequence;
c. a third country, event, party, person or thing. An anagram of *tiers.*
2. Departure. From L. *iter* = 'a walk', 'a journey', 'a going'.
3. The Danube. By anagram of Ister, this river's ancient name.

Iudée. III 97.
(Judee.)
1. Israel.
2. The southern part of Palestine.
3. Jewish. From Gk. *Ioudaios* and L. *Judaeus* = 'Judah'/'Judea'.

Iupiter. I 51, VIII 48, IX 55.
See *JUPITER.*

Jardin. X 49.
1. Garden.
2. Iraq. The Garden of Eden, of Genesis, was traditionally between the rivers Tigris and Euphrates, an area now in Iraq.
3. Temptation. The Garden of the Hesperides (see *HESPERIES*) contained trees bearing the golden apples stolen by Hercules/*HERCLE.*

Jeux. VII 22, X 74.
(Ieux.)
Games, sports. The first Olympiad was in 776 BC. Pliny the Elder tells of a games in honour of Venus Genetrix at which a comet/*COMÈTE* appeared

in the northern sky. The legendary founder of public games for prizes, a Greek institution between the 12th and 7th centuries BC, was Lycurgus. He is named by Nostradamus in his dedication to Henry II. Homer's Iliad features a funeral games.
(See *HERCLE* and *HERODDE).*

Jupiter. I 51, VIII 48, IX 55.
(Iupiter,
IOUË,
Ioue.)
1 Jupiter, the largest planet.
2. Jupiter, or Jove, the Roman sky god equivalent of the Greek Zeus. Originally a god of agriculture, but later variously entitled Fulgar the wielder of lightning; Imperator the supreme commander; Invictus the invincible; Praedator the predator, pillager and booty-snatcher; Tonans the thunderer (see *TONNERRE);* and Triumphator the triumphant. His counterparts are *NEPTUNE* in the sea and Pluto on and beneath the earth. In Ovid's Metamorphoses it is Jupiter disguised as a bull who kidnaps Europa/*EUROPE* and with her sires Minos the founder of the first great European civilization. In later literature Caesar notes that Jupiter is the king of the gods of *GAUL;* and in Dante's Inferno it had been Jupiter who slew Typhon/*TISON.*

In astrology he rules over zodiacal *PISCES* and Sagittarius/ *SAGITTAIRE,* and also the first hour of Thursdays; his attributes are a throne, a crown, an eagle and a thunderbolt. In alchemy, as the master of judgement and will, Jupiter is a higher development of Venus, and he has a full understanding of the material world when he is linked with the moon/*LUNE.*

Langues. III 95.
1. Languages, speech, tongues. Much of the Old French used by Nostradamus is *langue d'oc,* a low Latin brought to southern France by Roman soldiers.
2. Promises.
3. Branches of a religious or military organisation, as in that of the Knights Hospitallers.
4. National and racial divisions.

Larisse. V 90.
Larissa/Larisa.
1. A city in N. E. Greece.
2. Ancient coastal town North West of Sardis in Asia Minor, now Turkey. Mentioned by Xenophon in The Education of Cyrus.

Latin. V 50, V 63.
1. Where Latin was spoken;-
a. Italy;
b. Europe.
2. Those who spoke Latin, and their descendants.

3. Originally the inhabitants of Rome's southern neighbour, Latium. (See *LATINE).*

Latine. II 5.
See *LATIN.*

Latona. I 62.
(Laton.)
The moon/*LUNE.* In Greek mythology, Latona was the mother of Apollo and *DIANE,* but in Egyptian, according to Herodotus, only their nurse and preserver. In Book Two of his Histories he describes a temple to Latona situated in the city of Buto beside the Nile, at which the oracle is said to be the most accurate in Egypt.

Lebron. III 99.
1. The Lubéron mountains. A narrow wooded range running East to West, twenty five miles long and 3690 feet high, close to the river *DURANCE* in S. E. France. In Nostradamus' lifetime the fundamentalist Vaudois sect living there in a dozen villages was convicted of heresy and massacred.
2. *Le brun* = 'the brown'.
3. Hebron, eighteen miles from Jerusalem and the Dead Sea, is sacred to both Jews and Moslems.

Leman. IV 94, VI 81.
(Lemam.)

1. Geneva. From its Latin name *Lemannus*.
2. Disarmament. (See *GENEVE*).

Leo. II 98.
1. The zodiacal Leo 'The Lion', 23 July to 22 August.
2. The lion symbol of sun-gods such as Mithras.
3. In astrology Leo:-
a. is ruled by the sun/*SOL;*
b. marks the detriment of Saturn/*SATURNE* and the fall of Mercury/*MERCURE;*
c. is connected with emotions;
d. is associated in tarot cards with force and strength.
4. In alchemy Leo is:-
a. the fire element;
b. corresponding to sulphur.
5. The Gulf of Lion, off S.E. France.
(See *LION* and *LYON*).

Leon. I 73.
1. City and region of N. W. Spain. Brewing and wine trades.
2. Léon. Village in S. W. France.
3. Sicily. In his History of the Peloponnesian War Thucydides refers to a Leon North of Syracuse.

Lettres. I 41, I 62, II 5, III 27.
1. Documents, letters.
2. Knowledge.

Levant. II 91.
1. Eastern part of the Mediterranean, with its islands and the lands along its shores.
2. a. Dawn, morning;
b. figuratively, rising power. Both from *soleil levant* = 'rising sun'.

Libide. VIII 14.
Depravity, greed. From L. *libidinosus* = 'lust', 'longing', 'violent desire'. Livy connects this with obscenities.

Libra. IV 50.
1. The zodiacal *BALANCE* or 'Scales', 23 September to 22 October.
2. Justice, legality.
3. Inner harmony and self control; Libra is ruled by *VENUS*.
4. Self-destruction released by guilt.

Libyque. I 9, III 27, V 14.
(*Libinique*.)
North African. From L. *Libycus* = 'African','Libyan'.
(See *BARBARE*). The Tripolitan region of Roman Africa/*AFFRIQUE*. But the meaning varied. To the early Greeks it meant all Africa West of Egypt. But from the mid-3rd century BC both Greeks and Romans used 'Libyan' only for Africans controlled by Carthage. Note that the *SERPENT* guardian of the golden apples in the garden of the Hesperides (see *HESPERIES)* had a 'dark spine' and was 'a son of the Libyan soil'; and also that the garden

itself was according to Apollonius, "near the Tritonian lagoon" which was a salt lake on the coast of Libya.

Lion. I 35, V 25, VIII 2.
See *LEO* and *LYON*.

Ligue. II 100.
(Ligne.)
1. United Nations Organisation, as successor to the League of Nations.
2. Alliance. Both the above from L. *ligare* = 'league'.
3. Line.

Lis. V 50.
1. Lily.
2. France. From its pre-Revolutionary emblem, the fleur-de-lis.

Loeil. I 35.
(Yeux.)
See *YEUX*.

Logmion. V 80.
Ogmios, by cryptogram. Ogmios was the Celtic version of Hercules/*HERCLE* and a Gallic god of eloquence. There is a carving of him in an Aix-en-Provence museum. He is portrayed as an old man with a swarthy skin, armed with a bow and club. In the 2nd century AD Lucian recorded seeing a picture of Ogmios in Gallia Narbonensis/ *NARBON*. And Nostradamus

mentions "The Gallic Ogmion" in his Epistle to Henry II.

Loi. I 53, III 95, III 97, IV 43, V 80, VI 5.
(Lois,
Loix,
Loy.)
1. Law.
2. Ethics, standards of behaviour.
3. Control, hegemony, influence, power.

Londres. IV 46, IX 49, X 40, X 66.
(Lonole.)
1. London.
2. England, Britain.
3. The British government.

Loy. I 53, III 95, III 97, IV 43, V 80, VI 5.
See *LOI*.

Luminaires. III 5.
1. Lights. And figuratively, 'knowledge', 'intellectual, moral or spiritual light', from O.F. *luminarie.*
2. Stars, planets.
3. Wise men.

Lunaire. I 49, III 4.
1. Pertaining to the moon/*LUNE*.
2. Islamic.
3. Religious zeal.

Lune. I 56, VI 98.
The moon, from L. *luna.*
Whether full or crescent, the

symbolism attached to the moon has parallel origins and many meanings. The Nemean lion slain by Hercules/*HERCLE* began its life in the moon. To represent a crusade King Richard I's royal seal showed on each side of his head a crescent moon and a star. Western use of the crescent moon as a symbol goes back to the ancient Greeks who put it on coins to represent Artemis/ *DIANE*. The use of a similar crescent shape also originated in the up-swept horns of a bull, representing power and strength, as in the symbol of the moon-goddess Hêrê. Luna, from L. *lunaris,* was the Roman goddess of the moon. From these beginnings the crescent moon sign passed to Byzantium (see *BISANCE*). And in the mid-fifteenth century, when Byzantium fell to Moslems, it was adopted by both Ottoman and Seljuk Turks. But the crescent moon had already been a sacred symbol in the Middle East, - in the Assyrian empire since at least the 9th century BC. Symbolising growing brightness, it has now become the accepted and official emblem of Islam. To Moslems it represents protection from evil, as does the cross for Christians. In astrology, the moon represents the colour silver; and Monday, from *lundi,* is the moon's day. In Joel II 31 the moon will turn into blood/*SANG*.

Lusitanie. IX 60, X 100.
1. Portugal.
2. Spain.
In the Classical World the Lusitani were an Iberian people living in what is now Portugal. But in both his Annals and his Agricola and Germania Tacitus includes western Spain in Lusitania; and in his The Civil Wars Caesar treats it as a part of Hispania Ulterior which consisted of a portion of western Spain and only that part of Portugal lying South of Oporto.
(See *LUSITAINS*).

Lusitains. X 100.
See *LUSITANIE*.

Lyon. III 93.
See *LEO* and *LION*.

Mabus. II 62.
1. A cryptogram of Magus (see *MAGUES*).
2. A cryptogram of **Megabyzus**. Herodotus tells of two men by this name, both Persians. Gobrayas Megabyzus was one of the conspirators who overthrew the magus who had usurped the throne of Persia. He favoured the abolition of monarchy, but remained loyal to his co-conspirator Darius who became king. (See Chapter Fifteen for the full story). Afterwards, as the Persian governor in Europe, Megabyzus dealt harshly with all

opposition to Persian rule. His successful strategy against the Paeonians involved attacking them from within rather than from outside their own country. He was the father of Zopyrus (see *RAYPOZ*), and grandfather of the Megabyzus who became Persian governor of Egypt.

3. The cryptogram of *Mabus* is also found in *kometus AENOBARBE* (see *COMÉTE*).

Macedoine. II 96.

1. Macedonia.
2. Greece.
3. Europe.
4. Turkey.

Alexander the Great's Greek army was basically Macedonian. In the Classical Age, at the greatest extension of the Roman Empire, Macedonia consisted of what are now Albania, southern Yugoslavia, South-western Bulgaria, European Turkey and northern Greece.

Magnes. IV 23.

1. Magnesia. A region in S. E. Thessaly, Greece.
2. Ancient city of Lydia, founded by Magnesians from Greece, and now Manisa in Turkey; 'Magnesia on the Meander' in Tacitus' Annals.
3. A magnet or loadstone. From L. *magnes magnetis* and Gk. *magnes - etos* and O.F. *magnete*. Also referred to by Greeks as

'ironstone' and as 'the stone of Hercules' (see *HERCLE*); Pliny, quoting Nicander, says Magnes was the name of the discoverer of its properties. And, figuratively, 'enticing', 'seductive'.

4. A probably petroleum-based incendiary projectile such as that used by Byzantine warships. From *magnésie* = 'Greek fire'.

5. Brooding, threatening. As in this description of a sea cliff in Spenser's Faerie Queene:-
"On th'other side an hideous Rocke is pight,
Of mightie Magnes stone, whose craggie clift
Depending from on high, dreadful to sight,
Ouer the waues his rugged armes doth lift,
And threatneth downe to throw his rugged rift
On who so cometh nigh;"

Magues. X 21.

A cryptogram of maguses.

1. Iranian priests. The maguses, or magi, were originally priests in Media, a part of Persia now Iran, who interpreted dreams and prophecies. It was a magus who warned Alexander the Great that if he entered *BABYLON* he would die there: before he did enter it and did die there. But Pliny the Elder returns continually to their deceitfulness. The magi enjoyed killing any living thing; though the killing of dogs and men, who

might fight back, they left to others. Herodotus tells of two magi who were brothers, one of whom had already had his ears cut off for committing a crime. These two persuaded the king to have his brother and heir murdered. Then, while the king was out of the country, hiding his earless state and pretending to be the murdered heir whom he resembled and whose name he happened to share, one of these two magi usurped the throne. This was the magus overthrown by Megabyzus (see *MAGUS*).
2. Arab priests.
a. In Acts VIII 18 - 24 Simon Magus (see *ANTECHRIST*) is a native of Samaria in Palestine;
b. Aeschylus' The Persians features 'Magus the Arabian'.

Mahomet. I 18.
The Prophet Mohammed, founder of Islam.

Mahometiques. III 64.
1. Moslems.
2. Islamic.

Main. I 2, I 16, I 91, VI 33.
1. Hand. To both Berbers (see *BARBARE*) and Romans, this signified authority, power and protection.
2. A large area of land or water, from O.F. *megen-*, *megn*.

Mal. I 26, II 2, III 93, V 47,

V 62, VI 100.
1. Sick, unhealthy.
2. Evil, wicked.
3. Damage, harm.
All from L. *male* = 'ill'.

Maling. I 51.
(Malin.)
Common sense. From *malin* = 'shrewd'.

Malte. V 14.
(MALTHE.)
Malta. This island has been an outpost for, in turn, Phoenicians, Greeks, Carthaginians, Romans, Byzantines and Arabs. But since 1090 AD it has uninterruptedly been a bulwark of Christianity against Islam. In 1522, during Nostradamus' lifetime, the Knights of St. John of Jerusalem moved there from Rhodes and further strengthened its defences for that purpose.
(See *MELITES*).

Mandragora. IX 62.
1. Narcotic drugs.
2. Drug trafficking.
The mandrake or *Mandragora officinarum* plant has a narcotic root. In Book Twenty-five of his Natural History, Pliny describes mandrake as an anaesthetic, but warns that an excess leads to loss of speech and then to death.
3. Internal destruction. In primitive magic, mandrake represents the negative and

minimal aspects of the soul.

Marbre. VIII 28.
1. Marble. Widely used for inscriptions, especially over graves. (See *RANG*).
2. Coldness.
3. Opulence.
4. Deceit, fraud. While concealing poorer materials, marble is used in architecture to impart an impression of stability and wealth. Book edges, cake, soap and other objects are marbled to resemble what they are not.
5. Official corruption, loss of national identities, moral collapse, and pillaging of the planet. All these things Pliny associates with the use of marble, here in Book Thirty-six of his Natural History. "Nature is levelled. We carrry off materials which were meant as barriers between nations....but no law was passed that prohibited the import of marble....the authorities said nothing. Indeed, they made concessions in the interests of pleasing the populace! But why this excuse? How do vices infiltrate other than through official channels? How else have ivory, gold and precious stones come to be used by private persons? ....The moral considerations were naturally disregarded because standards had already collapsed."

Marmande. VIII 2.
Town on the river Garonne in S. W. France, thirty miles from Agen.

Marnegro. V 27.
(*Mer Negro.*)
The Black Sea. From L. *mare* = 'sea' and *negro* = 'black man'. Also It. *mare* = 'sea' and *nero* = 'black'.

Mars. I 94, III 5, IV 67, IV 84, V 14, V 23, V 25, V 59, VIII 2, VIII 46, VIII 49, IX 55, IX 73, X 72.
1. a. War;
   b. protection and survival.
Mars was the Roman god of war, the counterpart of the Greek Ares, and, according to Tacitus, of the German Tiu. In legend, Mars was the father of Romulus and Remus the founders of *ROME*. In its theology, creation can only occur through sacrifice, and what has already been created can only be preserved through war and sacrifice. In astrology, Mars rules over the zodiacal *ARIES,* and over the first hour of Tuesday which, as *mardi,* is Mars' day. The exaltation of Mars is marked by Capricorn, 22 December to 20 January. (See *CAPER).* The law of Mars demands a life for a life, and also elevates that which is criminal to serve good ends. It fuses hate with love in order to renew life,

and is identified with Silvanus the Roman god of trees and husbandry. Iron is the metal of Mars, and in his Natural History Pliny traces the idea of luck in a horseshoe to its being made of the metal of protection.

2. March, the month of Mars, links the zodiacal *PISCES,* 19 February to 20 March, with *ARIES,* 21 March to 20 April.

Mary. IX 34.
(Mari.)
1. Partner. From *mari* = 'husband'.
2. In difficulty. From O.F. *marir* = 'to be afflicted', 'to be vexed'.

Mastin. II 41.
(Mâtin.)
1. a. Mastiff;
    b. watchdog. Both from O.F. *mastin.* An ancient breed of dog used in Europe and Asia since 3,000 BC for bull and bear baiting, and to fight in wars. Two thousand years ago it was a main export from England for these purposes.
2. Disagreeable or sly person.

Mede. III 31, III 64.
Media. Previously a province in the Assyrian empire, in about 700 BC Media became independent. But by about 550 BC it became part of the Persian empire. In 36 BC Media Atropatene in N. W. Persia was the scene of a major

defeat of a Roman army by the Parthians (see *PARTHE),* after which Roman activity in the Middle East was drastically reduced. And in the line, "For peace the Median archer sighs", in his ode on Contentment, Horace equates 'Median' with 'Parthian'. Media now forms part of N. W. Iran. The magi (see *MABUS* and *MAGUES)* were Medes.

Melites. I 9.
(Mellites,
Temples.)
1. Malta, Maltese. (See *MALTE).*
2. Temples. Note: also a cryptogram of *Melites.*

Mensolee. VIII 46.
1. Noon. The point at which the sun/*SOL* reaches its highest position. From L. *mens solis* = 'the astrological meridian'.
2. a. Arch;
    b. keystone. Both from the archaic French *mensole* = 'keystone of an arch'. (See *ARCHE).*

Mercure. IX 55, IX 73.
(Mercu.)
1. Communication, information, mediation. Mercury was the Roman version of the Greek Hermes, Messenger of the Gods. He represents the power of the spoken word. As the son of heaven and light, god of roads and potentialities, he represents

sense and intellectual energy. He wears a winged hat and sandals, and carries a club. In mythology, it is Mercury's job to conduct the souls of the dead to the hereafter. In astrology, Mercury's fall is marked by *LEO*. Tacitus identifies Mercury with Wodan, and, from 'Wodan's day', Mercury rules over the first hour of Wednesdays.
2. Disinformation. According to Ammianus, a leader of those who did most to undermine integrity and morale in Rome, prior to the collapse of the Roman Empire, was a man named "Mercury ....a Persian by origin".

Mer Negro. V 27.
(Marnegro.)
See *MARNEGRO.*

Mesnie. III 31.
(Mesgnie.)
1. Establishment, following, retinue. From O.F. *mesgnie* = 'household'.
2. Sphere of control or influence. From O.F. *demeine* = 'estate'.

Mesopotamie. III 61, III 99, VII 22, VIII 70.
Mesopotamia. From Gk. *meso-potamus* = 'between rivers'. Traditionally, specifically the land between the rivers Euphrates and Tigris, in what is now Iraq.

Methelin. V 27.

Mytilene/Mitilini. From Methymna, port on Lesbos and chief town in the Aegean islands.

Mine. I 13, I 53.
1. A mine. From O.F. *mine* = 'source'.
2. Underground.
3. Secret.
4. Erode, subvert. From *miner* = 'to undermine'.
5. Danger. From L. *mina* = 'threat'.

Mirande. VIII 2.
Town in S. W. France.

Mitré. IX 34.
(Mittre.)
1. Surrounded. From Gk. *mitra* = 'girdle'.
2. Mitre, as in a mitre hat. The usually tall mitre hat is a stiffened version of the earlier soft, stocking-like headdress which became an emblem of revolutionaries in late 18th century France.

Moine. IX 20.
Friar, monk. Or someone appearing to be such.

Monet. IX 42.
(Monaco.)
1. Monaco. From Monoikos, originally an Ionian Greek trading settlement established shortly after 474 BC. (See *HERCLE* and *PHOCEAN*).

2. Money. From *monétaire* = 'monetary'.

Morique. III 95.
(Moricque.)
Moorish, North African. From Gk. *Mauros,* L. *Maurus* and O.F. *More* = 'Moor'. The Moors are the Arab-Berber Moslems of N. Africa. (See *BARBARE).* 'Mauretania' was a Roman province between the Atlantic ocean and Numidia, described by Strabo. It fell to the Vandals in the 5th century AD, to Byzantium (see *BISANCE)* in the 6th, and to Islam in 698 AD. Now Morocco and western Algeria.

Mur. III 7, V 81, VIII 2, IX 99.
1. Wall, barrier, defence-work.
2. Border. In the ancient world and the Middle Ages a wall and a border were often effectively synonymous.

Nantes. IV 46, VI 44.
Port on river Loire and largest city in western France. Industries include aircraft equipment engineering, oil-refining and ship-building. In 1598 the Edict of Nantes granted civil liberties to Protestants; and its revocation in 1685 led to an exodus from France of half a million people.

Narbon. III 92, IV 94, IX 34.
(Narbonne.)

1. Gallia Narbonensis was the first Roman colony in Gaul. The birthplace of Tacitus, it stretched across southern France from the Pyrenees to the Alps, with Narbo, now Narbon, its chief town. Also known as Provincia Romana, its eastern part is still called Provence. But even before the region fell to Rome, it was the westernmost outpost of Greek learning, and an ally of *ROME* at the beginning of the Punic Wars. Taken by Arabs in 719 and retaken by Franks (see *FRANCHE)* forty years later, it is now Narbonne city in southern France. Its port having silted up in the 14th century, it is connected to the Gulf of *LION* by canal. Its industries include processing uranium, barrel-making (see *BARRIQUES),* and sulphur refining (see *SOUFRE).*
2. Compte Louis de Narbonne (1755-1813) was Louis XVI's half-brother and Minister of War from December 1791 to March 1792 during the French Revolution. Of noble birth but believing in constitutional monarchy, Narbonne tried to reconcile king and Assembly. But his enemies at court convinced the king that Narbonne was a traitor. And in dismissing him, Louis brought about his own end.

Naves. IX 100, X 2.
Navy, ships. In common usage,

ships in general. But often, as in the *'Liburnae' naves* mentioned by Caesar, fast warships specifically. From L. *navis* = 'ship' and O.F. *navie* = 'ship' or 'fleet'.

Nef. I 18, V 62, IX 43, IX 100, X 2.
(Net.)
Ship. In archaic and poetical usage.

Neige. II 29, X 70.
1. Snow.
2. Snow-blindness from ultra-violet radiation. (See Chapter Twenty-eight).

Neptune. VI 90.
Sea power. Neptune is the Roman equivalent of Poseidon the Greek sea god. With his trident (see *TRIDENTAL*) which is equated with the thunderbolt (see *TONNERRE*) he releases storms in his role of the Destroyer. Earlier, he had been the god of fresh and fertilising water/*EAU;* and before that, of clouds and rain/*PLUIE*. In astrology, he occupies the throne of *PISCES*. His counterpart on land is Pluto.

Nimes. V 59.
(Nymes,
Nîmes.)
City in southern France. Founded by the Romans in the 1st century AD, the Gallia Nemausus mentioned by Caesar in The Civil Wars, (see *VOLSQUES),* its Roman arena is still in use.

Nocturne. I 26, V 81.
1. At night.
2. Each night, nightly.
Both from L. *nocturnus* and O.F. *nocturne.*
3. As in 'night birds', or birds of prey.

Noir. VI 33, VIII 70, IX 20, IX 60.
(Nois.)
1. King. By cryptogram of Roi.
2. Black, dark, African, Moor.
3. Angry, macabre, sinister, portending trouble.
4. Bruised.
5. Dirty, soiled.
6. Islamic. Mohammed's banner was black, the colour of vengeance.
7. Iraqi. The Abbasid dynasty which ruled Islam from Baghdad from 750 AD adopted the black flag.
8. Assertion of identity.
C. G. Jung told of a German myth in which a black knight tries to defend a tree/*ARBRE* from a white knight who annually cuts it down. But one day the black knight will be successful and the tree will grow. And when it is large a great battle will bring about the end of time.

Norneigre. VI 7.
(Norvege.)

1. Norway. From L. *Norvegia*.
2. Scandinavia. A composite cryptogram from *nord* = 'North'; *Nordique* = 'Nordic'; and *neiger* = 'to snow'.

Nuict. I 1, I 41, II 35, II 41, V 8, VI 44, IX 20, IX 100.
(Nuit.)
Night.
a. As in darkness;
b. as in marking passage of time.

Objet. X 70.
(Object.)
Something not fully described.

Occident. III 27, V 34, VIII 59, IX 55, IX 100.
1. Europe.
2. The West. A common term, as in Tacitus.
3. Sunset. All from L. *occidens - entis* = 'where the sun sets'.
From mankind's sun-worshipping past, a place of cold, darkness, death, decay and evil; as different from the dawning light and righteousness of the East in which the sun/*SOL* rises. (See *OCCIDENTAL*).
4. The South of France. From Occitania, an area of 12th century southern France ruled by several powerful families as different from a king.

Occidental. V 62.
Western. From L. *occidentalis* and O.F. *occidental*.

(See *OCCIDENT* and *SATURNE*).

Oeil. III 92, X 70.
1. Eye.
2. Vision, sense.
3. Luck. Since ancient Egypt the eye has been a symbol of providence.

Oiseau. V 81.
(Oyseau.)
1. Bird.
2. Aeroplane, air force.

Olchades. III 64.
1. Spain/*ESPAGNE,* Spanish.
2. a. S. E. Spain;
   b. Cartagena. The Olcades were a people of S. E. Spain, round Cartagena the capital of Carthaginian Spain. They were conquered by Hasdrubal the brother-in-law of Hannibal/ *ANNIBAL*.

Olestant. IV 82.
1. Concerned with oil. From L. *oleum* = 'oil', and L. *oleo* = 'to smack of' in Cicero.
2. Overconfidence. In medieval literature Oliphaunt/Olivant was the horn blown too late by Roland at Roncesvalles.
3. Destroying. From Gk. *oles.*
4. Container. From L. *olla* = 'a pot' (see *ROND).*
5. A substance. From L. *holus* = 'pot herb' (see *TARRACONNE).*

Onde. I 2, I 63, V 27, VI 5.
(Unde,
Onae,
Une.)
1. Sea.
2. A temporary increase.
3. Ripple, as in an effect.
4. A wave on water.
5. An air wave, radio.
All from L. *unda* and O.F. *unde*
= 'moving water', 'a wave'.
6. Of unknown origin. From L.
unde = 'whence?', 'where?', in
Caesar, Cicero and Virgil.

Oppi. IX 62.
1. Opium. From Gk. *opion.*
2. A reddish brown (see *SIENNE)*
addictive narcotic drug or opiate.
From L. *opium.*

Or. I 35, I 53, III 13, VIII 14.
1. Gold, golden.
2. Wealth.
3. Oil. Known as 'black gold'
and also 'liquid gold'. That the
'gold' can be a liquid is shown by
its being described in verse III 13
as *fondu* = 'melted', 'molten'.

Oracle. III 4.
1. Prophet, oracle, seer.
2. Prophecy.
3. Nostradamus himself.
The main oracles of the ancient
world, and their locations, were:-
that of the Pythonesses of Apollo
at Delphi in Greece; the temple
of Apollo at Dodona at Epirus in
Greece; of the Branchidae at

Didyma in Asia Minor; of Amon
at Siwa in Egypt; of Clarus
Apollo at Miletus near Colophon
in Asia Minor; of the Paphian
Venus on Cyprus; and of the
sibyls of Apollo at Cumae in
Italy.

Orgon. V 62.
A village on river *DURANCE* in
S. E. France, sixteen miles from
AVIGNON and close to the
Lubéron range (see *LEBRON*).

Orient. I 9, I 49, V 62, V 81,
VI 21, VIII 59.
1. East. From O.F. *Orient.* Also
from L. *oriens* = 'the East' as in
Cicero, Tacitus and Virgil.
2. Dawn. From L. *oriens - entis.*
3. Identified in verse V 62 with
the sun/*SOL.*

Oriental. II 29.
Eastern. (See *ORIENT*).

Orra. I 64, II 91, II 100.
Will hear. From O.F. *ouir* = 'to
hear'.

Ours. VI 44.
Bear.
a. Russia, of which it is an animal
emblem;
b. in mythology, associated with
DIANE;
c. in alchemy, the primitive,
perilous aspect of the
unconscious, and what is cruel
and crude in man.

Pache. V 50, VII 18.
1. Pact. From L. *pactum.*
2. Agreement, treaty. From L. *pacisci* = 'agree'.

Paix. I 63, II 43, IV 20, VI 90, VII 18.
Peace, peacefully.

Pannonois. V 47.
See *PANNONS.*

Pannons. V 48, VIII 15.
1. Eastern Europe. Specifically the area of Eastern Europe between Epirus in the South, the Adriatic to the West, the Rhodope mountains in the East and the Danube in the North. This now includes northern Greece, part of European Turkey, S. E. Bulgaria, Albania, Yugoslavia, Hungary and much of Austria. The ancient tribes living there had few fixed boundaries, and the Romans periodically created new provincial ones, so no name was permanently applicable even to its parts. And in their literature the Romans often lumped most of its peoples together as Illyrians. The main tribes of Illyricum were the Dalmatians (see *ALMATIE*) and the Pannonians. When Nostradamus writes of the Pannons and Pannonoise he alludes to the characteristics of the Pannonii and what they did in the Classical World, judged from Roman

literature. Velleius Paterculus thought them untrustworthy, their civilized appearance only superficial. And Ammianus speaks of "their cunning and versatility". Disorders in Pannonia tended to spread, and as troops from elsewhere became involved to deal with them, further disorders arose as far away as what is now France. And these distracted Western attention away from growing threats from the Middle East. The Pannonian revolt of 6 AD had to be dealt with by troops from Germany. But it still simmered, and for 9 AD Tacitus records, "A desperate revolt against Roman rule in Illyricum and Pannonia". Next, in 14 AD, again in Tacitus, "Mutiny broke out in the regular army in Pannonia". This followed the death of Augustus, when the army sensed weakness and division in the civil authority. And "At just about this time, and for the same reason," continues Tacitus, "the regular brigades in Germany mutinied too. They were more numerous, and the outbreak was proportionately graver". Western involvement in the Balkans continued to bring troubles with it until Rome abandoned the territory to the Huns in 395 AD. Ammianus describes what are now called guerilla tactics, used in Pannonia shorty before the Roman departure. "Illyricum was being overrun by the fury of our foes ....while we were away defending Italy and Gaul. ....They did not pin their hopes on pitched battles but on their usual surprise attacks." And in the Middle Ages a threat to the concept of a united Europe was still associated with Pannonia. For in the 9th century the Magyars, a nomad tribe of mounted archers from the Steppes, swept across Europe reaching down into Italy and S. W. France. And when defeated at Lechfeld in 955 AD they settled on the Pannonian plain where they are now Hungarians. In that same period the Slav tribes, mostly Serbs and Croats, introduced to the region a policy of planned resettlement and conversion of its inhabitants to Christianity.

2. Exhausted, failed. From *panne* = 'broken down'.

Both *Pannons* and *Pannonoise* having the initial syllable *'Pan'*, corresponding with the Gk. *pan* = 'all', 'whole', the 'all Europe' historical dimension has a linguistic parallel. (Also see Chapter Fifteen).

Parfondrees. V 62.
Sunk, sunken. From O.F. *parfondrer* = 'to sink to the bottom'.

Paris. III 93.
1. Paris.
2. The French government.
3. France. In Homer's Iliad, Paris elopes with Helen. In many versions of the story Paris also loots the Mycenean treasury; an act which alienates the Egyptians when they learn the full facts. The greed and duplicity of Paris brings complete destruction on his homeland.

Parque. I 70.
1. Lenient, sparing.
2. To pen in, or be stopped. From *parquer* = 'to park'.

Parthe. III 64
1. Iran. Parthia, now Khurasan, was a province in the Persian empire. Horace's "For peace the Median archer sighs" equates Media with Parthia. (See *MEDE*).
2. Divisions between Iraq and Iran. In the 2nd century BC the Parthian empire included Babylonia and Persia. Parthian expansion westward was delayed by the breaking away of southern Babylonia/*BABYLON*/*MESOPOTAMIE,* but it later reached into Syria (see *ARETHUSA)* and Armenia/*ARMENIE.*
3. Hit and run tactics. Before its decline in the 3rd century AD, ending in a Persian coup, Parthian armies inflicted two major defeats on *ROME.*

Shakespeare's line, "Or like the Parthian I shall flying fight" refers to the Parthian tactic which involved the firing of missiles while appearing to be in retreat, as does Ovid's "Like the swift Parthian, wheel your steed about".
4. The Parthini were a tribe in Dalmatia/*ALMATIE* which warred against Rome in the 1st century BC.

Pellices. X 53.
1. Whores. From L. *pellex - icis* = 'concubine'. (See *ADULTÈRE*.)
2. Syria, Iraq and Iran, the three states which as Assyria, Babylonia and Persia/*PERSE* exchanged between them possession of *BABYLON* at their centre.
3. An appearance of unity. Figuratively, from L. *pellis* = 'skin'.

Peloponnesse. V 90.
(Peloponese.) The southern peninsular of Greece.

Pelte. X 53.
1. Protection. From L. *pelta* = 'a leather shield.'
2. Appearance. From L. *pellis* = 'skin'.

Pempotan. X 100.
(*Pempotam.*) See *POMPOTANS*.

Perinthe. V 90.
(*Perinthus,*

Corinthe.)
1. Perinthus. A settlement founded in about 600 BC by the Sea of Marmora, and mentioned by Ammianus. Now a village in Turkey.
2. Turkey.
3. Corinth.
a. Town in N.E. Peloponnese and maritime power in 8th century BC, twice destroyed by earthquakes;
b. Isthmus between the Peloponnese/*PELOPONNESSE* and central Greece.
4. Greece.

Pers. I 70, II 96, III 64, III 77, V 25, V 27, V 86, VI 80, X 21.
(*Perse,*
Perce.)
1. Blue. From O.F. *pers/perse* = 'a shade of greyish blue'.
2. Iran, the modern Persia. (See *PERSIENS*).
3. In mythology, Perse was the wife of Helios/*SOL,* and daughter of Ocean the god of the waters. Perses was father of the goddess Hecate (see *DIANE*).

Persiens. I 73.
Iranians. From O.F. *Persien* = 'Persian'. (See *PERSE*).

Pertinax. IX 62.
1. Habit-forming, addictive. From L. *pertinax* = 'tenacious'.
2. a. Greedy;
   b. internally destructive.

Having killed him, the palace guards of the emperor Pertinax auctioned the Roman Empire to the highest bidder.

Peste. I 16, I 55, II 46, V 90, VIII 17.
1. Pest. An animal which is destructive, especially to food supplies.
2. Pestilence, sickness, epidemic disease especially bubonic plague the cause of which is pasteurella pestis.
Both from L. *pestis* = 'plague'.
(See *PESTIFÈRE, PESTILENCE* and *PESTILENTE*).

Pestifère. I 26, VI 5.
1. Harmful, troublesome, deadly. And, figuratively, 'pernicious', 'morally mischievous'.
2. Disease-bearing.
Both from L. *pestiferus.*
(See *PESTE, PESTILENCE* and *PESTILENTE*).

Pestilence. VIII 62, IX 55.
Fatal epidemic disease, especially bubonic plague. From L. *pestilentia.* In Homer's Iliad pestilence is brought by missiles fired from Apollo's bow.
(See *PESTE, PESTIFÈRE* and *PESTILENTE*).

Pestilente. VII 21.
Pestilential.
a. Physically or morally destructive, harmful, dangerous, troublesome;
b. bearing serious disease, especially bubonic plague. Both from L. *pestilentus.*
(See *PESTE, PESTIFÈRE* and *PESTILENCE*).

Phalange. II 22 .
1. Phalange.
a. Battle standard;
b. a Right-wing political group.
2. Phalanx.
a. A composite mass in a line of battle;
b. a group banded together for a common purpose.
All from Gk. *phalagx.*

Phatos. V 27.
1. Pharos. Peninsular at Alexandria, Egypt.
2. Paros. Island in *CYCLADES.*

Phebés. III 97.
(Phoebus.)
1. Phoebe. Roman moon/*LUNE* goddess, associated with *DIANE.* Also known as Artemis, Hecate and Selene (see *SELINE*).
2. Phoebus, meaning 'bright', 'pure', 'shining'. The sun god *SOL*, associated with Apollo. The twin brother of Phoebe.

Phocean. III 90.
1. Phocis, central Greece.
2. Phocaea, settled by Greeks in about 1,000 BC, was one of twelve cities along the coast of western Anatolia, now Turkey,

and adjacent islands in the Ionian League. (See *IONIQUE*). The League traded along and colonised the European and African coasts from the Black Sea to Spain. In about 600 BC Phocaea was swallowed into the Persian empire.
3. Lebanese/Phoenician. By 1250 BC a Semitic people from Tyr/Tyre now Sur, and from Sidon and Saida, in modern Lebanon, were trading and colonising along the Mediterranean. In the 9th century BC they founded Utica, later Carthage and now part of *TUNIS;* and in the 7th century BC they founded Oea, later Tripoli and now Tarabulus in Libya. (See *LIBYQUE)*. Phoenicia became a part of the Assyrian, Babylonian, Persian, Greek, Roman, Byzantine and Turkish empires, but is geographically and historically most closely associated with Syria.
4. Marseilles. At about the time their homeland fell to Persia, Ionian Greeks founded Marseilles. And Thucydides records that "The Phoceans, while they were founding Marseilles, defeated the Carthaginians in a sea battle". That conflict continued when Marseilles/Massilia supplied *ROME* with a fleet and spied on Hannibal's (see *ANNIBAL)* overland advance on Italy during the Punic Wars. Though losing its

independence in 49 BC, for choosing the wrong side in a Roman civil war, Massilia produced some of the earliest copies of Homer and remained a centre of Greek culture, with a university attended by leading Romans.

Phocen. I 18, III 79.
See *PHOCEAN*.

Phoebus. III 97.
(Phebés.)
See *PHEBÉS*.

Picquer. VII 38.
(Piquer.)
See *PIQUER*.

Piege. IX 99.
1. Trap, ambush. From *piège*.
2. Worse. From O.F. *piegi* = 'harmful'.

Pierre. II 18, II 47, V 35, IX 20.
1. Stone.
2. Weight.
3. Occupation.
4. Diamond.
5. Missile. It was a stone with which David killed Goliath. And this passage from Hesiod's Theogony tells of the use of stones in the war between the gods and giants.

   "Three hundred rocks from their stalwart hands they discharged in a volley, darkening the Titans' sky with missiles."

And the Crau, near where Nostradamus grew up, is a desert strewn with rocks. These were stones which, as Nostradamus the boy would have read in Strabo, had been supplied by *JUPITER* to Hercules/*HERCLE* for him to throw at the Ligurians when he had run out of arrows. The use of stones as missiles is long established, both in practice and in literature.

6. Chemicals, especially sulphur/ *SOUFRE*. From brimstone, as in "Then will fire, brimstone and asphalt be cast upon those men", in the Gnostic Apocalypse of Adam. Scriptures abound with such references; as in Luke XVII 29.

7. Danger.

a. From the black stone with which a vote for the death sentence was cast, as referred to by Aeschylus in Seven Against Thebes;

b. from the Tarpeian Rock from which persons condemned to death were thrown;

c. from the practice of stoning to death;

d. from the loadstone (see *MAGNES*).

(See *PIERREUSE*).

Pierreuse. II 18.
See *PIERRE*.

Piquer. VII 38.
(*Picquer*).

Stick into, spur. From *piquer* = 'to prick'.

Pisces. VIII 91.
1. Fish.
2. The zodiacal Pisces 'The Fish', 20 February to 20 March.
3. In astrology:-
a. the universal solvent;
b. the ambiguity of the beginning as the end and vice versa;
c. the geographical area around Palestine;
d. ruled by *JUPITER*.
(See *POISSON*).

Plaignant. VII 38.
(*Pleignant,*
Pliegnant.)
1. Alas. Expression of regret, sorrow.
2. Protesting.
Both from O.F. *plainte,* past participle of *plaindre* = 'to protest'.

Plays. I 35.
(*Classes.*)
Passes, strokes.

Pleurs. VI 81.
1. Tears.
2. Grief, regret.

Pli. I 41.
(*Plic.*)
1. Crease, fold, pleat. From L. *plicare* = 'to fold'.
2. Disease. Lice, which spread typhus, are carried in the hems of

clothing.

Pluie. I 70, II 1, II 18, II 46,
IV 67, VI 5, VI 44, IX 99.
(Pluye,
Plui,
Pluys.)
1. Rain.
2. Matter descending from the
sky, especially that resembling
rain. (See *ADUST, CONNISSE* and
GRÊLE).
3. Mist, spray. (See *BRUINE*).
4. Anything arriving more than
singly, as in 'a rain of blows'.
5. Associated with the
rainbow/*IRIS*, a traditional
symbol of war. (Also see
AQUARIUS and *EAU*).

Poison. I 41, II 47.
Poison. (See *SERPENT* and
VENINS).

Poisson. II 5, II 48.
1. Fish. (See *PISCES*).
2. Torpedo, in naval slang.
3. Submarine.

Pol. VIII 46.
1. Paul.
2. A Pole.
3. Cut off.

Pole. VI 5, VI 21.
(Polle,
Pôle.)
1. Axis, pivot.
2. Extreme.
3. Sky.

4. The Pole, as in North Pole.
All from Gk. *polos* and L. *polus.*
(See *POL*).

Polemars. II 48.
1. Thread. From O.F. *polomar* =
'twine'.
2. a. Northern;
  b. the North or Pole Star,
Polaris;
  c. the Polaris weapons system.
All the above by cryptogram in
which 'i' replaces 'em'.
3. War. By cryptogram in which
'e' replaces 'u' in Gk. *polu* =
'much', with *MARS* the Roman
god of war.
4. War leader. By cryptogram in
which 'cho' is inserted for Gk.
polemarchos = 'one who leads in
war'. In ancient Greece a
Polemarch was commander-in-
chief.

Pompotans. VIII 97.
1. a. Glory, pomp, splendour;
  b. power;
  c. empire. All from L. *pompa*
and O.F. *pompe* = 'splendid
display', with L. *potens* =
'power'.
2. All-powerful, especially on the
water. A hybrid word from Gk.
pan = 'all', L. *potens* = 'power',
and Gk. *potamos* = 'river'.
(See *PEMPOTAN*).

Ponteroso. VIII 49.
(Ponterose.)
1. Redbridge.

2. Red or pink bridge.
Both the above from L. *pontis* =
'bridge', and L. *roseus* = 'pink'.
3. The bridge (see *IRIS*) of the
poisonous dust and mist. From
pont in L. *pontis* = 'bridge'; *ter* in
L. *terra* = 'earth'; *roso* from *rose*
= 'pink' and *rosée* = 'dewdrop'.
(See *RHOSNE* and *SIENNE*).

Ponts. III 81, VIII 21, VIII 55.
(Pontz.)
1. Bridges. From L. *pons pontis*.
2. Connections.
3. Routes.
4. Entrances.
5. Sea. From L. *pontus*.
Sometimes used to denote
'abroad', 'overseas', as by
Aeschylus. In Hesiod's Theogony,
all other sea-gods are descendants
of Pontus.
6. Area of Asia Minor adjacent to
the Black Sea, as in Caesar and
Tacitus.

Pontife. II 41, II 97.
Pontiff, pope. From L. *pontifex*
maximus.

Porceau. I 64.
(Pourceau.)
Pig, piglike.

Port. VIII 21.
Port, harbour.

Portes. V 81.
Doors, gates.

Porteur. I 26.
1. Bearer, carrier.
2. Tanker.

Postulaire. I 26.
1. Demand. From *postuler* = 'to
ask for', and L. *postulare* = 'to
claim', 'to demand', 'to request'.
2. With a religious connection.
A 'postulant' usually belongs to a
religious organisation.

Poudre. V 8.
1. Dust, powder.
2. Rubble.
(See *ADUST, CONNISSE* and
POUSSIÈRE).

Poussière. IX 99.
See *ADUST, CONNISSE* and
POUDRE.

Predateurs. II 100.
(Prediteurs.)
Carpet-baggers, looters, pillagers,
predators. From L. *praedator* =
'plunderer'.

Preme. X 1.
1. First;
a. in importance;
b. in order or time. From L.
primus = 'first'.
2. Close, next. From O.F. *preme*
= 'near'.

Primat. X 70.
1. Archbishop, Church primate.
2. Man, mankind.
3. Primate. Member of highest

order of mammals. All from L.
primatis = 'highest'.

Profanum. VI 100.
1. Uninitiated.
2. Irreverent.
3. Foul-mouthed.
All from L. *profanus* and O.F.
prophane = 'profane'.

Promontoire. IX 60.
1. A lump on body.
2. Headland.
3. Outpost, salient, Trojan horse.
All from L. *promontorium* =
'promontory'.

Prophète. II 28.
1. Diviner, prophet, soothsayer.
2. Mohammed.
3. Nostradamus.

Prospérer. I 1.
(Proférer.)
1. Successful. From *prospérer* - 'to
prosper', 'to thrive'.
2. To pronounce, to issue. From
proférer = ' to utter'.

Pugne. IX 100
Battle. From L. *pugnare* = 'to
fight'.

Punique. I 9.
1. Punic, North African. Relating
to ancient Carthage. From L.
punicus, poenicus = 'Phoenician'.
(See *PHOCEAN*).
2. Treachery. As in 'Punic faith'.

Pyrenees. IV 94.
The Pyrenees mountains, between
France and Spain.

Ranc. IV 50, IX 62.
See *RANG*.

Ranes. IX 60.
1. Iranians. From Aryans,
prehistoric inhabitants of Iran.
2. *ARIES*.
3. Ares/*MARS*, gods of war.
Cryptograms.

Rang. IV 50, IX 62.
(Ranc.)
1. Ring.
2. Grade, position in pecking
order. From O.F. *ranc* = 'rank'.
3. Marble/*MARBRE*. In the 16th
century 'rance' was a kind of
marble, red with blue and white
veins.

Raugon. IX 62.
(Rougon.)
Turkey. By cryptogram of Agron,
a king of Lydia which is now in
Turkey. Agron is mentioned by
Herodotus in The Histories.

Raviere. IX 43.
Dash, élan, suddenness, rashness.
From O.F. *raviere* =
'impetuosity'.

RAYPOZ. IX 44.
(Faypoz.)
1. A cryptogram from Gobryas
Zopyrus, a Persian noble and son

of the Megabyzus (see *MABUS* and *MAGUES*) who was one of the seven conspirators who killed the magus. When *BABYLON* was holding out against a Persian siege, Zopyrus cut off his own nose and ears and lashed himself. Presenting himself in this bloody state to the Babylonians, with a tale of Persian ingratitude and cruelty, he was admitted to the city as a Persian deserter. He later opened the city gate to the Persian army. According to Herodotus, Zopyrus was well rewarded by the Persian king. (See Chapter Fifteen).
Xenophon's version of this story is different. But his The Education of Cyrus in which it is told is largely fictitious; and, in his How to Distinguish a Flatterer from a Friend, Plutarch has accepted Herodotus' account.
2. To clear away. From Fay from N. *faegja* = 'to clear away'; with *poz* as the abbreviation of *positif.*
3. A cryptogram of Zophar. In the O.T. Book of Job, God forces Zophar to pay compensation to Job for having unlawfully imprisoned him.

Rege. X 70.
(Rhege.)
1. King. From L. *rex regis.*
2. Leader, 'establishment'.

Regne. I 55, II 95, IV 20, IV 50, IV 95, IV 96, V 11, V 25, VI 2,
VIII 97, IX 49, IX 73, X 40, X 66, X 72.
(Regner,
Regnera.)
Authority, control, hegemony, king, kingdom, kingship, power, realm, reign, rule. From L. *rex regis* = 'king' and L. *regere* = 'to rule'.

Reims. I 26, IV 46.
Rheims.
1. City in Northern France.
2. France, French government. Since King Clovis of the Franks was baptised there in 496 AD, Rheims has been associated with the consecration or crowning of French kings.

Reines. IX 20.
1. Queens.
2. a. King and queen;
    b. realm. From O.F. *reigne* = 'kingdom'.

Remort. I 94.
1. Regret. From *remord* and O.F. *remors* = 'remorse'.
2. Attack again, counter-attack, react, respond. From L. *mordere* = 'to bite', with L. *re-* = 'again', 'back'.

Respers. II 98.
(Resperse.)
Splashed, wet. From L. *respergere* and O.F. *respers* = 'sprinkled'.

Révélera. IV 39.
(Revalera.)
1. Reassess. From O.F. *revaler* =
'to lower one's price'.
2. Will provide or see an
opportunity. From L. *revelare* =
'to unveil', 'to uncover', 'to
reveal'.

Rhege. X 70.
(Rege.)
See *REGE*.

Rhodanes. VIII 91.
The Rhone. From L. *Rhodanus,* as
in Caesar.
(See *RODES* and *RHODIENS*).

Rhodes. V 47, VI 21.
(Rodes.)
See *RODES*.

Rhodiens. IV 39.
1. People of Rhodes. From L.
Rhodiensis = 'Rhodian', and from
L. *Rhodii* = 'Rhodians', as in
Cicero.
2. Western forces. Occupied
from 1310 until 1522 - in
Nostradamus' lifetime - by the
Knights Hospitallers/Knights of
Saint John of Jerusalem, and only
twelve miles from Turkey, the
island of Rhodes was a Western
Christian outpost against militant
Islam.

Rhosne. II 96, IV 94, VII 22,
VIII 46, VIII 62.
(Rosne.)

1. River Rhone.
2. Disarmament. The river Rhone
rises at Geneva/*GENEVE*.
3. Pollution. From *rose* =
'reddish', and *rosée* - 'dew'; in
cryptograms of *rosne*. (See
PONTEROSO and *ROUGE*).

Rochers. I 87, V 62.
1. Rocks, stones. From O.F.
ro(c)que and *roke,* and Med. L.
rocca. (See *PIERRE*).
2. Blocs.
3. Islamic states. From "the black
stone which fell from heaven in
the days of Adam", now in the
Ka'ba, the 'house of God' in
Mecca.
4. Destruction, ruin. Rocks have
long been associated with
shipwreck. In Homer's Odyssey
the White Rock marks the way
to the underworld. Other rocks
in classical literature were the
Symplegades or Clashing Rocks at
the northern end of the Bosporus
and the Wandering Rocks near
the straites of Messina.

Rodes. V 47, VI 21.
(Rhodes.)
Rhodes. Largest of the
Dodecanese islands in the Aegean
Sea. From L. *Rhodus* and *Rhodius*.
(See *RHODANES* and *RHODIENS*).

Rogie. VIII 77.
(Rougie.)
See *ROUGIE*.

Roi. I 13, II 2, III 77, V 84, VIII 62, IX 49, IX 73, X 21, X 22, X 66, X 72, X 86.
(Roy.)
1. King, Shah.
2. Leader.
3. Government.

Romain. II 30, II 97, II 99, IV 82, V 14, VI 7.
(Romaine.)
1. Italian.
2. European.
3. Romanian/Rumanian. See *DACE*.
(See *ROME* and *ROMANIE*).

Romanie. V 50.
(Romanis.)
See *ROME* and *ROMAIN*.

Rome. V 62.
1. Rome.
2. Italy.
3. Europe.
(See *ROMAIN* and *ROMANIE*).

Romulides. I 9.
Romans (see *ROME*). A reference to Romulus, legendary co-founder of Rome. Virgil referred to Romans as "Romulidae".

Rond. II 91.
1. A round object. See *GLOBES*.
2. Note: a pun here on *un vent rond* = 'a brisk wind'.

Rosne. II 96, IV 94, VII 22, VIII 46, VIII 62.

(Rhosne.)
See *RHOSNE*.

Rouan. V 84.
1. Rouan. Ancient Rotomagus, city of Roman origin in northern France. Industries include chemicals, oil-refining and ship-repairing.
2. a. Paris;
   b. French government;
   c. France. On the river Seine, Rouan is the port of *PARIS*.

Rouges. X 86.
1. Red.
2. Coloured, as different from white.
3. Danger.
4. Contamination, pollution. (See *SANG* and *SIENNE*).
5. Battle. As in a 1666 London Gazette.
6. Blood. As, symbolically, on lance pennons.
7. Anarchy, Left-wing revolution. (See *ROUGIE, ROUGIR, ROUGIRA* and *RUBRICHE*).

Rougie. VIII 77.
(Rogie.)
See *ROUGES, ROUGIR, ROUGIRA* and *RUBRICHE*.

Rougir. IV 94, VI 98.
1. Redden.
2. Spread fever to.
(See *ROUGES, ROUGIE, ROUGIRA* and *RUBRICHE*).

Rougira. I 87.
See *ROUGES, ROUGIR, ROUGIE*
and *RUBRICHE.*

Rougon. IX 62.
(Raugon.)
See *RAUGON.*

Roy. I 13, II 2, III 77, V 84,
VIII 62, IX 49, IX 73, X 21,
X 22, X 66, X 72, X 86.
(Roi.)
See *ROI.*

Rubriche. IX 100.
1. Red, redden. From L.
rubefacere = 'to make red'.
2. Red ochre. From L. *rubrica*
terre = 'red earth'. (See *SIENNE).*
3. Pollution. For 100,000 years
red ochre has been mined to
represent blood/*SANG.*
4. Of a new type. From *rubrique*
= 'rubric', which draws attention
to a part of a text.

Sacrés. VIII 62 .
1. Holy, sacred, sacrosanct. From
L. *sacrarium* = 'a place where
holy things are kept'.
2. Principles. From L. *sacrosanctus*
= 'cherished', 'inviolable'.
3. Decadent, sham. Figuratively,
as in 'sacred cow', an institution
unworthy of the faith placed in it.

Sacrifiée. II 98.
(Sacrifice.)
1. Given up, sacrificed.
2. Slaughtered.

Sagittaire. I 16.
(Sagitaire.)
Sagittarius.
1. The zodiacal 'The Archer'/
'The Centaur', 23 November to
22 December. Ruled by *JUPITER.*
2. Guardians of Iraq. In the
Babylonian Epic of Gilgamesh,
Sagittarius is represented by
Scorpion Men "whose aura is
frightful and whose glance is
death", who guard the gate to the
East.
3. Centaurs are fabulous beasts,
therefore invented to convey a
range of characteristics in a single
word. These are half-man and
half-horse, in their mythology
born of Centaurus and the
Magnesian mares. Though
Chiron, (see *FLÈCHE)* wisest of
the centaurs, taught gymnastics,
hunting, music and prophecy, and
healing to Aesculapius, and they
are able to avert bad luck and to
resist evil influences, centaurs
also represent dominion over the
spirit by baser forces.

Sainte. I 53, IV 43, VIII 62,
IX 83, X 31.
(Sainct,
Faincte.)
1. Saint.
2. Christian, holy, religious.

Samarobryn. VI 5.
(Samatobryn.)
1. Sam R. O'Bryan. An anagram.
2. Amiens. This is the modern

name for the town of Samarobriva mentioned by Caesar.

Sang. I 18, I 55, II 46, II 97, II 98, III 59, IV 94, V 27, V 62, V 63, VI 7, VI 21, VI 81, VI 98, VII 18, VIII 17, VIII 77, IX 20, IX 55, IX 60.
Blood.
1. a. Battle. Blood is symbolised by the red on lance pennons;

b. anarchy or revolution, in which the red flag represents the blood which will be shed if necessary;

c. danger. The antiquity of the colour red in symbolising blood can be traced back to, for example, the blood-red ore mined at Ngwenya Ridge in Swaziland over 100,000 years ago.
2. In eschatology blood is the accompaniment of;-
a. sacrifice;
b. death;
c. irremedial misfortune. In these, especially when connected with *LIBRA,* it is often associated with self-chastisement.
3. a. Contamination, pollution;

b. disease, infection. Only after Noah's flood were men allowed to eat meat at all (Genesis IX 3 and 4; Leviticus XVII 14 and 15; Deuteronomy XII 16 and 23). And after that it remained punishable by death to eat blood or bloody meat

(Genesis IX 4; Leviticus XVII 12). Animals which had died naturally or had been mauled by wild beasts were taboo. In priestly thought, not just eating but any contact with body fluids or with the dead produced an uncleanness which was infectious. And the links between such contacts and sickness, clear from the instructions to wash afterwards, and from the periods of quarantine which were to follow the ritual cleaning, continue today in other guises. The washing is now called 'hygiene', and the periods of quarantine imposed closely resemble the incubation periods allowed by modern doctors for symptoms of disease to appear. (See *ROUGES, SANGUIN* and *SANGUINAIRE*).

Sanguin. X 10.
1. Confident, hopeful.
2. Blood-red. As in heraldry. Both from O.F. *sanguin* = 'sanguine'.
(See *SANG* and *SANGUINAIRE*).

Sanguinaire. II 89, VI 33.
1. Bloody.
2. Blood-thirsty.
Both from L. *sanguinarius*.
(See *SANG* and *SANGUIN*).

Satur. VIII 49.
(Saturn.)
1. a. Lustful, wanton;

b. unprovoked. These are attributes of the satyr, part-human and part-horse or part-goat god of the wild to Greeks and Romans. From Gk. *saturos* and L. *satyrus*. Though unpleasant, and often drunken, satyrs are, if tested, cowardly.
2. Having plenty. From L. *satur* = 'full'.
3. Saturn/*SATURNE*.

Saturne. I 51, II 48, III 92, IV 67, V 11, V 14, V 62, IX 44, IX 73.
(Saturn.)
1. The planet Saturn.
2. Crops. Saturnus was the Roman god of agriculture.
3. December. The month of Saturnalia, the festival of Saturn.
4. Lead. In alchemy, the metal of Saturn.
5. Coldness and gloom. In astrology, the characteristics of Saturn.
6. Cutting and devouring. Represented by Saturn and its attribute the Scythe, traditionally symbolic of Time devouring all its creations.
7. Death. As in many allegories. In European, and particularly in French folklore, Saturnalia is associated with the ass, sacred to the Egyptian god Set whom the Greeks knew as Typhon (see *TISON*). A sandy brown colour like Typhon, it is annually slain in retribution for murder.

8. The West. From the line *"Sol Orient, Saturne Occidental"* = "Sun the East, Saturn the West" in verse V 62.
9. Saturday. In astrology Saturn rules over 'Saturn's day'; as over the zodiacal Capricorn (see *CAPER*).
(See *SATUR*).

Saulce. IX 34.
1. Sauce. By cryptogram of L. *salsus* = 'sauce'.
2. Jean Baptiste Saulce, the grocer at *VARENNES* in whose house Louis XVI was lodged on the night of his arrest.

Saxe. VI 44.
1. Saxony. From L. *Saxonia*.
2. Germany.
3. Saxon, Anglo-Saxon.

Sceptre. I 62, V 14, V 48.
(Scepter.)
1. Sceptre. A staff representing sovereignty. From L. *sceptrum*.
2. Power. From Gk. *skepto* = 'to lean on'.

Secille. IX 42.
(Sicille.)
Sicily. From L. *Sicilia*.

Secret. I 13, I 70, IV 67.
1. Disguised, hidden, secret.
2. A retreat. From L. *secretus* = 'set apart' and *secretum* = 'retired place'.

Sel. V 34, IX 49.
1. Salt.
2. a. Taxation;
   b. government. Historically, salt taxes such as the gabelle levied in pre-Revolutionary France, have widely been sources of revenue. As a preservative, salt also represents another function of government; that of maintaining social cohesion.
3. Friendship.
4. Poison. To signify that Carthage would not rise again, after sacking it in 146 BC the Romans ceremonially cursed and sprinkled its site with salt.

Selin. I 94, VI 58, X 53.
See *SELINE* and *SELYN*.

Seline. V 35.
1. Selim.
a. Sultan Selim I (1467-1520) was a Sunni Moslem who slaughtered 40,000 of his Shiite subjects who sympathised with Iran;
b. Selim II (1524-1574) captured *TUNIS* and Cyprus from Western forces, but was defeated by them at sea at Lepanto in 1571;
c. Selim III (1761-1808) tried to westernise his administration and was murdered by his own men.
2. Selene. Greek goddess of the moon/*LUNE,* she was sister of Helios the sun/SOL. She is identified with Artemis/*DIANE* in such as Ovid's Heroides, and with the death-loving Hecate the

Greek goddess of the night. She is also associated with Lilith in which form she is a despised mistress/*ADULTERINE*. She is most active at the new crescent and full moons.

Selyn. II 1, IV 23.
(Selin.)
See *SELIN* and *SELINE*.

Sempiternel. III 79.
(Sempiternal.)
Eternal, never-ending. From O.F. *sempiterne* from L. *semper* = 'always' and *aeternus* = 'constant'. Used by Rabelais in Gargantua and Pantagruel.

Senoise. I 18.
See *SIENNE*.

Serp. V 25.
SERPENT. An abbreviation.
(See *SERPENT*).

Serpent. II 43.
1. Snake. From L. *serpens* = 'serpent'.
2. Betrayer, traitor.
3. In traditional symbolism the serpent is largely interchangeable with the rainbow/*IRIS*. And it represents;-
a. poison;
b. lightning;
c. chaos, death and destruction;
d. force, on any scale;
e. what is dark, unreasoning, unpredictable and primitive in

man's character - that which has now become recognised in Jungian psychology as the creative unconscious;

f. any Eastern area.

4. In Book Three of his Histories, Herodotus notes that the trees of Arabia "are guarded by winged serpents, small in size, and of varied colours, whereof vast numbers hang about every tree. They are of the same kind as the serpents that invade Egypt." (See *SERP*).

Seville. I 73.
1. City in southern Spain.
2. Spain/*ESPAGNE*.

Sicille. IX 42.
(*Secille*.)
See *SECILLE*.

Siccité. III 4.
(*Sicite*.)
Dryness. From L. *siccare* = 'to dry'.

Siècle. I 16, I 51, I 62, II 46, III 94, III 97, VI 2.
1. *CYCLE*.
2. Age, century, period, time. Both from Gk. *kuklos* and L. *cyclus* = 'cycle'. Aeons or cycles, recurrent rounds of events or time, are a major theme in mythology. They are symbolised in *ARIES* and completed by Aquarius. Each cycle ends in catastrophe, - as in the 13th century Christian hymn Dies Irae, in fire, - in flood/*DELUGE* or war. But only to clear the way for another cycle to begin. Always, as in all of the nearly worldwide flood legends, there are survivors, as Virgil's fourth Eclogue confirmed. "And the cycle of the ages recommences, ...The iron race shall vanish, and across the world another golden age shall see the light".

Siège. I 41, II 29.
1. Base. From O.F. *sege* = 'seat'.
2. Besiege. From O.F. *asegier* = 'siege'.

Sienne. VI 58.
1. Siena. City in central Italy. Industries include chemicals and wine/*VIN*.
2. Italy.
3. Red earth. *Terra di Sienna*/ Siena earth is a pigment from earth which is orange-red or reddish brown when burnt.
(See *CONNISSE PONTEROSO, POUDRE, POUSSIÈRE, RHOSNE, ROUGES, SANG, SENOISE, SIENS* and *TERRE*).

Siens. II 2.
See *SENOISE* and *SIENNE*.

Simulacres. VIII 28.
(*Simulachres*.)
1. Copy, image. From L. *simulare* = 'to simulate'.
2. Fake, fraud, pretence, sham.

From L. *simulacrum* = 'deceptive substitute'.

Simulté. VI 58.
1. Hostility, rivalry. From L. *simultas* = 'enmity'.
2. Quick, simultaneous, sudden. From L. *simultaneus.*

Sol. II 35, IV 84, V 25, V 27, V 62, VI 58, VI 98, VIII 2, IX 73, IX 83.
1. The sun. From L. *solaris.*
2. The East. From the line *"Sol Orient, Saturne Occident"* = "The sun East, Saturn West", in verse V 62.
Note: Selene (see *SELINE)* the Greek moon goddess was the sister of Helios the Greek counterpart of Sol the Roman god of the sun.
(See *SOLAIRES* and *SOLEILS*).

Solaires. V 11, V 81.
1. Solar.
2. Eastern.
(See *SOL* and *SOLEILS*).

Soleils. I 64, II 41, II 91, III 34.
See *SOL* and *SOLAIRES.*

Soliman. III 31.
Turkey. From Suleiman I the Magnificent (1497-1566). Born at Trebizond/*TREBISONDE,* and greatest sultan of Ottoman Turkish empire. The chief enemy of Charles V the Holy Roman Emperor. An alliance with Suleiman established France for three centuries as the chief Western trader with the Middle East.

Solus. IX 34.
(Soluz.)
1. Alone. From L. *solus.* Particularly as in a person separated from his or her marital partner.
2. Free, single, untied. From O.F. *solu.*

Sorgues. VII 21.
Sorgues sur l'Ouvèze, a town in S. E. France near which Petrarch settled, and noted for a natural gunpowder plant. The river Sorgue is mentioned in Dante's Paradise.

Soufre. IV 23, X 49.
(Soulphre.)
Sulphur.
1. Explosive. In chemistry, sulphur is a constituent of gunpowder.
2. In astrology, sulphur symbolises a desire for positive action.
3. In Gnosticism, sulphur is associated with the end of an aeon/*SIÈCLE.*
4. Punishment, purification. In Genesis XIX 24 God used sulphur - in the archaic form brimstone - to destroy Sodom and Gomorrah. A purpose also referred to in Luke XVII 29 and

in Revelation IX 17.
5. In alchemy, sulphur
corresponds to the zodiacal *LEO*.

Soustenant. X 21.
1. Encourage. From *soutenir* = 'to
support'.
2. Subvert, undermine. From *sous*
= 'under' and *tenir* = 'to hold'.

Sparte. V 90.
Sparta.
1. Ancient militaristic state in the
Peloponnese/*PELOPONNESSE,*
southern Greece.
2. Greece.

Sperant. IV 20.
(Sperants,
Aperant.)
Desiring, expecting. From L.
sperans = 'wishing' and *aspirant* =
'aspiring'.

Succombé. III 11.
See *SUCCOMBERA.*

Succombera. V 25, X 70.
(Succumbera.)
Will succumb. From *succomber* =
'to die', 'to fall', 'to be
overcome'.

Superée. IX 100.
Conquered, defeated, overcome.
From L. *superator* = 'conqueror',
'one who overcomes'.

Taincte. V 63, VI 21, VI 98.
(Teinte,

Taints.)
See *TEINTE.*

Tarraconne. VII 22.
1. Tarragona, a town in Spain.
2. Spain/*ESPAGNE.* Tarraconensis
was a Roman province in Spain.
Its capital was Tarraco, now
Tarragona, mentioned in both
Caesar's The Civil Wars and
Tacitus' Annals.
3. Pollution. Tarragon, or
wormwood, is a bitter herb from
the plant Artemisia dracunculus,
a native of eastern Europe and
also of southern Russia in which
its name, in Russian, is
'Chernobyl'. The significance of
this is supported by Revelation
VIII 10 and 11. "And there fell
from heaven a great star, burning
as a torch, and it fell upon a
third part of the rivers, and upon
the fountains of the waters; and
the name of the star is called
Wormwood: and the third part of
the waters became wormwood;
and many men died of the
waters, because they were made
bitter."

Tarasc. VIII 46.
(Tarare.)
Tarascon. An abbreviation.
1. The town and castle of
Tarascon in southern France.
2. A monster/*MONSTRE.* In
legend the Tarasque or Tarasca
was an amphibious monster, part
lion and part crocodile, which

was tamed by Saint Martha.
It haunted the river Rhone (see
RHOSNE) round Tarascon.

Tardeigne. VIII 49.
(Tardaigne.)
1. Area near Soissons, France.
From Tardenois.
2. To do too late. From *tard* =
'late', and *deigner faire* = 'to
deign to do'.

Taurus. IX 83.
1. The zodiacal The Bull, 21
April to 20 May.
2. A winter constellation of the
Northern Hemisphere.
3. a. *EUROPE;*
b. Crete. In mythology, Taurus
   was the white bull involved in
the kidnapping of the Phoenician
princess Europa to Crete, where
the emblem of the Minoan
civilisation was a bull. Also the
Cretan bull with which Minos'
wife Pasiphae fell in love. (See
BOEUF).
4. Turkey.
a. The Taurus mountains are in
southern Turkey;
b. in the Classical World
Tauraunitis lay in what is now a
part of eastern Turkey.

Teinte. V 63, VI 21, VI 98.
(Taincte,
Tainte.)
1. Bad quality.
2. Corrupt, decayed.
3. Diseased, ill, infected.

4. Stained, tainted.
All from *teindre* from O.F. *teinte,*
L. *tingere* = 'to deprave', 'to
putrify', 'to contaminate', 'to
stain'.

Témoins. VI 2.
(Tesmoings)
See TESMOINGS.

Tempiera. X 66.
(Empiera.)
1. Soften. From L. *temperare.*
2. At the rates, speeds, times.
From L. *tempi* = 'times', with *ère*
= 'era', 'epoch'.
3. At the time of the stones
(PIERREUSE). From L. *tempi* =
'times', and *piera* a cryptogram of
PIERRE = 'stone'.

Temple. I 9, VI 98, VIII 62.
1. Church, synagogue, temple.
2. Sacred place.
3. The Christian Church,
Christendom.
(See *MELITES*).

Terre. I 18, I 55, I 63, I 87,
II 5, II 18, II 43, II 89, III 7,
III 31, III 90, III 97, IV 20,
IV 95, V 48, V 80, VIII 70,
VIII 77, IX 83, X 31, X 100.
(Serre.)
1. Earth, soil.
2. Country.
Both above from L. *terre* =
'land'.
3. Abode. From L. *territorium* =
'territory'.

(See *TERROIR*).

Terroir. II 1, II 41, II 99.
See *TERRE*.

Tesmoings. V 12.
(Témoins.)
Confirmation, evidence. From L.
testis = 'testimony', 'witness'.

Testes. II 2, II 28, V 86.
(Tête.)
See *TÊTE*.

Tête. II 2, II 28, V 86.
(Testes.)
1. Head.
2. Chief, leader.
3. Command, unit.

Théâtre. IX 83.
1. Arena, theatre. See
AMPHITHEATRE.

Thunis. I 73, IX 42.
(Tunis.)
See *TUNIS*.

Tierce. VIII 21.
A third. In sequence or as a
fraction. (See *ITERS* and *TIERS*).

Tiers. III 59, III 77, IX 62.
(Iters.)
A third.
(See *ITERS* and *TIERCE*).

Timbre. II 43, V 63.
(Tymbre,
Tybre.)

See *TYMBRE*.

Tison. III 11.
(Tyson,
Tyfon.)
1. Brand, firebrand,
revolutionary.
2. Internal conflict.
3. a. Whirlwind. From Gk.
tuphon and Arabic *tufan* =
'typhoon';
b. Typhon was a wind which the
Greeks treated with suspicion
until it helped them defeat the
Persians at the battle of Salamis;
c. a monster/*MONSTRE*. In Greek
mythology the Typhon was a
wind-and-fire breathing monster
with a hundred heads who,
according to Herodotus, was
vanquished by Orus/*PHEBÉS*.
And storm winds were the
daughters of Electra and Typhon.
In his Inferno and again in his
Paradise, Dante identifies
'Typhoeus' as a hundred-headed
giant, for whose part in the
titans' rebellion against the gods
he has been imprisoned under
Mt. Etna in Sicily. This theme
was inherited from Ovid's letter
from Sappho to Phaon in
Heroides, and also from his
Metamorphoses V in which Etna's
volcanic eruptions are caused by
Typhon's attempts to escape. In
Hesiod's Theogony, 'Typhoeus',
father of Typhon who is
identified with the evil Egyptian
god Set, is associated with the

East wind *BOREAS*, which carries moisture and dust. By that association with Set, Typhon is sandy brown in colour. He also has the ears of the ass which, in the Saturnalia (see *SATURNE*) of European and especially French folklore, is annually slain in retribution for murder. (See also under *GRIFFON*). Pliny the Elder tells of a king named Typhon who gave his name to a comet/*COMÈTE*.

4. Revenge by terrorism. In another version of the Typhon story, the creation of the monster is an act of revenge by a side which has been defeated on the battlefield. Apollonius says, "It was there" - on the slopes of the Caucasus, by the rock (see *ROCHERS*) of Typhaon - "that Typhaon, when he had offered violence to Zeus ....made his way to ....where he lies to this day in the waters of the Serbonian Lake". The latter place, referred to by Milton as "A gulf profound as that Serbonian Bog, where Armies whole have sunk", is Lake Serbonis in Lower Egypt, a once marshy but now dry tract of ground covered with shifting sand.

Tochsain. VI 81.
(Frofaim,
Fromfaim.)
See *FROFAIM*.
Tonant. II 98.

(Venant.)
Thunder. See *TONNERRE*.

Tonneaux. VIII 55.
Barrels, casks, tuns.
(See *BARRIQUES).*

Tonnerre. V 81.
1. Thunder. From Tonans, the Roman god of thunder.
2. *JUPITER* was known as The Thunderer.

Topique. X 40.
1. Subject, theme. From L. *topica* = 'topic'.
2. Gossip.
3. Controversy. From O.F. *topiquer* = 'to dispute', 'to quarrel'.

Tours. IV 46.
1. City in West Central France.
2. Battle in 732 AD at which a Western army halted an Islamic conquest of Europe.

Trafic. VII 21.
(Traffique.)
Dealing, trading, trafficking, usually illegally. From *trafic* = 'traffic'.

Trahi. V 47.
(Trahy.)
See *TRAHIR* and *TRAHIRA*.

Trahir. IX 34.
(Trahye.)
1. To give away, to reveal.

2. To commit treason. Both from *trahir* = 'to betray'.

Trahira. I 70.
See *TRAHI* and *TRAHIR*.

Trainé. VII 38.
Dragged. As in *être à la traîne* = 'to be in tow'.

Translat. III 92.
1. Translate.
2. Shift.
3. Hand over.
All from L. *translatus*.

Trebisonde. V 27.
Trebizond. Town on the Black Sea coast of Turkey. An ancient route and depot for trade with Persia. By 1450 Trebizond, and part of the *PELOPONNESE*, were all that remained of the Byzantine empire.

Trejection. IV 67.
1. Meteor.
2. Missile. Both from L. *trajectorius* = 'trajectory', the path of missile.

Tremulente. II 43.
(*Tremulante.*)
1. Trembling. From L. *tremulare* = 'to shake'.
2. Vacillating. From L. *tremulus* = 'tremulous'.

Trestous. X 66.

Everyone, every single one. From O.F. *trestous* = 'all'.

Tricast. III 93.
The three avengers. A hybrid word. *Tri* from Gk. *treis* = 'three'; *cast* from L. *castigare* = 'to punish' and also as in *castor* = 'bearer'. Literally, 'The three punishment bearers'.

Tridental. V 62.
1. Of a trident.
2. Lightning.
3. Sea power. Both Poseidon the Greek sea god and *NEPTUNE* his Roman counterpart are pictured holding a trident. Both gods release storms of destruction in which the trident usually represents the thunderbolt. (See *TONANT* and *TONNERRE*).

Troche. II 46.
(*Trouble.*)
1. Trouble. From GK. *trukos* = 'misery', 'unhappiness'.
2. Trochée or choreamania, an epidemic of contortions and convulsions, probably hysterical, which spread across 15th century Europe.

Trois. II 43, III 31, IV 95, V 86, VI 2, VIII 17, VIII 21, VIII 46, VIII 77, VIII 97, IX 97, X 53, X 100.
Three.

Trouble. II 46.

(Troche.)
See *TROCHE*.

Truie. VI 44.
1. Sow.
2. The Roman people. As represented on coins.
3. Greed. A characteristic of pigs.

Tuile. IX 34.
(Tuille,
Thuille.)
1. Tile.
2. The Tuileries Palace, so named because it was built on the site of an old tile-yard. Its construction was ordered by Catherine de Medici in 1564.
3. A spot of bad luck. An idiom.

Tunis. I 73, IX 42.
(Thunis.)
1. Tunis.
2. Carthage. Now a suburb of Tunis. (See *PHOCEAN*.)
3. Tunisia. In 146 BC Rome established a province in what is now Tunisia. And later extended it along the Tripolitan coast to include most of what is now Libya/*LIBYQUE*. (See *BARBARE*).

Turban. IX 73.
(Turbao.)
1. Turban. Headdress of Moslem and Sikh men. Symbolically, any headdress represents the thoughts within the wearer's head.
2. Mob. From L. *turba* = 'an uproar caused by a crowd' as in

Cicero and Livy; and from L. *turbamentum* = 'an excuse for a commotion' as in Tacitus.

Tyfon. III 11.
(Tyson,
Tison.)
See *TISON*.

Tymbre. II 43, V 63.
(Timbre,
Tybre.)
1. River Tiber.
2. Italy.
3. Europe. The Tiber flows through *ROME,* capital of Christendom.
Note: As the crest on a helmet or shield, the *tymber/timbre* is that which identifies a participant in a conflict.

Tyran. VII 21.
Dictator. From O.F. *tiran* = 'tyrant'.

Tyrannisant. VIII 70.
Tyrannising. From GK. *turannikos,* L. *tyrannicus* and O.F. *tyrannique* = 'tyrannical'.

Tyrren. III 90.
(Tyrran.)
1. Tyrrhenian Sea. Between Corsica, Italy, Sardinia and Sicily/*SECILLE*.
2. Of Tyr or Tyre ancient city in Lebanon.
3. Syrian. (See *PHOCEAN*).
4. Italian. The Tyrrheni were a

people of northern Italy. (See
ETRUSQUE and *VOLSQUES*). In
his Theogony, Hesiod too
connects the Tyrrhenians with the
LATIN region.

Tyson. III 11.
(Tison,
Tyfon.)
See *TISON*.

Uberté. IV 20.
(Vberte.)
Plenty. From L. *ubertas* and O.F.
uberté = 'abundance'.

Undans. II 43.
Flooding/*DELUGE*. From L.
inundare = 'to inundate', 'to
overflow', 'to swamp'.

Unde. I 2, I 63, V 27, VI 5.
(Onae,
Onde,
Une.)
See *ONDE*.

Une. I 2, I 63, V 27, VI 5.
(Onae,
Onde,
Unde.)
See *ONDE*.

Unique. V 80.
(Estenique.)
See *ESTENIQUE*.

Univers. VIII 15.
1. Universe.
2. Everywhere, universal.

Urne. IX 73.
See *HURNE*.

VAR. VIII 97.
(Var.)
1. River and coastal region in S.
E. France between Marseilles and
Cannes. The river 'Varus' in
Caesar, and the border between
Languedoc and Provence since
the early Middle Ages. Dante
drew attention to the 'river'
aspect of this name.
    "From Var to Rhine, the
Seine,
Isère and Loire beheld and every
vale
whose waters flow to fill the
river Rhone."
2. From O.N.F. *var* = 'war'.

Varennes. IX 20.
Varennes, or Varennes en
Argonne. A village on river Aire
in N. E. France, where, in 1791,
Louis XVI and Marie Antoinette
were arrested while trying to flee
from France. (See Chapter
Twenty).

Varneigne. III 99.
Green and snow-capped. A
composite word. From *ver* as in
vert = 'green'; and *neigne*, a
cryptogram of *neigeuse* = 'snow
covered'.

Vaultort. IX 20.
(Voltorte.)
See *VOLTORTE*.

Venant. II 98.
(Tonant.)
See *TONANT.*

Venins. II 48.
1. Poisons.
2. Trouble-making; malicious actions or words.
Both from O.F. *venin* = 'venom'.

Venise. IX 42.
Venice. City on Adriatic coast (see *ADRIE*) of northern Italy. Its one hundred and eighteen islands are linked by four hundred bridges/*PONTS*. A city state at its zenith in the 14th and 15th centuries.
(See *VENITIENS*).

Venitiens. I 73.
1. Venetians.
2. Italians.
3. Europeans.
(See *VENISE).*

Vent. IV 67.
Wind. From L. *ventus* and O.F *esvent*.
1. In the Classical World many winds were associated with gods and spirits and all had names. Roman literature is full of these, as for example in the letter from Canace to Macareus in Ovid's Heroides, which reels off;
   "Notus and Zephyr and Thracian Aquilo,
as well as your guills, reckless Euros."

To the Greeks the North and North East wind was *BOREAS,* and the South and South East wind was Euros. To the Romans the North and North East wind was Aquilo, and the South West wind was Africus. The Greeks treated winds with suspicion, especially the one they called Typhen (see *TISON*); until it helped them to win a major naval victory. According to Hesiod's Theogony the latter would have been *BOREAS.* Other winds include Bora in the Adriatic, Hippalus (see *ALUS*) in the Persian Gulf and Levanter in the eastern Mediterranean. The harpies of classical literature were storm winds born of Electra and Typhon (see *TISON*). Aeolus (see *ALUS*) was the king or god of winds in Greek mythology.
2. Chance, luck.
3. Need for care. When Aeolus gave Odysseus a bag of winds, one of his crew carelessly released them with the result that the ship was blown back to Aeolus/*ALUS*.
(See *AURE*).

Venus. IV 84, V 11, V 25.
1. The planet Venus.
2. The Roman counterpart of Aphrodite the Greek goddess of beauty and love.
3. War. In astrology, Venus is connected with *MARS*.
4. Hostility concerning Lebanon

and Syria. In mythology, Aphrodite loved the Syrian god Adonis, the incestuous son of the king of Lebanon. And she quarrelled over him with Persephone the queen of the dead.
5. The moon. In astrology, Venus is also connected with the moon/*LUNE*.
6. Friday. In addition to ruling the zodiacal *LIBRA* and *TAURUS*, in astrology Venus rules over the first hour of Fridays.

Ver. V 25.
1. Real. From L. *verus* = 'true'.
2. a. Springtime;
b. of life.
Both from L. *vernare* = 'to grow green'.

Verbine. III 11.
(*Vermine.*)
1. Peace . From L. *verbena* = 'sacred olive branch'.
2. Vermin.

Verifique. IV 96.
(*Verrifique.*)
Evidence, proof. From *vérifier* = 'to confirm', and L. *verificare* = 'to verify'.

Vers. I 16, I 91, II 1, II 91, III 4, III 97, VIII 15.
1. About, around, towards, with.
2. Maggots, worms. From L. *vermis.*

Vestales. IV 95.
1. Religious. fanatics.
2. Fire.
Both from L. *vestalis* = 'pure'.
Vestal Virgins were priestesses who maintained the fire sacred to Vesta the goddess of the hearth.

Vides. I 9.
(*Vuides.*)
Deserted, empty, evacuated.

Vin. V 34, IX 49.
1. Wine.
2. Taxation.
3. Government.
Wine is one of the oldest sources of customs and excise revenue.

Vindications. I 56.
1. Excuses, exonerations.
2. Revenge. From L. *vindicare* = 'to avenge'.
(See *VINDICTE*).

Vindicte. I 94.
See *VINDICATIONS*.

Voguera. IX 83.
(*Voquera.*)
See *VOQUERA*.

Voile. X 2.
Screen. From O.F. *voile* = 'veil'.

Volsques. VI 98, VII 21.
(*Volsicque.*)
1. Central southern France. From Volcae Arecomici a Gallic tribe living along the coast between the

Pyrenees and the river Rhone, whose chief town was Nemauses/*NÎMES* - mentioned by Caesar in his The Civil Wars - the ancient inhabitants of Languedoc.
2. Italy. From Volsci, early inhabitants of the Liris river valley in Italy. Volci later became one of the city states of Etruria (see *ETRUSQUE*), but fell to the Romans in the 4th century BC.

Voltigeant. VII 38.
Playing. From *voltige* = 'trick-riding'; and *voltigeur* = 'tumbler'.

Voltorte. IX 20.
(Vaultort.)
1. Dawdle. From *voltiger* = 'to flutter', 'to hover while in flight'.
2. Roundabout. From *volte* in *volte-face* = 'about turn'; and *tort* from L. *tortum* = 'wrong'.
3. Twisting. From L. *torquere tort* = 'twist'.

Voquera. IX 83.
(Voguera.)
Will call upon, will pray. From L. *vocare* = 'to call'.

Vuides. I 9.
(Vides.)
See *VIDES*.
Vulgus. VI 100.
Coarse, low, vulgar. From L. *vulgus* = 'the common people'; 'the mob' and 'the rabble' in Cicero, Livy and Vergil.

Yeux. I 35.
(Loeil.)
Eyes.

Yres. VII 22.
(Irez.)
See *IREZ*.

FURTHER READING

The following are among books on Nostradamus which have been published in the past fifty years. Those containing a full edition of Les Prophéties, are marked with an asterisk.

Nostradamus Speaks. Rolfe Boswell, NEW YORK, 1941.

Nostradamus, The Man Who Saw Through Time. Lee MacCann, NEW YORK, 1941.

Nostradamus Sees All. André Lamont, PHILADELPHIA, 1942.

Nostradamus. The Future Foretold. James Laver, LONDON, 1942.

Nostradamus. Herman I. Woolf, LONDON, 1944.

The Complete Prophecies of Nostradamus. Henry G. Roberts, FIRST PUB. 1947, REVISED EDITION LONDON 1985.*

Prophecies on World Events by Nostradamus. Stewart Robb, NEW YORK, 1961.

Nostradamus. Life and Literature. Edgar Leoni, New York, 1961.*

The Prophecies of Nostradamus. Erika Cheetham, LONDON, 1975.*

Nostradamus. Countdown to Apocalypse. Jean Charles de Fontbrune, LONDON, 1983.

The Final Prophecies of Nostradamus. Erika Cheetham, LONDON, 1990.*

SKETCH MAP OF SOUTHERN FRANCE

LEGEND	Agde	12	Marseilles	20
	Agen	4	Mirande	7
	Auch	6	Monaco	22
	Avignon	16	Montpellier	13
	Béziers	11	Narbonne	10
	Bordeaux	2	Nîmes	14
	Condom	5	St. Rémy	18
	Foix	9	Salon	19
	Léon	1	Sorgues	15
	Lyons	21	Tarascon	17
	Marmande	3	Toulouse	8

THE INDEX

NOTES: A location reference in italics indicates that there is also a dictionary reference for that index entry. If the dictionary reference is spelt differently the alternative spelling is shown in parentheses.